Hardware/Firmware Interface Design

Best Practices for Improving
Embedded Systems Development

Gary Stringham

AMSTERDAM • BOSTON • HEIDELBERG • LONDON
NEW YORK • OXFORD • PARIS • SAN DIEGO
SAN FRANCISCO • SINGAPORE • SYDNEY • TOKYO

Newnes is an imprint of Elsevier

Newnes is an imprint of Elsevier
30 Corporate Drive, Suite 400, Burlington, MA 01803, USA
The Boulevard, Langford Lane, Kidlington, Oxford, OX5 1GB, UK

Notices

Knowledge and best practice in this field are constantly changing. As new research and experience
broaden our understanding, changes in research methods, professional practices, or medical
treatment may become necessary.

Practitioners and researchers must always rely on their own experience and knowledge in
evaluating and using any information, methods, compounds, or experiments described herein. In
using such information or methods they should be mindful of their own safety and the safety
of others, including parties for whom they have a professional responsibility.

To the fullest extent of the law, neither the Publisher nor the authors, contributors, or editors,
assume any liability for any injury and/or damage to persons or property as a matter of products
liability, negligence or otherwise, or from any use or operation of any methods, products,
instructions, or ideas contained in the material herein.

Library of Congress Cataloging-in-Publication Data
Application Submitted.

British Library Cataloguing-in-Publication Data
A catalogue record for this book is available from the British Library.

ISBN: 978-1-85617-605-7

For information on all Newnes publications
visit our Web site at *www.elsevierdirect.com*

Typeset by diacriTech, Chennai, India

Printed in the United States of America
08 09 10   10 9 8 7 6 5 4 3 2 1

Contents

Preface

You can find books written by hardware engineers teaching hardware engineers how to design hardware. You can find books written by firmware engineers teaching firmware engineers how to write firmware. This book is written by a firmware engineer but is directed primarily to hardware engineers.

Many engineers have experienced problems when trying to get firmware working on hardware. They are designed generally in isolation from each other and then are expected to work when brought together. But problems and defects appear. At times it is unknown where the defect is located—in hardware or firmware, or maybe the documentation.

There is very little written about how to get hardware and firmware to work well together. This book attempts to fill that niche. It addresses the interface between the hardware and firmware domains and provides practices that will reduce the time and effort required to produce an embedded systems product. It covers all aspects of development surrounding the hardware/firmware interface, including the process of development, the high-level design, and the detailed design.

A key feature of this book are the 300+ Best Practices that give detailed instructions for various aspects of the development process and design. These best practices apply perfectly, but only for a given situation. They should be scrutinized for applicability in a given situation. Throughout this book, the emphasis is for engineers to develop their own set of best practices. They may start with these 300, but the set should evolve to be made their own, as this increases the likelihood of success within their organization.

To help engineers understand the 300+ Best Practices, and to help them create their own set, Seven Principles are presented that provide overarching guidelines and direction. These principles, when internalized, will help engineers work in the right direction, even if there is no specific best practice for that situation. Following the Seven Principles and 300+ Best Practices will improve the design teams' ability to produce successful embedded systems products.

Chapter Summaries

The following chapter summaries provide an overview of the book and help the reader to navigate through the book.

1. **Introduction:** This chapter establishes the foundation for the book. It discusses various types of hardware and how they impact the hardware/firmware interface. It defines principles and best practices, the target audience, and the product life cycle. It also presents a case study used throughout the book.

2. **Principles:** This chapter presents the Seven Principles and provides a high-level view and reasoning for the direction of this book. Understanding these principles is key to understanding why the best practices are stated as they are.

3. **Collaboration:** Of key importance to the success of an embedded product is the proper and sufficient collaboration between hardware and firmware engineers. This chapter defines roles and processes in such an effort.

4. **Planning:** Before starting a project, planning must be done to determine and agree what direction should be taken with the new product. This chapter covers several areas that should be visited when planning a new project.

5. **Documentation:** Most engineers assigned to write documentation do not like the task. And most engineers reading documentation get frustrated with incomplete and incorrect documentation. This chapter discusses the types of documentation, when to write them, how to review them, and what types of details to include in them.

6. **Superblock:** This chapter introduces the concept of a block that can do everything within its own domain. It discusses why a superblock is good and how to set it up to be used where needed. But it also discusses the reality of practical limitations and how to handle those.

7. **Design:** Various design aspects are discussed in this chapter, such as events, power-on sequences, communication, and control.

8. **Registers:** Registers are the fundamental interface between hardware and firmware. This chapter discusses them in great detail, including addresses, bit locations, and types of bits.

9. **Interrupts:** Given a lack of consistency among interrupt designs used in the industry, this chapter focuses in great detail how interrupts from hardware into firmware should be managed. This chapter also contains a proposal for an interrupt standard and discusses the proposal in detail.

10. **Aborts, etc.:** Too often very little thought is given to errors and how to recover from them. This chapter discusses design elements necessary to allow firmware to abort hardware operations, recover, and resume processing.

11. **Hooks:** Logic analyzers cannot probe the internals of a chip but knowledge of what is occurring inside is important when trying to get firmware working on hardware. Having firmware-accessible hooks inside the chip allows firmware to retrieve information for engineering analysis. This chapter contains many possible hooks that could be included.

12. **Conclusion:** This chapter wraps up the book. It also contains a couple of cartoon illustrations used to help illustrate the concepts in the book.

   Appendices

   A. **Best Practices:** This appendix collects all the best practices in the book into one place.

   B. **Block Specification:** This appendix is a documentation template as explained and described in Chapter 5, Documentation.

   C. **Using This Book in a University:** This appendix provides suggestions on how to use this book to teach hardware and firmware engineering students that have to work together on a project.

   D. **Glossary:** Given that this book addresses two different engineering disciplines, hardware and firmware engineering, it covers terms from one domain that might not be understood by the other.

Conventions Used in This Book

The bulk of the text in this book discusses the concept at hand. Interspersed in the text are one or more of these elements: figures, listings, register maps, best practices, and tales from the trenches.

Figures

Figure 0.1 is an example figure.

Firmware Listings

Listing 0.1 shows an example listing of firmware source code written in C.

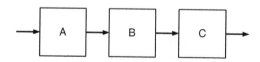

Figure 0.1: Example figure.

Listing 0.1: Example C code listing.

```
/* Read the current list of pending interrupts */
interrupts = *interruptRegister;
```

Hardware Circuits

A few hardware circuits are illustrated in the book. Both a schematic drawing and its equivalent Verilog listing will be given. Figure 0.2 is the schematic and Listing 0.2 is the corresponding Verilog code for an example circuit.

Register Maps

This diagrammatic form is used in discussions about registers, how various bits are mapped into the register, and the mode of operation and reset values of these bits. A detailed explanation of this format is given in Chapter 5, Documentation.

	MSB					Daily Register – 0x0004				LSB
Bits	31 30 29 28	27 26 25 24	23 22 21 20	19 18 17 16	15 14 13 12	11 10 9 8	7 6 5 4	3 2 1 0		
R/W	- - - -	- - - -	- - - -	- - - -	- - - -	- - - -	- - - -	- C B A		
Reset	0 0 0 0	0 0 0 0	0 0 0 0	0 0 0 0	0 0 0 0	0 0 0 0	0 0 0 0	0 0 0 0		

A This bit means one thing.

B This bit means another.

C And this bit means something else.

Best Practices

The book contains 300+ Best Practices related to the concepts being taught. In addition to presentation throughout the book, these practices are collected in Appendix A, thereby

Figure 0.2: Schematic for example circuit.

Listing 0.2: Verilog code for example circuit.

```
// A simple AND gate.
assign c = a & b;
```

providing a concise checklist that can be used during chip design projects. They are also provided in a spreadsheet available online at the publisher's website, elsevierdirect.com/companions, and at the author's website, garystringham.com/hwfwbook.

Each best practice has an ID number, X.Y.Z, which is used in the body of the book, in Appendix A, and in the spreadsheet.

☑ **Best Practice**

1.1.1 Best Practices of Hardware/Firmware Interface Design.

Like the book, the Excel spreadsheet database is copyrighted material. Purchasers of this book are entitled (and encouraged) to start with the database and modify it to suit the needs of their design team, but some restrictions apply. See Appendix A for more details on the database and its copyright permissions.

☑ **Best Practice**

1.1.2 Copyright © 2009, Gary Stringham & Associates, LLC. All rights reserved. Do not distribute beyond your team.

Tales from the Trenches

Scattered throughout this book are real-life stories that help illustrate the impact of the topic at hand. These are stories from real engineers (mostly me) in the trenches, working away designing and solving problems. The following is an example tale (not a real one).

📖 **Tales from the Trenches**

I remember hearing a story from a friend of a friend, who heard that an engineer had said that he heard a manager tell her subordinate that–according to the rumor she had heard–it was already broken to start with.

Companion Website

This book has a companion website at elsevierdirect.com/companions/9781856176057, where you will find links to the spreadsheet database for the 300+ Best Practices, the document template discussed in Chapter 5, Documentation, and other related content. Please visit the author's website at garystringham.com/hwfwbook for the same tools, plus additional links to his work in this area and details of how to contact him directly.

How to Contact Me

If you have any questions about the content of this book or about your hardware/firmware interface design, feel free to contact me at gary@garystringham.com.

Acknowledgments

I would like to thank Jack Meador and Mike Merrell, the two unlucky hardware engineers who had to put up with my constant questions, issues, and requests as we worked through the project that was the catalyst for this book. They provided valuable insight and help from within their hardware domain. They, along with other hardware and firmware engineers within the organization and from other companies, provided much of the input used in many of the best practices and tales from the trenches in this book.

I would also like to thank my immediate managers at the time, Warren Johnson and Tracy Sauerwein, and managers above them, Sandy Lieske and Von Hansen. The book is finally published—your unwarranted support, while tracing my progress from sandy to smooth, was not in vain.

Me badly english writin' was greatly improved through the patient tutelage of my technical writing coach, Joel Saks. He has a gift with words that is way beyond my abilities. In addition, he was a valuable resource for critical analysis of my concepts, pushing me to clearly articulate and justify what seemed obvious to me.

I would also like to thank John Blyler, Clive "Max" Maxfield, Jack Meador, Mike Merrell, Joel Saks, and three others (who wish to remain anonymous) for reviewing all or parts of my book. Your comments provided valuable input and suggestions, making the book better than otherwise. Thanks to Mike Merrell for his help with the Verilog code and to Kevin Falk for drawing the car illustrations. And thanks to the many others who have given me suggestions and enthusiastic encouragement during the 5 years it took me to complete this project.

Most of all, I want to thank my wife and children 👪 for their patience and long suffering as I spent evenings and weekends working on this book instead of making repairs on the house, driving the children to their activities, and vacationing with the family.

CHAPTER 1

Introduction

Hardware and firmware engineering design teams often run into problems and conflicts when trying to work together. They come from different development environments, have different toolsets, and use different terminology. Often they are in different locations within the same company or work for different companies. The two teams have to work together but often have conflicting differences in procedures and methods. Since their resulting hardware and firmware work has to integrate successfully to produce a product, it is imperative that the hardware/firmware interface—including people, technical disciplines, tools, and technology—be designed properly.

Because of the nature of embedded systems, hardware design will always precede firmware design. While some tools and techniques are available to permit a more parallel effort, in the end, the hardware must be created before the firmware team can carry out its final development and testing efforts. Although a significant amount of effort is expended to ensure correct design at the hardware/firmware interface, problems will still appear when hardware and firmware are integrated as a system.

Problems found in firmware are relatively easy to fix compared to problems found in hardware. Respinning an application-specific integrated circuit (ASIC)[1] can take up to 4 months and cost several million dollars, depending on the process node at which the chip is being developed, such as 90 nm, 65 nm, and so on. So pressure is put on the firmware teams to try to work around any hardware problems to avoid the delay and cost. As Jack Ganssle, an embedded systems expert, humorously stated, "Quality is firmware's fault—because it is too late to fix it in hardware."

Chips are expensive and hard to design and build; getting them "right" is a business necessity. Designing chips for firmware engineers is a key enabler. This book provides a rigorous study of common sense approaches to chip design based on years of experience in writing firmware for chips. It captures practical and sensible ideas and applies structure and

---

[1] For the purposes of this book, the term ASIC will also be taken to encompass application-specific standard products (ASSPs), system on chips (SoCs), and field-programmable gate arrays (FPGAs). (See also the definitions later in this chapter.)

DOI: 10.1016/B978-1-85617-605-7.00003-4.

rigor to the design. The goal of the book is to provide principles and best practices that allow hardware and firmware engineers to improve the development and integration of embedded systems. This book is most useful during the development phase of the product, specifically during the development of both the chip and the firmware for a product.

This first chapter provides background into the subject matter and lays the groundwork for the remainder of the book. The second chapter discusses seven principles of hardware/firmware interface design. The rest of the book contains over 300 best practices. Obviously the list of best practices presented here cannot be an exhaustive one in this area. As you read through the following chapters, you will think about best practices that you use and will get ideas for others. Write them down so you can apply them to your work and share them with others.

1.1. What Is the Hardware/Firmware Interface?

The hardware/firmware interface is the junction where hardware and firmware meet and communicate with each other. On the hardware side, it is a collection of addressable registers that are accessible to firmware via reads and writes. This includes the interrupts that notify firmware of events. On the firmware side, it is the device drivers or low-level software that controls the hardware by writing values to registers, interprets the information read from the registers, and responds to interrupt requests from the hardware. Of course, there is more to hardware than registers and interrupts, and more to firmware than device drivers, but this is the interface between the two and where engineers on both sides must be concerned to achieve successful integration.

The terms "hardware" and "firmware" vary in scope and meaning in the industry, so let's define how they are used in this book.

1.1.1. What Are Hardware, Chips, and Blocks?

In the electrical engineering context, the term "hardware" includes all electronic circuits in an embedded product, including printed circuit boards, passives like resistors and capacitors, and chips. It can also refer to nonelectrical, mechanical components, such as bolts, spacers, and housing/enclosures. Meanwhile, the term "chips" includes any devices made from silicon or other semiconducting materials containing multiple transistors that implement digital or analog functions. They can be simple, single-function devices or complex, multi-function devices containing processors, memory, interfaces, and other functional circuitry.

For the purposes of this book, "hardware" and "chips" refers to just a subset of devices (such as ASICs and FPGAs): specifically, the components that interact with firmware via registers and interrupts. It does not include microprocessors, microcontrollers, or memory. Furthermore, "hardware" and "chips" are used almost interchangeably in this book; for example, "The hardware team designs the chips."

A "chip" will contain one or more functional "blocks," such as a USB communications function, an MPEG compressor, and a memory controller. There may be more than one instantiation (copy) of a particular block, such as two UARTs. Blocks within a chip typically communicate with each other and with external memory via a shared bus. Each block is typically designed as an individual unit. When a new chip is designed, it may comprise a mixture of blocks used in previous designs and new blocks.

Within the scope of "chips," are several general families of integrated circuits, each with their own minor differences with regard to the context of this book, but the concepts generally apply to all.

ASICs

ASICs (application-specific integrated circuits) are designed to be used in a specific product of a specific brand. It contains a customized mix of standard and/or proprietary blocks. ASICs are high-volume chips optimized for power, performance, and cost. This means that there are many different ASICs in use, each with its own hardware and firmware design teams. These hardware and firmware teams continue to work together as they produce variations of the ASICs for various product families and multiple generations of the products.

Both of the teams may be working for the company producing the product; alternatively, one or both of the teams might be working for other companies hired to do the work. Whatever the case, close coupling between the teams must still be present so as to provide the hardware team with more opportunities to make changes and improvements because they can collaborate with the firmware team in advance.

ASSPs

ASSPs (application-specific standard product) are like ASICs except that they are designed for a specific application area and are sold to more than one customer—hence the name "standard product." By contrast, an ASIC is designed and built to order for a specific customer. ASSPs have only standard functionality, allowing them to be used in a variety of embedded systems by a variety of companies. This means that one company generates an ASSP, while potentially many companies generate firmware for that ASSP. Device drivers are typically needed for a variety of operating systems (OSs) and versions; these device drivers will be specific to the firmware of the target embedded system. Thus many different firmware teams from multiple companies are typically involved. The firmware teams generally do not have ready access to the hardware team that designed the ASSP. There is no one-to-one relationship as found in ASIC teams.

This puts the burden on the hardware team to try to please many different firmware teams without being able to collaborate with each and every one. In this scenario, the hardware team should select one or two firmware teams to partner with to help develop the chip while it is still in the design phase. This is commonly the case, with the end result that the company selling the chip has a few device drivers already written that other companies can use to leverage into their products.

The contents of some ASSPs are standard enough that they are produced by multiple companies that allow the same device driver to work on any brand. Examples include EHCI (enhanced host controller interface)-compliant USB (universal serial bus) controllers and 16550-compatible UARTs (universal asynchronous receiver transmitters). This means that the registers, bits, and functionality are fairly identical. This allows the same device driver to run on diverse brands of ASSPs. Maintaining this compatibility restricts the hardware design team even further by not allowing them much freedom to improve on other brands.

FPGAs

FPGAs (field-programmable gate arrays) have the flexibility of having their functionality changed through reprogramming, but they typically use more power, have slower performance, and cost more per part.

FPGAs can be programmed with a customized mix of content. This custom mix makes it similar to ASICs in that typically one firmware team is paired with the one hardware team. However, because FPGAs can be modified in a matter of hours, it is possible for many versions of the FPGA programming to exist. This requires close collaboration between the hardware and firmware teams to ensure that the version of firmware paired with the version of FPGA code will work together.

FPGAs are also used when changes to the design are needed after the product has been deployed to customers. A new programming file can be distributed and downloaded to the product.

FPGAs can also be programmed with a standard mix of content. This is similar to ASSPs in that companies can sell the same package to many customers. This means that there could be many firmware teams writing device drivers for this standard, FPGA-based content. Companies use this method to sell small quantities of their designs without incurring the NRE (nonrecurring engineering) expenses associated with sending the design to a foundry for fabrication as is the case with non–FPGA-based ASSPs.

References in this book about the time and expense required to respin the chip do not apply to FPGAs. Firmware cannot tell the difference between an ASIC/ASSP or FPGA, as the register/interrupt interface is the same.

SoCs

An SoC (system on chip) is similar to an ASIC and ASSP, but in addition to its mix of blocks, it also contains one or more processors and possibly some memory. It may be a customized mix (ASIC + processor) or it may be a standard mix (ASSP + processor). It may be sent to the foundry for fabrication or it may be programmed into an FPGA.

For the purpose of this book, SoCs are synonymous with ASICs, ASSPs, and FPGAs. The processor and memory parts of SoCs are not discussed; instead, the focus is on the rest of the chip—the functional blocks that are accessed by firmware. While firmware is executed on the processor and resides in and accesses memory, this book is not about how to design processors or memory.

Table 1.1 is a three-part table that summarizes the differences among these types of chips.

Other Chips

Other families of chips exist, such as DSPs (digital signal processors) and CPLD (complex programmable logic devices), but the basic fundamentals are still the same. Firmware needs to interact with, control, and respond to these devices.

Table 1.1: Summary of Differences among Types of Chips

Part 1	ASIC	ASSP
Content mix	Custom	Standard
Target customers	One	Many
Firmware teams	One	Many
Design optimization	For one	For all
Design changes/improvements	Possible	Difficult
Part 2	**Fabricated Parts**	**Programmable Parts (FPGAs)**
Programmability/flexibility	No	Yes
Respin costs	High	None
Relative power	Low	High
Relative speed	Fast	Slow
Relative per-part cost	Low	High
Relative up-front NRE cost	High	None
Sales volume	High	Low
Part 3	**Non-SoC**	**SoC**
Microprocessors	None	One or more

1.1.2. What Are Firmware and Device Drivers?

Firmware is software that is built into an embedded systems product and stored in nonvolatile memory, such as ROM, EPROM, E²PROM, or FLASH. The memory could be located on-chip or off-chip. Firmware is also known in the industry as "embedded software" or "low-level software." Major firmware components optionally include an operating system (OS), kernel, device drivers, and application code.

The term "firmware" has other meanings in the industry that are not used here. For example, to some people, firmware refers to the microcode running in processors that is executed because of an assembly language instruction. In other sections of the industry, firmware is the content downloaded into an FPGA to program it. Firmware in this book does not refer to such microcode or FPGA programming code.

Firmware might contain an OS. This might be an RTOS (real-time operating system). The OS may be a commercial product, such as Embedded Windows®, Linux®, and VxWorks®, or it may be developed in-house. Some lightweight embedded systems do not use an OS, but instead execute the firmware directly.

Device drivers are the specific firmware components that interact with chips. On some systems this is called the BIOS (basic input/output system) or low-level code. Device drivers read from and write to registers and respond to interrupts. Applications in firmware go through device drivers to access the hardware.

The term "driver" has other meanings for hardware engineers, such as current drivers or buffer drivers. In the computer world, "driver" also refers to software modules installed on a computer to work with peripheral devices, such as a printer driver. In this book, the term "driver," by itself, refers specifically to "device driver."

Typically there is one device driver for every block on the chip as illustrated in Figure 1.1. This figure shows the firmware and a chip. The chip consists of several blocks and the firmware consists of several applications and device drivers.

As an example, I will use Figure 1.1 to describe how a page is printed in a laser printer. Suppose Block A is a USB block that receives the packets of data for a print job. Driver A reads the incoming packets from Block A and hands them to Application A. Application A assembles all the packets and when enough packets arrive for a page, hands it to other applications, such as a print job interpreter which may use a rasterizing application, a data compression application, and others. Eventually Application B is given the raster data, which hands it to Driver B, which then sets up the registers in Block B to use that data to control the laser.

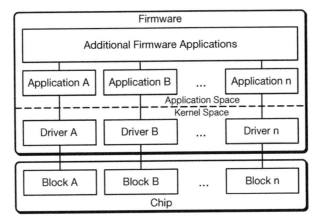

Figure 1.1: Relationship between applications and device drivers in firmware and functional blocks in the chip.

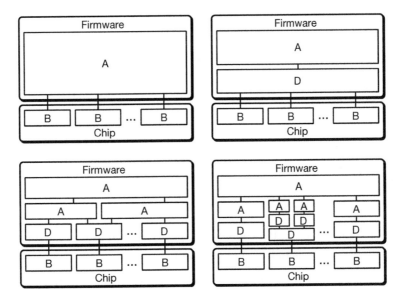

Figure 1.2: Other examples of possible firmware architectures for applications (A), device drivers (D), and blocks (B).

The firmware architecture presented in Figure 1.1 offers just one possible scenario; Figure 1.2 illustrates other possible architectures.

1.2. What Is a Best Practice?

The term "best practice" has a few different meanings in the industry. The following definition is used for this book and conveys what and how best practices should be treated.

A "best practice" is the most balanced or optimized way to do something in a given situation.

An article by Ivar Jacobson, et al., in *Dr. Dobb's Journal* states that "A 'practice' provides a way to systematically and verifiably address a particular aspect of a project." It also says the following:

- A practice does not attempt to address the entire problem. Rather, a practice attacks a particular aspect of the problem.

- A practice is systematic in that someone can articulate it. It is not a black art. A practice has a clear beginning and end, and tells a complete story in usable chunks.

- A practice includes its own verification, providing it with a clear goal and a way of measuring its success in achieving that goal. Without verification, the practice is not complete.

The term "best practice" also invokes negative connotations among some. In a recent article in *CIO*, Michael Schrage wrote, "Best practice isn't. Best practice is a fiction, a lie, and a con job . . . . Never, ever allow [your operations] to be determined by anyone else's best practices."

The problem is that too many people forget that a "best practice" applies only in a given situation and within a certain context. They try to apply a practice in a different situation without giving it any thought. A wrench is the best tool for turning a bolt but not for pounding a nail into the wall.

A best practice is not as rigid as a standard. Everybody has to abide by the standard or things will break. Standards, once set and in place, rarely change. Best practices need to constantly be evaluated and modified as necessary.

Schrage continues, "Effective implementation [of practices] requires companies to constantly assess the trade-offs between adoption and adaptation."

For each best practice in this book, I explain why it is a best practice. If the "why" applies in your situation, then the best practice might apply too. As you go through each best practice in this book, this is what you should do:

- Pick and choose the ones you want to use.

- Modify them if necessary to better fit your situation and organization.

- Decide together (both hardware and firmware teams) if and how to use them.

- Broadcast your list to the rest of the engineers in your hardware and firmware teams.

- Repeat as necessary.

Included with the purchase of this book is a Microsoft® Excel® spreadsheet database containing all of the best practices presented in this book.[2] This is a good place to start as you develop your own list of best practices. The list of best practices in this book does not pretend to be an exhaustive list of all known best practices in this domain. In addition to what is in this book, look for best practices within your organization or elsewhere as possible candidates to add to your own list of best practices. Look at lessons learned from past projects, especially those that were less than successful.

1.2.1. What Is a Principle?

Several times I mention "principles" and "practices" of hardware/firmware interface design. The terms are not interchangeable.

> *A "principle" is a fundamental concept that guides what is or is not a best practice.*

To better illustrate the differences among principles, practices, and standards, consider the following example:

- **Standard:** "The data bits in an RS-232 start with the least-significant bit first." This is a specific design criterion that devices must follow to ensure interoperability. This is not allowed to change.

- **Principle:** "Prepare for Contingencies." This is a fundamental guideline but has no specific design action to follow. This will remain true, no matter what the product being designed is used for.

- **Best Practice:** "Make the DMA address readable by firmware as the DMA transfer progresses." This is a specific design criterion within the principle of "Prepare for Contingencies" because it allows firmware to diagnose potential DMA transfer problems. But there may be conditions under which this practice is not advisable, such as a chip with a security requirement to not allow reads, thereby preventing rogue firmware from sniffing DMA transfers. In this case, the best practice does not apply but the principle, "Prepare for Contingencies," still remains true.

Over 300 best practices are presented in this book but only seven principles. These seven principles will be discussed in more detail in Chapter 2, Principles.

---

[2] The best practices spreadsheet is available at the publisher's website, elsevierdirect.com/companions/ 9781856176057, and at the author's website, garystringham.com/hwfwbook.

1.2.2. Benefits of Principles and Practices

Several benefits exist for implementing and using principles and best practices:

- **Reduce chip respins:** A chip respin can incur up to four months of delay and millions of dollars in cost. Surveys published by John Blyler and Geoffrey Ying in *Chip Design Magazine* indicate that 45 to 70% of chip respins are due to functional/logical errors. Following these best practices will reduce the number of chip respins due to logic mistakes and functional errors. It also reduces the cascading impact of extra costs incurred, and loss of engineering productivity waiting for new chips, product release delays, and reduced market share.

- **Increase product quality:** When following these design practices, many errors will never be introduced into the chip, which increases the quality of the final product. And the errors that are introduced will more easily be diagnosed and worked around, again allowing the product to have a better quality than otherwise. Mike Barr wrote that "a coding standard can help keep bugs out. It's cheaper and easier to prevent a bug from creeping into code than it is to find and kill it after it has entered."

- **Earlier time to market:** Avoiding respins of fabrication-based chips is one means for allowing products to be released to market sooner. In addition, following these design practices for fabrication-based and FPGA-based chips will allow firmware engineers to develop their firmware sooner, again allowing the product to be released sooner.

- **Reduce variations of chip designs:** By following best practices regarding design, features, and performance, each chip designed and produced has the potential of extending its life by being usable in future products that otherwise would require a new variation in the design of chip with its associated design, verification, masks, and testing costs.

1.3. "First Time Right" Also Means...

The industry uses a term, "first time right," to mean that the first run of chips that come back from fabrication are perfect. This is extremely important since defects that cause respins have a significant impact on schedule and costs. Wolfgang Rosenstiel states that "first time right" is the most important goal and it requires that engineers ensure a perfect design before the production is started. One engineering manager in the industry told me that he had been given quotas that a certain percentage of his team's chips have to be "first time right."

Significant effort is put into the design of a chip, from the front to the back end, to reduce the risk of errors. Many simulations and tests are executed. Design verifications are carried out. Many products and techniques exist that are designed to help ensure correct functionality and achieve "first time right."

But no matter how hard engineers try, it is nearly impossible to make perfect chip designs. We cannot think of all the possible use cases in advance. We cannot foresee system interaction problems. We cannot assure that 100% of the defects have been found. Chips do become better as the designs mature and stabilize but for new designs, it is difficult.

However, by expanding the definition of "first time right" to include more in the case of imperfect design, we can make "first time right" more achievable. The expansion of the definition includes other aspects that will aid in that effort, such as creating the chip in such a way as to make the design:

1. Easier to program.

2. Easier to debug.

3. Easier to work around defects.

This expansion gives firmware engineers a greater probability of making the chip usable in products in spite of defects that sneak in, thus allowing the chip to be used without a respin.

1.3.1. Easier to Program

Chips can be designed to ease the efforts required by firmware engineers who write the code to control the chip. By helping firmware engineers do their job, the chip becomes more usable, especially when it comes to learning about the chip and solving problems that arise while developing the firmware.

Reviewing the design of the chip with firmware engineers increases the chance that the design will work with the firmware itself. Improving the documentation will help the firmware engineers learn and understand the chip. Judicious layout of the register formats will help the firmware engineers program and control the chip without complicated interactions. Consistency in how similar functions operate throughout the chip will reduce errors as existing firmware code is leveraged.

1.3.2. Easier to Debug

Designs frequently have defects and flaws. The challenge is for engineers to be able to diagnose them when they come across them.

When (not if, but when) defects are found in chips, the first task is to diagnose the root cause of the defect. It is only after the root cause of the defect is found and clearly understood that a fix or workaround can be developed and implemented.

Anything that can be done to aid the diagnosis of defects will be of help. Since it is unknown beforehand where any defects will occur, placing debugging hooks throughout the chip will increase the likelihood that some will be in the right place when defects are encountered.

1.3.3. Easier to Work around Defects

Once defects are found and well understood, the next step is to find a way to work around them. If firmware can be written to work around the defects, it will save the expense and delay of having to respin the chip.

Working around defects may mean being able to disable or bypass a portion of the block, use extra registers to allow firmware to peek into the block for possible anomalous conditions, or use other means to allow firmware to poke a portion of the block.

While using such back-door methods is not preferable, it does give the option of making the chip functional enough to ship products without incurring an expensive respin.

- - - ঙ - - - - - - ঞ - - -

The principles and practices in this book support "first time right" by making the chip easy to program, to debug, and to work around defects.

> **Note:**
>
> My expansion on the phrase, "first time right," is not to be used as an excuse for lazy designs that "should work just fine." Engineers should still do the best design work they can. By following the principles and practices in this book, they will have greater success in producing chips that can be used in products the first time, even though there may be flaws in the design.

Many of the concepts in the book should be applied to the design of a chip even though it is not known in advance if they will be required. Applying them will increase the probability that the chip will succeed the first time. If just one of these concepts saves a chip from a respin, then all the work to employ the many concepts is worth it to achieve "first time right."

1.4. Target Audience

Since this book addresses the interface between hardware and firmware, the target audience is the engineers on both sides of the hardware/firmware divide. However, because of the nature of the business, the hardware engineers produce something that firmware engineers must use. This means that the bulk of the work on the hardware/firmware interface as discussed in this book lies primarily on the shoulders of hardware engineers. Firmware engineers have a role in the design of the chip, but they are not as involved.

1.4.1. Hardware Engineers

Within the hardware engineering community, this book targets more specifically those working on the front-end of chip design, and in particular, those working on the interface between the chip and firmware, which is primarily realized in the form of registers and interrupts.

It is expected that the hardware engineering reader is familiar with basic digital logic and chip design practices. Examples in this book use Verilog, but only a cursory knowledge of the language is required. Similarly, only cursory knowledge of C is needed in order to understand the firmware examples presented in the book.

In particular, this is not a book on Verilog (or VHDL, System C, System Verilog, or other HDL derivatives or extensions). It does not give specific instructions on how to implement the concepts; instead, it describes how the chip should present itself to firmware.

1.4.2. Firmware Engineers

Within the firmware engineering community, this book targets those writing the lower-level code; that is, those portions of code—such as device drivers—tasked with dealing directly with the hardware. While the bulk of the best practices are implemented by hardware engineers, it is beneficial for firmware engineers to also know the concepts so they can be on the same page with respect to the problems being addressed and the methods that will be agreed upon to address those problems.

It is expected that the firmware engineering reader has some familiarity with firmware development, can read C code, and has some awareness of the chip development process.

Firmware readers should also be able to read Verilog and VHDL code well enough be aware of the general concepts of the design, but not necessarily understand all the nuances of the language and its syntax.

Note:

While it is possible for firmware engineers to read Verilog and VHDL files, they must remember that in specific contexts, the lines of code are being executed concurrently in parallel (all at once,) as opposed to firmware code that is executed in serial. Consider the following example:

    X = Y;

    Y = X;

In C/C++, both variables will end up containing the original contents of Y. In Verilog/VHDL, the contents of the variables will be exchanged.

1.4.3. This Book in a University Setting

This book has application in a university setting, such as a senior design project where electrical engineering students and computer science students have to work together. An example curriculum and exercise method is available at the publisher's website, elsevierdirect.com/companions/9781856176057, and at the author's website, garystringham.com/hwfwbook.

1.5. Project Life Cycle

Each design organization has its own terminology and phases for the various steps in their product development life cycle. Many of the hardware and firmware life cycles that organizations have developed are focused on either the hardware or the firmware but not both. Other life cycles are system-level and are focused on the entire life of the product, including manufacturing, sales, customer support, and obsolescence. I will describe a life cycle consisting of the hardware and firmware development phases and its terms that will be used in this book.

Figure 1.3 shows the phases of the hardware and firmware life cycles. The height of the lines indicates the relative number of engineers involved in the project at that time.

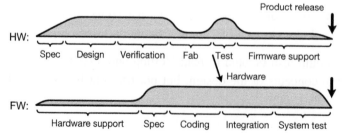

Figure 1.3: Life cycles and phases of hardware and firmware development.

The hardware team is more heavily involved at the beginning with the specification, design, and verification, while the firmware team is more involved later in the project with the coding, integration, and system testing. In the beginning, the firmware team supports the hardware team by collaborating on the design. Near the end, the hardware team supports the firmware team as they get the hardware and firmware working together as a complete system.

Tools are available that allow co-development activities where firmware engineers are able to develop code before hardware is ready. Such tools include co-simulation, virtual prototypes, and FPGA prototypes.

1.6. Case Study

Case studies are useful to learn something via an in-depth examination of an event, individual, or activity. Some case studies are set up in advance to take detailed notes throughout the activity. Others examine an unusual event from the past to learn from it. Consider the following example.

1.6.1. Monochrome Video Block in the Unity ASIC

The Unity ASIC was developed by Hewlett-Packard engineers for use in some of their LaserJet® printers. It contains several blocks, including standard I/O and data compressors. One of the blocks is the monochrome (mono) video block for use with HP's monochrome LaserJet printers. Its job is to take compressed raster data from memory, decompress it, perform some print quality enhancements, and control when the laser is on and off. Figure 1.4 is a block diagram of the mono video block.

The mono video block on the Unity ASIC had an unusually high rate of defects, which made it very difficult for the mono video device driver to carry out all the necessary tasks for printing an image on paper. Because this particular block had such an unusually high occurrence of errors, it is an excellent candidate for this case study because much can be learned from this example.

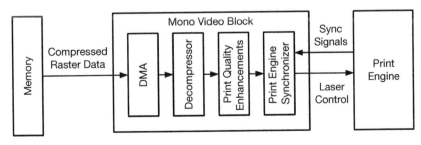

Figure 1.4: Modules and operation of the HP LaserJet mono video block.

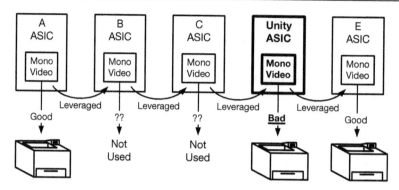

Figure 1.5: History of the mono video block.

A look into the history of the block indicates why this block had so many defects (Figure 1.5). The previous monochrome printer used an ASIC with a good and functional mono video block, illustrated as the A ASIC in Figure 1.5. That mono video block was leveraged to the next two ASICs, the B and C ASICs, with some features added and changed but neither was used in monochrome printers. When the B and C ASICs were turned on, a basic (but limited) test was performed on their mono video blocks to verify that they were functional. But since they were not used in a product, they were not thoroughly tested, allowing the defects that were introduced to escape detection.

One might ask why the mono video block was in the B and C ASICs if it was not used. The answer is that there was a possibility that it might be used. Given the long lead-time required for ASICs, and given the ever-fluctuating future forecasts for printer products, it was deemed prudent to include the block in these devices.

The block was then leveraged into the Unity ASIC, which was deployed in the next monochrome printer. Again, the basic test showed that the mono video block was functional. But as I developed the device driver to handle more and more of the required use cases, I kept uncovering new defects.

It took me several months to encounter, diagnose, and work around the many defects and get the mono video device driver and the mono video block in the Unity ASIC to the point to where we had a shippable product. It required a lot of support from the hardware engineer assigned to the block. But we were able to ship Unity ASICs in monochrome printers without having to incur the expense and delay of a respin.

When that block was leveraged from the Unity ASIC into the E ASIC, I worked closely with the next hardware engineer to eliminate all known defects and to add a few enhancements. This includes implementing many of the best practices in this book. When I got the E ASIC back, I had the mono video device driver running on it in less than a week, much better than the months that were required for the Unity ASIC.

Many of the best practices and tales from the trenches in this book stem from that mono video block on the Unity ASIC.

In discussing the many problems of this particular block, let me make it clear that I do not do so to malign HP engineers. HP is well known for engineering excellence and these LaserJet hardware engineers are no exception. This particular case is an anomaly and was the result of a series of events over time. None of the other blocks on the Unity ASIC, nor any of the blocks on any other HP ASICs that I worked on, had anywhere near the level of problems exhibited by this Unity mono video block.

The reason I discuss this block is because there is much that can be learned from it. The lessons learned have been applied to other blocks in subsequent HP ASICs and have proved beneficial to HP. My experience with that block inspired me to write this book. HP has graciously allowed me to use this example for, in the words of one manager, "the betterment of the industry."

1.6.2. A Case Study of a Good Example?

The Unity mono video block is a case study with many negative examples. What could I use as a case study of positive examples? That is trickier, because it is difficult for people to identify good things that avoided problems.

For example, suppose you are driving a car on an icy roadway when another car slides through an intersection just ahead of you. You slam on your brakes. If your car has an ABS (automatic braking system), you are likely to keep control of your car and avoid an accident. How much time and money did you save by not crashing? You avoided going to the hospital with its associated costs, pain, and recuperation time. You avoided the time and expense of repairing the car or purchasing a new car. You avoided the disruption in your life and your work. What is a dollar figure for this? You cannot come up with it. However, if you had been driving a car without an ABS and crashed, it is easy to tally up the medical costs, the car repair or replacement costs, and the lost time at work.

Following the principles and practices in this book will help you avoid costly delays and respins, but you will have a difficult time calculating a dollar amount that you saved. However, if one day you are able to identify just one best practice that was implemented which avoided a million-dollar respin, then the effort to implement all of them will have been worth it.

1.7. Summary

Aside from laying the groundwork for this book, this chapter has two important messages. One is to define the hardware/firmware interface as the junction where the hardware and the firmware meet. This intersection is often ignored, hence the purpose of this book.

The second important message is the concept of "first time right," meaning more than just trying to get a perfect design. It also means putting design practices into place to avoid defects, putting in hooks to diagnose defects, and making it easy to work around defects.

This chapter also defined several terms in the context of this book, such as "chip," "best practice," and "firmware." These terms (and others) are also defined in Appendix D, Glossary.

The next chapter is devoted to the seven principles of hardware/firmware interface design that will provide the overarching guidance for the best practices described in the remainder of this book.

References

Barr, Mike. Bug-Killing Standards for Firmware Coding. *Embedded.com*, March 24, 2009. Available at: embedded.com/design/opensource/216200567.

Blyler, John. Chip Design Magazine. Devil in the Details: Trends in ASIC Prototyping. *Chip Design Magazine*, October 23, 2008. Available at: chipdesignmag.com/sld/blog/2008/10/23/devil-in-the-details-trends-in-asic-prototyping.

Ganssle, Jack. Managing Embedded Projects. Tutorial at Embedded Systems Conference. San Francisco, March 2005.

Jacobson, Ivar, Pan-Wei, Ng, and Ian, Spence. Enough of Processes: Let's Do Practices. *Dr. Dobb's Journal*, May 2007. Available at: ddj.com/architect/198800543.

Rosenstiel, Wolfgang. *Hardware/Software Co-Design: Principles and Practices*. Edited by Jørgen, Staunstrup and Wayne, Wolf. Norwell, MA: Kluwer Academic Publishers, 1997.

Schrage, Michael. Making IT Work: Don't Solve Problems with Best Practices. *CIO*, February 15, 2003. Available at: cio.com/article/31713/Making_IT_Work_Don_t_Solve_Problems_With_Best_Practices.

Ying, Geoffrey. Chip Design Magazine. Start at the Top to Reduce Re-Spins for Analog-Digital Chips. *Chip Design Magazine*, June/July 2005. Available at: chipdesignmag.com/display.php?articleId=117&issueId=11.

CHAPTER 2

Principles

As I was adding yet another best practice to my collection, I asked myself, "Why is this one important? Why does it belong?" I thought about it and then answered my own question, "It supports version independence." The term "version independence" had just popped into my head. (I have since replaced it with "compatibility.") But I realized it was a good way to describe why many of the best practices belong in the list. Then I realized that it was a guiding principle and that all of the best practices in the collection were there because of some fundamental principles that I was following, even though I had not verbalized them.

Just as a brief review from last chapter, "principles" and "practices" are not interchangeable terms:

- **Practices:** The best way to do something in a given situation.

- **Principles:** Fundamental concepts that guide what is or is not a best practice.

2.1. Seven Principles of Hardware/Firmware Interface Design

I had already realized that it would be impossible for anyone to remember the few hundred best practices in the collection, and it occurred to me that a few fundamental and guiding principles would be much easier to remember. Thus, I analyzed my collection and generated seven principles of hardware/firmware interface design as follows:

1. Collaborate on the Design.

2. Set and Adhere to Standards.

3. Balance the Load.

4. Design for Compatibility.

5. Anticipate the Impacts.

6. Design for Contingencies.

7. Plan Ahead.

These principles will help you understand why the best practices in this book are included.

DOI: 10.1016/B978-1-85617-605-7.00004-6.

2.1.1. Collaborate on the Design

Designing and producing an embedded product is a team effort. Hardware engineers cannot produce the product without the firmware team; likewise, firmware engineers cannot produce the product without the hardware team. Even though the two groups know that the other exists, they sometimes don't communicate with each other very well. Yet it is very important that the interface where the hardware and firmware meet—the registers and interrupts—be designed carefully and with input from both sides.

Collaborating implies proactive participation on both sides. Figure 2.1 shows a picture of a team rowing a boat. Some are rowing on the right side and some on the left. There is a leader steering the boat and keeping the team rowing in unison. Both sides have to work and work together. If one side slacks off, it is very difficult for the other side and the leader to keep the boat going straight.

In order to collaborate, both the hardware and firmware teams should get together to discuss a design or solve a problem. Collaboration needs to start from the very early stages of conceptual hardware design all the way to the late stages of final firmware development. Each side has a different perspective, that is, a view from their own environment, domain, or angle.

Figure 2.1: Both sides row to keep the boat going straight.
(Photo © iStockphoto.com/Steve Pepple Photography.)

Collaboration helps engineers increase their knowledge of the system as a whole, allowing them to make better decisions and provide the necessary features in the design. The quality of the product will be higher because both sides are working from the same agenda and specification.

Documentation is the most important collaborative tool. It ranges from high-level product specification down to low-level implementation details. The hardware specification written by hardware engineers with details about the bits and registers forming the hardware/firmware interface is the most valuable tool for firmware engineers. They have to have this to correctly code up the firmware. Of course, it goes without saying that this specification must be complete and correct.

Software tools are available on the market to assist in collaborative efforts. In some, the chip specifications are entered and the tool generates a variety of hardware (Verilog, VHDL...), firmware (C, C++...), and documentation (*.rtf, *.xls, *.txt...) files. Other collaborative tools aid parallel development during the hardware design phase, such as co-simulation, virtual prototypes, FPGA-based prototype boards, and modifying old products.

Collaboration needs to happen, whether it is achieved by walking over to the desk on the same floor, or by using email, phone, and video conferencing, or by occasional trips to another site in the same country or halfway around the world.

This principle, collaboration, is the foundation to all of the other principles. As we shall see, all of the other principles require some amount of collaboration between the hardware and firmware teams to be successful.

In this chapter, I will use the following Best-Practice-style box even though these are principles, not best practices. But this will help reinforce the principle and will be included in the electronic version of the best practices database.

☑ **Principle**

2.1.1 Collaborate on the Design.

2.1.2. Set and Adhere to Standards

Standards need to be set and followed within the organization. I group standards into industry standards and internal standards.

Industry standards exist in many areas, such as ANSI C, POSIX, PCI Express, and JTAG. Stay true to industry standards. Don't change them. Changing a standard will break the protocol, interoperability, and any off-the-shelf components, such as IP, device drivers, and test suites. For example, USB is widely known and used for connecting devices to computers. If this standard is adhered to, any USB-enabled device can plug into any computer and a well-defined behavior will occur (even if it is "unknown USB device installed").

Industry standards evolve but still behave in a well-defined manner. USB has evolved, from 1.1, to 2.0, and now 3.0, but it still has a well-defined behavior when plugging one version into another.

By internal standards, I mean that you have set standards, rules, and guidelines that everybody must follow within your organization. Modules are written in a certain fashion, specific quality checks are performed, and documentation is written in a specified format. Common practices and methods are defined to promote reuse and avoid the complexity of multiple, redundant ways of doing the same thing.

In the same way that industry standards allow many companies to produce similar products, following internal standards allows many engineers to work together and encourages them to make refinements to the design. It provides consistency among modules, creation of common test suites and debugging tools, and it spreads expertise among all the engineers.

Look at the standards within your organization. Look for best practices that are being used and formalize them to make them into standards that everybody abides by. There are many methods and techniques in the industry that help with this, such as CMMI (capability maturity model integration, an approach for improving processes; sei.cmu.edu/cmmi), ISO (International Organization for Standardization, international standards for business, government, and society; iso.org), and Agile (software development methods promoting regular inspection and adaptation; agilealliance.org). Adapt and change your internal standards as necessary. If a change needs to be made, it needs to go through a review and approval process by all interested parties. Once such a change has been approved, make sure that it is published within your organization. Apply version numbers if necessary.

There is no such thing as a "customized standard." Something is either a standard or customized, but not both. If you break away from a standard, be sure you have a good reason.

☑ **Principle**

2.1.2 Set and Adhere to Standards.

2.1.3. Balance the Load

Hardware and firmware each have their strengths and weaknesses when it comes to performing tasks. The challenge is to achieve the right balance between the two. What applies in one embedded system will not necessarily apply in another. Differences exist in CPU performance, bus architectures, clock speeds, memory, firmware load, and other parameters.

Proper balance between hardware and firmware depends on the given product and constraints. It requires studying what the tradeoffs will be for a given situation and adjusting as necessary.

An embedded system without a proper balance between hardware and firmware may have bottlenecks, performance issues, and stability problems. If firmware has too much work, it might be slow responding to hardware and/or it might not be able to keep hardware busy. Alternatively, hardware might have too big of a load, processing and moving data excessively, which may impact its ability to keep up with firmware requests. The quality of the system is also impacted by improper load balancing. The side with the heavier load may be forced to take shortcuts, fall behind, or lose some work.

A simple example to illustrate this point is to calculate the parity of a byte, a task often required in communication and storage applications. A firmware routine has to use a `for()` loop to look at each bit in the byte to calculate its parity. Listing 2.1 is an example in C of a `for()` loop to calculate parity by exclusive-ORing each bit.

Listing 2.1: C code for generating parity in firmware.

```
// Generate the parity of a byte
char generate_parity (char byte);
    {
    char parity;     // Contains the current parity value
    char bit;        // Contains the bit being looked at
    char pos;        // Bit position in the byte
    parity = 0;
    for (pos=0; pos<8; pos++)     // For each bit in the byte
        {
        bit = byte >> pos;        // Shift bit into position
        bit &= 0x1;               // Mask out the rest of the byte
        parity ^= bit;            // Exclusive OR with parity
        }
    return (parity);
    }
```

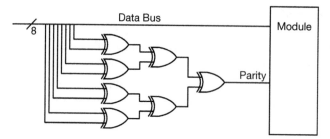

Figure 2.2: Schematic drawing of a circuit to generate parity in hardware.

Listing 2.2: Verilog code for generating parity in hardware.

```
module parity(
    Data,
    Parity
);
input [7:0] Data;
output Parity;
assign Parity = Data[0]^Data[1]^Data[2]^Data[3]^
                Data[4]^Data[5]^Data[6]^Data[7];
endmodule
```

The four-step `for()` loop translates into several assembly language steps that must be repeated eight times requiring multiple CPU cycles to do so. Other algorithms exist with various impacts on time and memory, but none can get close to the performance that can be achieved using a hardware implementation. Figure 2.2 and Listing 2.2 illustrate how hardware can exclusive-OR all eight bits together in a single clock cycle.

Like the firmware version, the hardware version has several steps (levels of logic) to it. But since it can access all eight bits at once, the parity is generated in a single clock cycle. In fact, the parity can be generated while the byte is being transferred on the bus.

Another example is the tradeoff for calculating floating-point numbers. It is faster to calculate them in hardware with a floating-point coprocessor but it adds to the material costs of the product. Performing the calculations in firmware is slower but reduces parts costs.

The lesson here is to consider the tradeoffs between the hardware and firmware tasks and to determine whether the balance needs adjusting. Do the I/O buffers need to be expanded? Do interrupt priorities need to be adjusted? Are there firmware tasks that could be performed faster in hardware? Are there hardware tasks that require the flexibility of firmware? Are there handshaking protocols between hardware and firmware that could be better tuned? Are there ways to reduce material costs by having firmware do more?

Balancing the load between hardware and firmware requires collaboration between the hardware and firmware engineers. Engineers understand the load impact associated with a task in their own domain but may not fully realize how it impacts the other.

A principle of economics applies here—two parties will be more productive if they work together, but with each working on the tasks that suits them best.

☑ **Principle**

2.1.3 Balance the Load.

2.1.4. Design for Compatibility

Designing for compatibility means to design in such a way as to facilitate, where possible, the ability for any version of firmware and any version of hardware to be paired up.

Cell phones are a good example of this. Many, many different models of cell phones exist but some are very alike. Different phones may have a variety of skins and colors but their hardware and firmware can be very similar. Cell phones can be upgraded with newer versions of firmware with new features; meanwhile, different (but similar) models of cell phones may be equipped with the same firmware.

In some cases, for example, firmware can be set up to support many features and then—through the use of configuration files, NVRAM settings, compile-time switches, and so on—only the required features will be enabled. The relevant hardware blocks would be designed with full support for all features, while the firmware would control which features are actually used. This allows the same hardware to be installed in different models of the product while still presenting different features to the outside world.

Designing for compatibility also means that when a new version of hardware is released with new features, it won't break when paired with older versions of the device driver, thereby allowing reuse of the old device driver. This is accomplished by following rules such as not moving bits and registers around. Compatibility is especially useful when multiple versions of hardware and firmware are deployed during product development and among customers. It reduces development time, saves costs, and gets the product out to customers sooner.

Firmware is becoming more and more expensive; in some cases, developing firmware can cost more than hardware. Also, it can be difficult to change firmware due to its many components, layers, and architecture. This increases the importance of striving for compatibility in hardware so as to minimize changes forced upon firmware.

Pairing any version of firmware with any version of hardware is ideal but not practical all of the time. However, it is a vision to strive for. Bearing compatibility in mind while designing from the beginning will lead to decisions that move toward that goal.

☑   **Principle**

2.1.4 Design for Compatibility.

2.1.5. Anticipate the Impacts

In the game of golf, the golfer selects the club, puts the ball on the tee, looks down the fairway, checks the wind, lines up the club to the ball, and checks his stance. He is anticipating the impact of his club on the ball. He does this because he does not want to miss or slice the ball, sending it into the rough.

Similarly, when creating a new hardware design or changing an existing design, you want to anticipate the impact on firmware. I chose the word "anticipate" because it implies a proactive effort. The dictionary lists "foresee" and "prevent" as synonyms. It is not enough to understand the impact or prepare for the impact; instead, you should anticipate, foresee, and prevent the impact.

When designing a new block, group bits into registers according to usage; don't mix different types of bits in the same register; and limit how many registers need to be accessed by more than one device driver. When making changes to an existing block, make the new version of the block work with the old device driver. Do not move bit locations and register addresses around.

Thus far I have been discussing the avoidance of negative impact. On the flip side, you want to look for positive impact. For example, providing a DMA with chaining capabilities or a larger I/O buffer will reduce the firmware load.

> 📖 **Tales from the Trenches**
>
> New monochrome printers were going to use an older, expensive SoC because there was no time or budget to develop a cheaper one. An opportunistic engineer took an existing SoC for color printers and replaced the color video block with the mono video block leaving all else unchanged.
>
> This saved time by avoiding much of the floor planning, timing closures, and verification activities that are typical with such a chip. Blocks that were no longer needed were left in to avoid turmoil. Even an ASCII string was left unchanged so that most test suites, simulation modules, and waveform files could remain unchanged. All pads and pins remained unchanged with the exception that the mono video block now used some of the pins that the color video block was using. This made the chip plug compatible on the printed circuit boards.
>
> He used only three to four engineers and had tape out in 2 months (in contrast to the more usual 15 engineers and 9 months to tape out). When the chip returned from fabrication it booted in 1 day.
>
> Because the lead engineer restricted all but the minimum change necessary, he had a positive impact in producing a new and cheaper SoC using significantly less money and time than normal. This provided a less expensive chip for the new mono printers, thereby saving the company millions of dollars in future parts costs.

The concept of collaboration is also applicable here because one of the best ways to determine if and how a hardware change is going to affect firmware is to talk to firmware engineers. They are best-suited to determine the impact.

Returning to the golf metaphor, the golfer does want to have an impact, but he wants it where the ball flies straight down the fairway. He may not get a hole in one, but he will be headed in the right direction with fewer strokes. As you anticipate the impact, your product development will be in the right direction without wasting time in the rough.

> ☑ **Principle**
>
> 2.1.5 Anticipate the Impacts.

2.1.6. Design for Contingencies

Why do you carry insurance on your car (beside the fact that in many places the law requires it)? Why pay the insurance premium? Do you want to collect on it? Are you going to purposefully get into an accident so you can collect? No. But when you do get into an accident, you will be glad you have it. You are prepared for that contingency.

Figure 2.3: JetBlue flight 292 landing with the nose gear stuck sideward.
(Top photo is copyrighted by the submitter, Andrewmarino, commons.wikimedia.org/
wiki/Image:JetBlue292Landing.jpg. Reproduced with the permission.
Bottom two photos are in the public domain.)

On September 21, 2005, JetBlue flight 292 with 139 passengers took off from Burbank, California. Unfortunately, the plane's nose gear got stuck sideward. After circling Los Angeles for 3 hours to burn off fuel, the flight crew came in for a successful landing (msnbc.msn.com/id/9430871; foxnews.com/story/0,2933,170076,00.html). It was amazing that the nose gear did not collapse. It was rugged. It was designed for contingencies, although no one anticipated what the gear would be called upon to do. Figure 2.3 shows the sparks from the plane when landing and how the wheels were ground down.

Designing for contingencies means that you do what you can to prepare for problems that may appear.

One manager of a young hardware design team told me how his team had informed him that they had completed their design. The manager then said, "Six months from now, you are going to get the chip back and it won't turn on. What are you going to need to debug that chip?" The team went off, thought about it, and added some test and debug hooks.

When you are trying to get a chip to work, you will need to know what is going on inside. If you are using a software simulator, you have clear view of every internal signal and flip-flop. Similarly, if you are working with an in-circuit emulator or JTAG, you have a good view as to what is going on inside your design. But when you are trying to get firmware working on a physical chip mounted inside the product, visibility inside the device is very limited.

Visibility inside the chip can be provided to firmware by adding test and debug hooks in the device. Adding additional read/write access to internal flip-flops and signals gives firmware "peek-and-poke" capabilities. It is like having a basic logic analyzer built into the chip. These added capabilities cost a little in terms of space on the silicon and time required designing and verifying them, but this is similar to paying insurance. You hope you don't have to collect, but if there are problems, you will be very happy that your premiums have been paid.

Furthermore, test and debug hooks in the chip are not solely for diagnosing and working around defects in the hardware. They are also very useful for locating and identifying defects in the firmware.

> ☑ **Principle**
>
> 2.1.6 Design for Contingencies.

2.1.7. Plan Ahead

People who look to the future toward retirement prepare now by putting away money. Those who are short-sighted spend their whole paycheck without any thought for the future. Businesses that plan ahead will take action today to get them to where they want to be 3 to 5 years from now. They don't focus solely on maximizing this quarter's results. They do have to produce good numbers for this quarter, but they don't lose focus on the future.

Making decisions based solely on current effort and time constraints, without regard to its impact on the future, is to simply postpone corrective action until later when it will be difficult and expensive to fix.

Similarly, when designing embedded system products, look ahead and make good decisions today that will pay off in the future while not sacrificing the current product. Put a framework in the design that will allow new features and expansion to occur. Modularity, abstraction, and reuse are techniques that support planning ahead.

Returning to cell phones, the manufacturers regularly put out newer models having slightly different versions of hardware and firmware. They are able to accomplish this because they look ahead and develop a framework to support this capability.

Someone once scrawled on a white board, "There is never enough time to do it right, but there is always time to do it again." Obviously this is not desired behavior. By taking the time now to plan ahead and do it right, you will save time and money in the future when developing your next product.

☑   **Principle**

2.1.7 Plan Ahead.

2.2. Summary

Although it will not be possible for you to memorize the 300-plus best practices discussed in this book, you will find that all of them are covered by one or more of the seven principles presented in this chapter. In addition, you may come across situations that are not covered by a best practice in this book. In this case, following the fundamental concepts of these seven principles will help you to make the right decisions.

The next chapter will start our journey toward better chip designs by encouraging hardware and firmware engineers to collaborate.

CHAPTER 3

Collaboration

Successful projects are the result of well-integrated teams with people working toward a shared goal. While many teams are necessary, the hardware and firmware teams are central to the successful development of embedded systems products. However, due to the realities of their differing development processes, life cycles, organizational structures, vocabularies, and cultural backgrounds, hardware and firmware engineers often have difficulties working together while developing the product.

This chapter focuses on improving the ability for hardware and firmware engineers to work as one team and to collaborate with each other. I will begin by discussing the roles of team members and the first steps that should be taken when the project commences, and then I will talk about formal and informal collaboration activities.

While there will be challenges in working together, following these best practices can dramatically improve the project development effort.

3.1. First Steps

While the number of engineers and the level of their involvement on a given chip will vary throughout the product development life cycle, identifying all team members and introducing them to each other are necessary first steps.

3.1.1. Roles

Each organization has its own list of roles and responsibilities with respect to the hardware and firmware teams. Some roles require more than one person and some people are assigned more than one role. Let's consider some of the roles that have hardware/firmware collaboration responsibilities. You might be using different names for these roles in your organization but you should be able to understand the intent. Some of these roles have a best practice associated with them.

DOI: 10.1016/B978-1-85617-605-7.00005-8.

Traditional Roles

These roles are common in the industry. I describe some of them as they pertain to the development around the hardware/firmware interface.

- **System engineers:** These engineers work with the system as a whole, composed of both the hardware and firmware components. Organizationally, they may be with the hardware team, firmware team, or on their own team. While several positions exist at the system level, I want to point out two of them as follows:

  System architects: These engineers design the embedded system product from the top level, taking into consideration the hardware and software components. They should review the design with both hardware and firmware architects.

  System test developers: These engineers develop tests to test the system as a whole. They understand how the hardware and firmware components are supposed to work with each other. In many cases, these are firmware engineers since they also integrate and test their firmware on the hardware.

- **Hardware engineers:** These engineers have several roles in the design of the chips and boards. I want to point out four of these roles, which may be assigned to the same or different persons as follows:

  Specification writers: As part of writing the hardware specification documents, these engineers assure that approved requests from firmware engineers for changes and features are captured in the documents, and that appropriate firmware engineers have a chance to review any such documents.

  Hardware architects: These engineers design the board and chips from the top level. They should have their high-level designs reviewed by the firmware architects to assure that firmware can implement the required features.

  Front-end chip designers: These engineers design the front end of their respective block or blocks. They should stay in contact with the corresponding firmware engineers regarding designs, features, and issues.

  Test developers: As part of developing the tests for the blocks and chip, these engineers confer with firmware engineers to ensure that the tests being developed reflect the actual firmware usage of the chip.

- **Firmware engineers:** These engineers have several roles in the firmware development. I want to point out two of them as follows:

  Firmware architects: These engineers design the firmware for the product from the top level. They need to have their high-level designs reviewed by the hardware architects to assure that hardware has the necessary features to support the firmware design.

  Device-driver writers: These engineers write the device drivers for their respective blocks. They should be in contact with the corresponding hardware engineers early in the specification and design cycle to make sure that the blocks are designed properly.

Collaborative Roles

These roles are not traditional but aid in the collaborative effort between the hardware and firmware teams. The persons assigned to these roles may have other roles and there may be more than one person assigned to each role.

- **Best practice champion:** This person should be a member of the hardware team since most of the best practices have to be implemented in that domain. This person leads the way to promote, inform, and monitor the progress of team members with regards to carrying out the best practices. Since this is a leadership role (though it may be informal), this person should have the respect of colleagues. Since the best practices list is a living document, this person handles requests for additions, changes, and deletions of the best practices in the list.

☑ **Best Practice**

3.1.1 Designate a member of the hardware team as best practice champion.

- **Hardware ambassador:** This person's job is to have regular contact with the firmware team, informing them of progress and issues with respect to the chip development, and delivering documents for review. This person occasionally sits in on the firmware team's meetings and is a resource to the firmware team with respect to addressing any of their hardware questions and issues, or to direct them to the appropriate member of the hardware team.

☑ **Best Practice**

3.1.2 Designate a member of the hardware team as ambassador to the firmware team.

- **Firmware ambassador:** This person's job is to have regular contact with the hardware team to monitor their progress. This person occasionally sits in on the hardware team's meetings and is a resource to the hardware team with respect to addressing any of their firmware questions and issues or to directing them to the appropriate member of the firmware team.

☑   **Best Practice**

3.1.3 Designate a member of the firmware team as ambassador to the hardware team.

The details of these roles listed here are intentionally limited. Existing organizations will have their roles and respective responsibilities already in place. These roles and responsibilities may need to be modified to take on the additional hardware/firmware collaboration tasks outlined here.

3.1.2. Kick-off Activities

Once their roles have been assigned to team members, the next thing to do is to have a kick-off meeting with both the hardware and firmware teams present. The following is a list of agenda topics, some of which might require advance preparation and/or a post-meeting follow-up.

- Introduce the product.

    Highlight its marketing features.

    Discuss major product components including relevant industry standards.

    Review the development schedule, budget, resource margins, and risk mitigation.

- Introduce the various team members.

    Collect contact information including spheres of responsibilities.

    Designate points of contact.

    Identify each team's counterparts in the other team.

    Establish contact protocols.

    Distribute contact and responsibilities information.

- Discuss project mechanics.

   Collect a list of tools needed, especially for hardware/firmware collaboration.

   Determine appropriate project-specific email groups, databases, wikis, forums, and other communication tools.

   Set and distribute schedule of meetings.

☑ **Best Practice**

3.1.4 Hold a project kick-off meeting between hardware and firmware teams giving introductions and discussing schedules and procedures.

☑ **Best Practice**

3.1.5 Collect and distribute contact information and spheres of responsibility of hardware and firmware team members across both teams.

3.2. Formal Collaboration

In this section, I discuss formal collaboration strategies and benefits. In the next section, I discuss informal collaboration techniques.

Formal collaboration consists of activities that follow established procedures and processes. These are designed to assure that the right connections are made and that the right information is being exchanged.

3.2.1. Regular Meetings

Though not enjoyed by all, meetings keep the hardware and firmware teams working together smoothly. The frequency, scope, and attendees of the meetings will vary through the life cycle of the project. Table 3.1 lists several example meeting subject matters and corresponding attendees during the life cycle.

These are just a few examples. You will have other topics that need to be discussed.

Do not force a meeting every week if there is very little to accomplish. Let engineers stay at their desk and get some work done. When there is a topic that needs some focused discussion, bring in those appropriate engineers. Ambassadors can represent the rest of their team for the minor notes and discussions, and then take it back to the appropriate team members.

Table 3.1: Sample Meeting Topics and Attendees

Phase	Topics	Attendees
Initial high-level specification	Look at the list of features that marketing requires. Determine if and how these features will be supported. Determine the hardware and firmware components required to support the features.	System, hardware, and firmware architects. Ambassadors. Other experts as needed.
Detailed design of each block	Discuss what features each block will have and how firmware will use these features to implement the requirements. Review several use-case scenarios, including error handling. Discuss interactions with other blocks.	Hardware and firmware engineers of the block(s) under discussion. Architects and other block engineers as needed.
Block verification and test plans	Review the hardware test and verification plans for each block to ensure that it will be tested according to how firmware will use it.	Appropriate hardware and firmware engineers.
Hardware test and hardware/firmware integration	When real hardware becomes available, hardware engineers will be bringing up and testing the system and firmware engineers will be integrating firmware with the real hardware. Problems and issues will surface that need to be understood by all.	Ambassadors and appropriate hardware and firmware engineers.
System test for full operation and performance tuning	Address problems in getting the whole system to operate properly and with the targeted performance. These issues appear toward the end of the development cycle prior to product release.	Ambassadors and appropriate hardware and firmware engineers.

☑ **Best Practice**

3.2.1 Hold regular (weekly) meetings on relevant topics with appropriate firmware and hardware engineers in attendance.

Ideally, hardware and firmware engineers are within a short walking distance from each other. But in today's outsourced world of global development, engineers are often not in close proximity to the rest of their team members. They may be in different locations within one or two time zones. Or they may be halfway around the world. They could also be in different companies. These barriers make regular meetings difficult. Overcoming these barriers require extra efforts by all team members, which may include meeting in the early morning hours or into the evening. Fortunately today's technology provides many useful tools as follows:

- Telephone/VOIP conferences

- Video conferences

- Email discussions

- Forums/blogs/wikis

- Presentations via internet meetings

- Translation tools

- Airline travel

☑   **Best Practice**

3.2.2 Apply extra effort to meet when hardware and firmware teams are in different locations, such as using emails, teleconferencing, and other means.

3.2.2. Initial Firmware Support

Due to the fact that most of the hardware development effort occurs without the involvement of firmware engineers, the firmware engineers may not be fully aware of the current state of the hardware with regards to schedules of upcoming milestones and checkpoints. Hardware engineers, then, need to notify their firmware engineering counterparts of upcoming events requiring their assistance.

After the initial kick-off meeting, hardware engineers will be working on the initial high-level architectural design of the chip, performing basic system tradeoff analysis to balance power, performance, area, and cost. They need to make sure that the appropriate firmware engineers are involved in that process to avoid surprises. The firmware ambassador is in a good position to monitor activity to make sure involvement occurs at the right time.

📖   **Tales from the Trenches**

Along with other firmware engineers, I was invited to a meeting set up by the hardware team to review the overall plan for the design of a new chip for a next-generation printer family. The hardware engineers presented their proposal for the chip and the firmware engineers made their recommendations. The conversation revolved around which blocks should be in the chip and whether defects in other blocks were worth the risk to fix.

Some of the firmware team comments and requests surprised the hardware team in that they were not anticipated. At times, the discussion was intense. But the hardware team walked away with excellent input and an agreement by all parties; they adjusted their plans accordingly.

☑   **Best Practice**

3.2.3 Start collaboration between hardware and firmware engineers during the initial high-level hardware design phase.

As the hardware design moves from high-level specification toward block-specific details, firmware engineers need to stay involved. As specifications and test plans are written, they should be reviewed by the appropriate firmware engineers. The formal way to encourage this is to have firmware representation sign off on reviews and checkpoints throughout the product development life cycle. The firmware ambassador can help make sure the appropriate firmware engineers are involved for the reviews and signoffs. This will help keep the firmware team current during the hardware development.

☑   **Best Practice**

3.2.4 Make sure that the firmware team is represented in the overall design of the chip, the detailed designs of the blocks, and the plans for testing.

☑   **Best Practice**

3.2.5 Make sure that the firmware team is represented in reviews and signoffs of hardware checkpoints throughout the life cycle.

3.2.3. Co-Development Techniques

An inefficient way to develop an embedded systems product is serially—first the hardware and then the firmware. Unfortunately, in some companies this is still the way things are being done today. A more efficient manner is to do as much in parallel as possible. Co-development tools allow firmware to be developed and tested while the hardware is still being developed and simulated, even before the physical chips arrive back from the fab.

Co-development helps collaboration because it gets hardware and firmware engineers working together earlier than otherwise. Getting firmware to run on the developing chip becomes an added bonus with regard to the chip verification phase. Any hardware/firmware integration issues are discussed by both teams early on. Chip design problems discovered early can be corrected before it is too late. Co-development techniques include using legacy hardware, FPGAs, co-simulation, and virtual prototypes.

Legacy Hardware

This works well for chips (or blocks inside chips) that do not change much in the new design. Hardware engineers can design new boards that use the old chips, allowing the boards to be put into prototype products for testing. Device drivers for these old blocks have already been put to use and are thoroughly tested. When the new chips arrive, changes are made to accommodate the differences and development effort can continue.

The problem with using old hardware is that it will not have the new features. In some cases, firmware stubs can be used to emulate the new features. For first-generation products, of course, there are no old versions that can be used.

FPGAs

FPGA-based prototype boards allow device drivers to be developed for new blocks or modified versions of existing blocks. The firmware can run at speed on a real processor. Errors found in the blocks can be corrected and new versions can be downloaded into the FPGA within hours. In cases of large ASICs, several FPGAs may be required. FPGAs can also be paired with legacy hardware to reduce the need to support as much in the FPGAs. Multiple FPGAs or FPGAs paired with legacy hardware may require temporary address changes for registers until the physical chip arrives.

FPGAs do have limitations with regards to speed and size. (These limitations are shrinking as next-generation devices become available.) Resynthesizing RTL to fit in the same prototype boards can be difficult given fixed pin assignments and partitioning across multiple FPGAs. In addition, in some cases, RTL code written for ASICs is not necessarily usable for FPGAs, although this limitation is shrinking too.

Co-Simulation

Co-simulators allow simulated firmware to run on simulated processors controlling simulated hardware. This technique is possible without first fabricating any hardware. Errors discovered in the block or device driver can be corrected and the simulation can be run again. Co-simulation has the advantage of being able to monitor internal signals, waveforms, and registers that are otherwise hidden on a real chip. Even after chips are back from the fab, co-simulation can be used to duplicate problems found so that the internal signals can be inspected.

However, co-simulation requires software models of internal and external behavior. It takes hours to run a few milliseconds worth of activity, even with a substantial amount of computing power. This allows only a limited number of test cases to be run. In some cases simulations are accelerated by using C models parts not specifically being tested.

Virtual Prototypes

Co-simulators are slow because they simulate every gate at every clock edge. Virtual prototypes take shortcuts by skipping ahead, emulating in C or other techniques. For example, a count-down counter starting at 1000 and then asserting a signal at count 0, will not simulate all the gate changes going to 999, 998, 997, and so on. It figures out that after 1000 clock cycles, the signal will assert. It then waits until the rest of the system catches up to that point in time and then asserts the signal.

Virtual prototypes are completely software based, making it easy to deploy to developers in remote locations. Changes in the design can be made and re-deployed.

- - - ✆ - - - - - - ✆ - - -

Even though limitations exist in these various co-development techniques, the advantages are clearly apparent to spending the time and money on these activities. Many companies are developing tools to aid co-development. Gabe Moretti in "Juggling Jobs: Hardware/Software Co-Design," discusses several such tools. See also John Blyler, "Devil in the Details: Trends in ASIC Prototyping."

Co-development activities lend themselves to getting hardware and firmware teams to work together sooner. Chip design problems caught early enough will help avoid million-dollar respins. Firmware developed sooner will allow the product to get to market months earlier than would otherwise be the case. While there are definite benefits to co-development, there will still be the need to integrate firmware with real hardware to conduct system testing and to verify proper performance and behavior.

📖　**Tales from the Trenches**

Two of my fellow firmware engineers were tasked with writing a new USB device driver for a new USB block on a new ASIC. They were given this task during the design phase of the chip and were able to use co-development activities. They developed the device drivers on FPGA-based prototype boards; this was a first for our team. They refined the design of both the device driver and the block.

When the chips came back from the fab, the two team members were successful and completed the porting and testing on the actual chip in a relatively short period of time. These results clearly illustrated to us the benefits of co-development.

☑　**Best Practice**

3.2.6 Use co-development activities, such as virtual prototypes, FPGAs, co-simulation, and old hardware to get firmware engineers involved in developing code and finding and resolving problems before the physical chips arrive.

3.2.4. End-Game Hardware Support

After the chips arrive from the fab and are mounted onto boards, hardware engineers bring up the boards and chips to run their tests and verify basic functionality. They cannot test all aspects of the hardware at this stage because the complete firmware system is required to get the hardware fully functional. Once the basic tests are done, the hardware is given to the firmware team for integration with firmware. The hardware engineers often move on to the next project.

However, hardware engineers still need to keep in touch with firmware engineers to help them solve problems during system integration and test. This is somewhat ad hoc since the discovery of problems cannot be scheduled. When problems are found that firmware engineers cannot solve, hardware engineers may be required to help diagnose and resolve these problems. The hardware ambassador can help monitor which problems the firmware team is dealing with and can notify appropriate hardware engineers as necessary. As part of this process, hardware engineers will also document any problems in the chip design with a view to fixing them in a future version of the chip.

📖 **Tales from the Trenches**

As I mentioned regarding the Unity mono video block (see Section 1.6, Case Study), I encountered several defects in the block, many of which required help from the hardware engineer assigned to that block to diagnose and resolve.

He was very patient with me and did not take it personally every time I found another problem. He took it as a new challenge to be understood and solved, even though he was busy working on his next ASIC. His collaborative assistance was instrumental in helping me successfully get that block to work, not just for that printer, but also for several subsequent monochrome printers using the same ASIC.

☑ **Best Practice**

3.2.7 Provide hardware engineering support to firmware engineers through to the end of firmware development.

3.2.5. Documentation

Imperative to the smooth operation of a collaborative relationship between the hardware and firmware teams is the flow of important information, and in particular, all necessary hardware specifications and known hardware defects.

This is a one-way information exchange. Hardware specifications and defect lists are needed by firmware engineers in order to do their jobs. But firmware specifications and defect lists are not generally required by hardware engineers. This places the burden on the hardware team to provide a means for their firmware counterparts to get the desired information when needed.

In the case of hardware specifications, several methods of storage, distribution, and management are possible, depending on the needs of the organizations involved; for example:

- The firmware engineer may simply walk over or send an email to the hardware engineer that wrote the specification and ask for a paper or electronic copy.

- The hardware team may have a centralized storage server or website from whence firmware engineers can retrieve the desired document. (This server or website may require a password for each person requiring access.)

- A central person may be in charge of producing and numbering paper copies and requiring firmware engineers to sign for the copies they receive.

- The firmware team, who are part of one company, may submit a formal request for specific documents to the hardware team who are part of another company.

As we see, many different methods are possible, depending on security needs and confidentiality of the specifications.

☑   **Best Practice**

3.2.8 Establish a repository for the hardware team's high-level and detailed design documents and provide appropriate access to it for firmware engineers.

Documents, once completed, are not likely to change very much. Having said this, defects are likely to be discovered—and the corresponding documents updated—throughout the whole development life cycle, possibly even after the product has been released. Due to the nature of physical components, defects found in hardware are very difficult to fix as compared to defects found in firmware.

Defects discovered in the chip before being sent off to the fab have a possibility of being fixed. But once the chip design is "frozen in silicon," it is too late to make any changes. (FPGAs, of course, are much more flexible.) In such a case, the firmware team will hopefully be able to work around any problems so as to avoid million-dollar chip respins.

In order for firmware to work around the chip's defects, the firmware team needs to be aware of all such defects that could possibly impact them. Therefore, the hardware team needs to provide a way to convey this information to the firmware team. Ideally this would be in some online, searchable database, especially for teams that are remotely located from one another. Again, depending on the security and confidentiality needs, various implementations are possible.

☑ **Best Practice**

3.2.9 Maintain a repository of chip defects that firmware engineers can easily access.

Once firmware engineers have examined the chip defect repository for pertinent defects, they may not see a need to go back and look again. So when hardware engineers discover a new defect, they need to "push" this information out to the appropriate firmware engineers to notify them of the newly detected problem.

Defects may be as simple as an incorrect register address or bit location, which firmware can easily accommodate. Alternatively, defects may be more severe, requiring firmware to perform complicated steps to work around them. Or defects may be that some features are broken and firmware cannot use them.

Letting firmware engineers know about defects as they are discovered will minimize wasted time by firmware engineers battling against defects that hardware engineers already knew about.

📖 **Tales from the Trenches**

I was asked to join a team consisting of several hardware and firmware engineers to diagnose a printer ASIC that was having intermittent problems. After 2 months of effort, we determined that the problem was in a block where the IP was purchased from a third-party vendor. Once we collected enough data, the IP vendor recognized it as a problem that they had known about for several months.

They had not told us about the problem because the ASIC had been in use for 6 months with no apparent problems. But it was an intermittent corner case error that did not occur all the time. The strange behavior had been observed but it was thought to be due to a defect in a different block in the ASIC.

The IP vendor apologized and admitted that they should have notified us earlier. Had we been aware of it sooner, we would have saved several engineering months and tens of thousands of dollars. Fortunately, we were able to design and implement a firmware workaround to the problem.

☑ **Best Practice**

3.2.10 Notify all applicable firmware engineers of chip defects as they are identified.

The hardware team needs to notify the firmware team when they discover hardware defects that are too late to fix so that the firmware team can work around them. By comparison, the firmware team does not need to notify the hardware team of firmware defects because there is nothing that the hardware team can do in the hardware to fix such defects.

3.3. Informal Collaboration

Aside from the tasks and actions to foster formal collaboration, informal collaboration is just as important. I have spent many hours at the desks of hardware engineers, and they at mine, discussing various topics (including the latest movies and sports scores). This established a good working relationship that paid off during product development. Whenever I was stuck, it was easy to walk over to their desks, call them, or email them with a few questions.

Someone once told me that 75% of the engineers are introverts. (A study by Luiz Capretz shows 61%.) It is true that, in many cases, engineers are content to stay put at their computer working away, designing logic, writing code, and solving problems. Initiating a conversation with someone else may be viewed as a chore, but it needs to happen. Depending on the personalities involved, the firmware engineer might be an extrovert while their hardware counterpart is an introvert, or vice versa. So it may be that one will initiate more conversations than the other. Managers can also play a role to ensure that conversations are happening.

3.3.1. Formal Organizational Structure

The informal nature that I have described above works very well in informally structured companies, even if the hardware and firmware teams are in different organizations. However, in many companies there is a very structured process where one must go up one management chain and down the other side to get a message to other engineers. I have had to operate in such circumstances and solving problems in a timely fashion is difficult.

Imagine the following real-world conversation (paraphrased) that actually took place between myself and a hardware engineer had we been required to go up and down the management chain.

Me: "I put the block in reverse mode and I can't get it to work. This is how it is supposed to work, right?" (Accompanied by a lot of hand-waving in the air.)

Him: "No, it doesn't work like that, it works like this." (More hand-waving in the air.)

Me: "How can it work like that? It is missing some information."

Him: "There is a register with that information."

Me: "What register?"

Him: "The line-size register."

Me: "Oh, that one? I didn't know it was being used in this case."

This type of dialog is very interactive. It cannot be done by writing an email with all the questions because the next question depends on the answer of the previous question. When difficult problems exist, it is critical to pull together all pertinent engineers to solve them quickly.

In some cases, however, the organizational structure must be accommodated. A few techniques that might help follow:

- Use email and include all appropriate managers on both teams.

- Write the email yourself but have your manager send it.

- Visit with each manager explaining how direct contact is critical for the success of the project.

- Appoint a well-respected but capable senior engineer to be a liaison.

- Accompany the managers as they do the talking, providing clarification and details as necessary.

- If approved, contact the other engineer directly but be sure to write up a report and send it to the relevant managers.

☑ **Best Practice**

3.3.1 Build bridges between teams to promote informal collaboration between hardware and firmware engineers.

3.3.2. Hardware Engineers' Initiative

As hardware engineers go through the specification and design process, there will be times when they are faced with design options or changes that could impact firmware. Not only should hardware engineers be aware of how much firmware might need to change, but they also need to be aware of how many firmware engineers are impacted. If the number of firmware engineers writing device drivers for the block is small (such as a custom ASIC to be used by one company), then consult with those firmware engineers with regard to the proposed changes. If there are many firmware engineers (such as for an ASSP used by many companies), then changes in the block will have a much greater impact and will affect many firmware engineers and device drivers. All firmware engineers cannot be consulted, but a representative number of them should be to obtain their input.

📖   **Tales from the Trenches**

One of my co-workers came to me with a stalled printer, which was leaving paper stopped inside. Upon investigation, I found a race condition when an interrupt occurred from a CAN block. An incoming CAN packet was slow getting to memory and the device driver missed it. I found a firmware workaround to detect and wait for the slow packet, but I also made a request to the hardware team to fix the race condition.

The hardware engineer assigned to that block determined that the fix required running a signal from one side of the silicon die to the other, which would have created routing and timing risks. She came to me and explained what would have to occur in the chip to meet my request. I could see that it would have added unnecessary complexity and risk to the block, especially since I had a workaround in firmware that was very robust and not complex. Based on this, I dropped my request for that fix.

☑   **Best Practice**

3.3.2 Consult with firmware engineers when contemplating changes to the hardware/firmware interface.

3.3.3. Firmware Engineers' Initiative

While the hardware engineers are busy doing the design work, the firmware engineers are typically working on some other project until the new project's hardware becomes available. However, firmware engineers need to take the initiative to visit with their corresponding hardware counterparts to monitor progress, discuss how each block will be used, and consider design options. It is while the hardware is still in the design cycle (or sooner) that the firmware engineers should discuss possible design enhancements, features, and other changes they would like to see.

☑   **Best Practice**

3.3.3 Firmware: Initiate contact with the hardware engineer early in the design of the block to discuss the block, its device driver, and their interactions.

If a firmware engineer has been through a design cycle already and has experience in the types of problems encountered, that engineer is in a good position to request possible test and debug hooks that would make sense to add to the design of the block. Chapter 11, Hooks, lists several ideas for test and debug hooks that might give the firmware engineer ideas on what to request.

☑ **Best Practice**

3.3.4 Firmware: Discuss with hardware engineers possible test and debug hooks to be added to the blocks that would assist firmware development. Review the best practices in the test and debug hook section for ideas.

As firmware engineers design their code, they may come across cumbersome and difficult interactions that are required to get the code to work on the hardware. For example, a register containing both interrupt bits and configuration bits require special handling to avoid inadvertent "acking" (acknowledging) of interrupts or changing configurations. Another example is requiring a sequence of register reads and writes to access each word in an internal buffer. Talk to the hardware engineers about the problems and see if a better solution can be designed.

☑ **Best Practice**

3.3.5 Firmware: Work with the hardware engineer to find solutions to hardware/firmware interaction problems when they are discovered.

3.3.4. Collaborative Problem Solving

The firmware engineers are the ones who are primarily involved with integrating hardware and firmware together and conducting system tests using near-final hardware and firmware. During this phase, they will occasionally encounter problems that require help from the hardware engineers. These problems will typically come as one of four generalized types as follows:

1. The firmware is incorrect because of an incorrect assumption by the firmware engineers as to the operation(s) of the block.

2. The firmware is incorrect because of erroneous or inadequate hardware documentation.

3. The firmware has a defect.

4. The hardware has a defect.

Determining the type of the problem can be a challenge, requiring effort from both hardware and firmware engineers. Sometimes it may take several guesses, but only after the root cause of the problem has been correctly identified can a solution be attempted.

For problems of the first two types, the documentation needs to be corrected or improved. Generally it is easy to fix these types of problems in firmware. Problems of the third type are also generally easy to fix in firmware. Problems of the fourth type are more challenging because the chip cannot be immediately fixed (unless it is an FPGA). In order to continue using the chip, hardware or firmware workarounds must be put in place.

Determining the root cause of a defect in the chip is only half of the battle; deciding on a firmware workaround is the other half. Determining a firmware workaround may require help from hardware engineers because they are familiar with the chip and its capabilities and know what possible solutions might exist.

📕   **Tales from the Trenches**

While I was integrating the device driver with the Unity mono video block, I discovered a problem with a use case on the particular printer under development. The image, when printed on the back side of the paper, was shifted down by about a quarter of an inch (6 mm). Working with several hardware and firmware engineers, I came up with six possible resolutions to this problem, but all of them were ugly.

After studying the problem for a few days, a hardware engineer had the seed of an idea, and together, we came up with a seventh solution which was much, much better than the previous six. My device driver put the block into test mode, caused the block to think that paper was moving, stopped it after a quarter of an inch, then froze it until the real paper came, and then let it resume. It was complicated but it worked. The point is that it required both of our domain expertise to derive this solution.

☑   **Best Practice**

3.3.6 Involve both hardware and firmware engineers to determine the root cause of complicated defects and to then design a firmware workaround.

3.4. Summary

This chapter stresses the importance of having the hardware and firmware teams collaborate in the design and development of embedded system products. It discusses a few key roles, including the best practice champion and the hardware and firmware ambassadors. It also discusses several activities for formal and informal collaboration. In particular, it stresses the importance of informal collaboration and how it is vital to understanding the system, influencing the design, and solving difficult problems. Furthermore, it encourages the removal of barriers that hamper informal collaboration, including the ability for hardware and firmware engineers to talk directly to each other, whether face-to-face, or via phone call, email, and so on.

3.4.1. Supporting Principles

The concepts of this chapter support the principles of hardware/firmware interface design as follows:

1. **Collaborate on the Design:** The primary focus of this chapter was on this principle—the collaboration of hardware and firmware teams.

2. **Set and Adhere to Standards:** Having a best practice champion helps ensure that your best practices are understood and followed.

3. **Plan Ahead:** Firmware engineers who work early in the development life cycle with hardware engineers are planning ahead and preparing for firmware integration on real hardware.

The next chapter will discuss activities that help plan the design of the chip. Proper planning at the beginning of the project prepares the way for a smoother development cycle.

References

Blyler, John. Devil in the Details: Trends in ASIC Prototyping. *System-Level Design Community (blog archive)*, October 23, 2008. Available at: chipdesignmag.com/sld/blog/2008/10/23/devil-in-the-details-trends-in-asic-prototyping.

Capretz, Luiz F. Is There an Engineering Type? *World Transactions on Engineering and Technology Education* 1(2), 2002: 169–172.

Moretti, Gabe. Juggling Jobs: Hardware/Software Co-Design. *EDN*, March 4, 2004. Available at: edn.com/article/CA382778.html.

Planning

Once the hardware and firmware teams have been identified and have started collaborating, the next activity is to plan what the requirements and specifications of the chip should be. Thoughtful planning early in the project sets the stage for the development and integration of hardware and firmware components into a successful product.

This chapter focuses on various activities and guidelines used to plan the requirements and specifications of the next chip to be developed. Planning involves looking back into the past at previous projects to carry forward good aspects and correct bad aspects. It involves looking forward into the future to determine the desired direction. And it involves looking sideward at other teams operating on similar projects in parallel to leverage and collaborate on the projects.

A long-term goal and direction for the product line helps determine the few steps that need to be taken for this particular chip. The long-term goal may change by the time you are ready to start on the next chip but unless the change was drastic, you will be headed in the right general direction.

4.1. Industry Standards

Many standards exist in the industry for a wide variety of interface protocols and data formats. Some examples include USB, PCI, TCP/IP, I^2C, JPEG, and MP3, each of which serves different needs. Those that are used in a particular application have supporting blocks placed into chips.

Often hardware architects and engineers wrestle with the decision of if and how to implement industry standards. Should a new interface or format be designed? Or should an existing standard be used? If so, to what extent should the standard be implemented? Here are a few points that will aid in the decision process.

DOI: 10.1016/B978-1-85617-605-7.00006-X.

4.1.1. Existing Standards

Existing industry standards have many advantages:

- The design is completed, tested, debugged, and documented.

- Hardware, IP, software, device drivers, and other components are available "off the shelf."

- Debuggers, sniffers, analyzers, documentation, and other support tools already exist.

- Fewer engineering resources are required to implement them.

- Expertise exists and is available.

Not only does using an industry standard provide benefit to engineers implementing the standard, but it also benefits other engineers, both hardware and firmware, who use that standard in later stages of the product development. Experience has shown that using standard protocols and formats saves many engineering months during implementation, development, testing, and debugging. The time spent in a learning curve is avoided when other engineers know the standard. And if they don't, books are already written that they can learn from.

The development process flows smoother when standards are used, just like driving a car. Traffic flows smoother when drivers stay on their side of the road and stop at red lights. Drivers who don't follow those standards literally run into problems.

Even though there are some good reasons to design something new, if possible, use an industry standard.

☑   **Best Practice**

4.1.1 Use existing industry standards where possible.

Industry standards are documented and formalized by a standards body. However, many de facto standards and conventions are in use. Many are in place because of market dominance by a product that others emulate, such as the "AT" syntax first put in Hayes modems. Following de facto standards increases the ability to leverage existing work, increases interoperability, and increases success in the marketplace.

☑   **Best Practice**

4.1.2 Use a de facto standard, if one exists, in the absence of an official standard.

Some standard blocks go so far as to have an official or de facto standard for its firmware interface in the layout, order, and position of its registers and bits. Many device drivers know how to deal with an EHCI-compliant USB host controller. (While there are standards for USB hosts, there are not for USB devices.) Standard blocks with standard register interfaces speed up development. Device drivers can generally be purchased for standard hardware. If there is not an exact fit, new device drivers can be highly leveraged from existing ones.

4.1.2. Implementing the Standard

Once a standard has been selected, the question is still asked as to how much of it should be implemented in the block. The degree of implementation falls into one of these four options:

- **Full standard:** In a full implementation of the standard, the block can do anything as specified by the standard, even though not all of its functionality is planned to be used in the target product. However, if the plan changes, a fully implemented block will allow changing how the block is used. An example standard is RS-232 and a full implementation will have support for hardware handshaking.

- **Standard subset of the standard:** Some standards allow and specify how a portion of the standard can be implemented. This permits partial implementation to reduce the silicon space or pins needed when the additional functionality is not needed. An example of a standard subset is an RS-232 block without support for hardware handshaking.

- **Non-standard subset of the standard:** A non-standard subset is when a portion of the standard is implemented that is not specified by the standard. Engineers implementing the block decide what portions to implement. This has the advantage of being able to implement and use a very specific portion. An example of a non-standard subset might be an RS-232 block that can only transmit but not receive.

- **Derivation of the standard:** A derivation of the standard might be implemented if some things need to be altered to meet certain design goals. Starting with a standard and then altering it may be better than starting with a whole design from scratch. An example derivation of the standard might be an RS-232 block that deals with 10-bit words instead of 8.

To take full advantage of compliance to a standard, blocks should be implemented using the full standard or a standard subset. Implementing a non-standard subset or a derivation is not recommended and could cause problems. There are valid reasons for doing so which are discussed in Section 4.1.3, Deviations or New Creations. But the following are reasons why the design should comply with the full standard or a standard subset:

- **Standard device drivers:** Standard device drivers are written assuming that the full standard is implemented in the chip. Even though some features are not being used, the device driver might access the unused portion as part of its normal startup tasks before it is aware of which portions to use or not use during normal operation. Using a standard device driver has the obvious benefit of being already written and tested. Standard subsets are also well known and device drivers exist which can support that as well. Depending on the block and the device driver, a particular version of a device driver may be able to support both the full standard and the standard subset. If the block implemented a non-standard subset or a derivation, device drivers need to likewise be modified. This requires implementing a new device driver or modifying an existing one, both of which are prone to introducing defects and causing delays.

- **Standard tests and tools:** Many standard blocks and device drivers already have test suites and development tools available on the market. Using what is already available aids in testing and developing designs for industry standards. Non-standard subsets and derivations will require that test cases be modified, rewritten, added, and deleted. It also forces new development tools to be developed, modified, and maintained. Again, this adds more time to the schedule and risks not being as thorough.

- **Change in intended usage:** Implementing the full standard leaves open the option of using any part of that standard. It may be that only certain portions of the standard are planned for the target or future products. However, it is not uncommon for plans to change due to product requirement changes, to provide necessary performance improvement, to solve problems encountered, or put in unplanned new products. Implementing a standard subset still uses standard device drivers, tests, and tools, but limit the options if changes in the plan are needed.

Aside from intentional changes to a standard, there are unintentional changes (defects) when the block was not implemented correctly. Or the changes are intentional, either to save time or gates, but the impact was not well understood, creating problems later.

> 📖 **Tales from the Trenches**
>
> Tale 1: A standard I²C block in our ASIC was implemented with only the byte-transfer mode. Block-transfer mode was not implemented, which was fine at first. But later more data needed to be transferred and it had to be done slowly, 1 byte at a time, resulting in performance problems. In the next version of the block, block-transfer mode was added in.
>
> Tale 2: Someone in another company told me of a configuration register hardcoded to a specific IRQ. It worked fine in the target product but had a conflict when the chip was put in a new product.
>
> Tale 3: One of our ASICs had a JPEG decompressor block that did not respond per the standard when it saw a certain marker in the compressed data. The workaround was to have the device driver go through the compressed data, hunt for that marker, and change it to a different marker. The decompressor was fixed for the next ASIC.

> ☑ **Best Practice**
>
> 4.1.3 Implement a standard exactly to the specifications of the standard.

> ☑ **Best Practice**
>
> 4.1.4 Implement the full standard or a standard subset of the standard.

4.1.3. Derivations or New Creations

As much as it would be desirable, there is not always an industry standard that fits the design requirements of the project at hand. This leaves two options, deriving from an existing industry standard or designing something new.

Taking an existing standard and deriving from it is an option if the exposure is limited. Making a USB device with deviations will not work when the device is expected to connect to many computers. Using deviations to the RS-232 standard to get just two components within the same system to talk to each other will work as long as other RS-232-based devices in the industry are not expected to connect in. In addition, deviations made could eliminate the possibility of using off-the-shelf IP, device drivers, development tools, and debuggers. If a standard with deviations is used, be sure to document all deviations to help those who know the standard be able to understand what changes were made. Explain the motivations and the reasoning why each change was made, and outline any risks that have been identified.

> ☑   **Best Practice**
>
> 4.1.5 Clearly document any deviations from a standard, including motivations, justifications, and risks for each deviation.

If it is not possible or practical to use an existing standard with deviations, then a new protocol or format needs to be designed that meets the requirements of the product. Another reason for developing a new protocol or format is to make it proprietary to protect new technologies. A new design makes it difficult for competitors to sniff, decode, break into, and understand.

Before starting on a new design, engineers need to do research to look for designs readily available that will suit the purpose. In other words, don't do what I did.

> 📖   **Tales from the Trenches**
>
> I needed to compress some printer raster data to reduce memory and bandwidth consumption. I was not (and am still not) an expert on data compression techniques. I knew a little about two or three other schemes but they did not meet my needs. So I "invented" a new algorithm. I ran some tests on it and discovered that it performed quite well, as long as it operated within certain parameters. For certain data patterns, it did not do as well and problems existed in the design. I then discovered industry standard compression schemes that worked better than mine did so I quit wasting my time on my design.

If nothing else can be found, only then start work on a new design.

4.2. Common Version

It is very common for firmware engineers to architect their modules to work on multiple versions of hardware. It solves the problem of first having to determine which version of the hardware is being used before knowing which version of the firmware to install. This task is easier for firmware engineers if the different versions of hardware are as much alike as possible.

Depending on how the hardware teams are organized, it may be that different teams are designing chips that use some of the same blocks. When putting together a new chip, look at other teams who may be using the same block for the latest version of each block. It may be that other teams have taken your earlier version and added enhancements and fixed defects. Picking up their latest version will save time and effort from repeating the same bug fixes and enhancements that they have already performed.

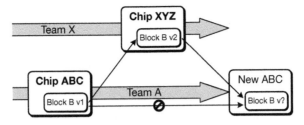

**Figure 4.1: Use the version of a block from the
neighboring team if it is more recent than the version
used by your team.**

Figure 4.1 illustrates how Team A made Chip ABC with Block B version 1. Then Team X took Block B, made some changes to make version 2, and used it in their Chip XYZ. When Team A is then ready to make New ABC, they should not use version 1 in their old chip, but use version 2 from Chip XYZ.

☑ **Best Practice**

4.2.1 Consult with other project teams to identify the latest version of the block to leverage for the next chip.

In some cases, firmware engineers are aware of later versions because they had to do the firmware for those versions and can point hardware engineers in that direction.

Once the latest version has been identified, the next question is to determine if and what new features and enhancements to add. Besides looking for requirements within your own team, consult with other partner teams that will be using the same block for requirements they might have. Also check with marketing to see what new features are needed that require support from the block.

☑ **Best Practice**

4.2.2 Consult with marketing and other partner teams to look into the near future for features that might be needed and add them to the block.

Once the requirements are identified, then the changes necessary to support those requirements need to be put into the block. By making changes to support other teams besides your own, you open to them the possibility of using your chip in their product, or using your block in their chip as is without further changes.

☑ **Best Practice**

4.2.3 Add in necessary changes to support new requirements and features when leveraging a common version block from one generation to the next.

The discussion has been with regards to commonality in context of whole blocks. Common versions also apply to sub-blocks, such as DMA controller and interrupt modules. It can even go so far as individual registers and how they are laid out.

Again, this ties in with providing a common and consistent interface for firmware. A firmware module written to handle DMA controller modules can be leveraged across all the device drivers provided that the various blocks in the chip instantiate the same IP for DMA. Many of the best practices in this book are geared toward providing this consistency. Chapter 9, Interrupts, is dedicated specifically to providing a consistent and common interrupt module for use by all blocks in all chips.

☑ **Best Practice**

4.2.4 Develop internal design standards for the style and format of register layout, register access, interrupt modules, DMA modules, and other common elements.

I will discuss more on this topic of a common version in Chapter 6, Superblock.

4.3. Compatibility

As a block is carried from one generation to the next, there will likely be new requirements and features that will be added in. Where possible, the new version of the block should be backward compatible with the old. This will allow a mix of old and new chips and device drivers. Old device drivers will work on both new and old chips. However, old device drivers are not aware of new features and therefore cannot take advantage of them in the new chip. New device drivers will be able to use the new features in the new chip but, when running on the old chip, will not try to use the new features and will still work with the old features.

☑ **Best Practice**

4.3.1 Make changes to the new version of a block to be backward compatible with the old version of firmware where possible.

4.3.1. Range of Backward and Forward Compatibility

The range of compatibility between versions of blocks is wide. At one extreme, changes to the bits and registers are very small such that the old firmware works without any changes. At the other extreme, everything changes; the register addresses and contents, the bit locations and meanings, the interrupts generated, and the block tasks. This forces a major overhaul, if not a complete rewrite from scratch, of the device driver. Typically though, changes from one block version to another are somewhere in between.

Even between one version and the next, there is a range of changes. Some changes have no firmware impact, some have major impact, and some are somewhere in between.

The following list indicates various types of changes with regards to its impact to firmware. It is in approximate order with the smallest impact on firmware at the top and the biggest impact on the bottom.

- **No impact:** Some changes can be made without causing a change in firmware. An example is an 8-bit register that contains an integer. If firmware is set up to read the 8-bit register as a 32-bit word, then the next version of the block could change the number of bits, such as making it a 12-bit register, and firmware will not need a change. Not only is this backward compatible, but it is forward compatible. It will work with other integer sizes (up to 32 bits).

- **Superset:** One version of the block may implement some bits from a superset while another version implements other bits from the same superset. For example, the old version supports bits A, B, and C, while the new version supports bits A, B, and D (where bit D is not in the same position that bit C was). Firmware is set up to support the superset, all four bits. Firmware does not need to know which version of the block it is running on; it will respond to any of the four bits at any time. On certain versions of the chip, certain bits will never be true. If the superset does not change in future versions, firmware supporting the superset does not need to change. But if more bits are added, then the firmware's superset would need to be updated.

- **Legacy mode:** Some block changes are designed so that when the new block powers up, it powers up in legacy mode, making it look like the old block. This allows old firmware to work on it. New firmware knows how to get it out of legacy mode and enable the new features.

- **Version number:** Sometimes firmware reads the chip version number to know which version of the block is in the chip, and can then operate accordingly. The down side of this is that version numbers of future chips are unknown to firmware, which forces firmware to be updated for every new version. This method is not forward compatible. It forces firmware to maintain a list of which chip versions match to which versions of the block.

- **Version clues:** In some cases, a version number may not be sufficient or available. Firmware can use other clues to determine the version. One way for firmware to determine which version is in the chip is for firmware to set a bit that exists in only one version. If the bit stays set, then it is the one version. If not, it is the other version. This technique will work, on future versions where the feature may or may not be implemented.

- **Incompatible:** The changes are too numerous and too drastic. It is better to write a new device driver from scratch.

The more the changes in the new version of the block fall near the top of this list, the greater the likelihood that firmware is easier to port and maintain. Analyze the changes that you are considering. Can the change be done differently so as to move it higher on this list?

☑ **Best Practice**

4.3.2 Minimize the impact on firmware when changes to a new version of the block cannot be completely backward compatible.

Chapter 6, Superblock, focuses on how to have variability between versions but still be high on this compatibility list.

4.3.2. Combinations of Old vs. New

Old versions of device drivers work on old versions of the block. And likewise, new versions of device drivers work on new versions of the block. But how well will mixed combinations of old and new work? It depends on how the changes in the block were made. Fewer problems with mixed combinations will arise by following the rules in this book and by making the versions as compatible as possible.

Table 4.1 illustrates what might happen with different combinations of old and new blocks and device drivers. This table discusses three types of blocks: an old block, a highly compatible new block, and an incompatible new block. And it discusses four types of device drivers: one to support just the old block, one to support just the compatible new block, one to support just the incompatible new block, and one to support both the old and the new blocks. The descriptions of each pairing are to be taken as relative generalities.

Table 4.1: Combinations of Old and New Blocks and Device Drivers

	Old Block	**Compatible New Block**	**Incompatible New Block**
Device driver for old block only	Works fine.	Will work fine. Block was designed to allow driver to be forward compatible, although it cannot take advantage of new features.	Will not work. Block design did not allow driver to be forward compatible.
Device driver for compatible new block only	It might work. The driver might be confused when new features do not work.	Works fine.	Not applicable.
Device driver for incompatible new block only	Will not work. Driver not backward compatible.	Not applicable.	Works fine.
Device driver for both old and new block	Works fine.	Works fine. Only a little code is required to handle version differences.	Works fine but a lot of code is required to handle version differences.

4.4. Defects

As much as we do not like it, defects are a part of embedded systems development. With regards to the hardware/firmware interface, the challenge is to minimize the impact that defects in the chip have on firmware. This section discusses planning activities with regards to documenting, fixing, and testing for defects.

4.4.1. Document Defects

Because of the nature of the hardware/firmware domains, defects in the chip impact firmware's ability to operate properly because a chip (excepting FPGAs) can require millions of dollars and months of delays to get fixed. This forces firmware engineers to attempt to modify the firmware to work around chip defects, and therefore, firmware engineers need to know the nature of defects in the chip. On the other hand, defects in firmware generally do not impact the chip because the firmware can more easily be fixed so hardware engineers do not need to know about firmware defects.

When chips are deployed to firmware engineers, information about any chip defects that firmware engineers might run into should also be given to the firmware engineers. Several pieces of information about the chip should be included:

- Behavior of the defect

- Conditions that will or may cause the defect to occur

- Impact of the defect

- Likelihood of the frequency of the defect

- Steps firmware should take to avoid or work around the defect

- List of versions of chips that contain the defect

☑   **Best Practice**

4.4.1 Document defects that exist in the chip, including description, chip version, how to reproduce, and workarounds.

Rarely Occurring Defects

There is a tendency to ignore rarely occurring defects because "they won't happen often enough to worry about." However, rare defects will always occur—eventually.

Always look for problems that might occur, no matter how rare they may seem. A classic case is when two asynchronous events happen to occur at the same time, causing a collision. Just because such an event is improbable does not make it impossible. Many of these types of problems appear while doing extended test runs near the end of the development cycle. Many units may run tests for hours while only one unit fails. These types of defects are very difficult to isolate and understand.

📖   **Tales from the Trenches**

One of our printers would occasionally hang. The control panel said it was working, but no pages came out. We didn't know if it was still processing a complex job or if it was really hung. Finally, after giving up, we would have to reboot the printer.

When I looked at the problem, I could see that my device driver had told the mono video block to print the page and was therefore waiting for the block to say it was done. But the block indicated that it was ready and waiting to be told to print. Somehow, the message to print got lost between the device driver and the block, thus hanging the printer with an appearance that it was working.

The hardware engineer and I dedicated several weeks to finding the root cause of this problem. He finally discovered that, on rare occasions, the device driver could set and clear the print bit without the block noticing it because a state machine in the block had been distracted by an asynchronous, external event. More than 99% of the time it worked fine, but not 100% of the time.

> The workaround was to have the device driver set the bit three times (write to the register three times) to guarantee that it was set long enough for the block to see it before the device driver cleared the bit.
>
> This workaround was useful for this given platform. However, given a different platform with different chips, processors, and clock speeds, setting the bit four times may be necessary. We fixed the block so that the device driver sets the bit and the block clears the bit when ready, completely eliminating the race condition.

Strive toward making something work 100% of the time, not 99%. That 1% will always occur. Looking for and eliminating such conditions will help save many hours of debugging time. If you cannot eliminate it, at least document it thoroughly so that firmware engineers are aware of it and might recognize it if they saw it.

A 1% occurrence is very hard to debug. As stated above, it might take many machines many hours to get one occurrence. There might not be enough information from that one occurrence to figure out what happened. This requires firmware engineers to make special firmware, deploy it, and run it for many hours to hopefully catch the defect in the act.

> ☑ **Best Practice**
>
> 4.4.2 Document all defects, even those deemed unlikely to occur and those for which cause and symptoms may be vague.

4.4.2. Fix Defects

When planning changes to make in the new chip, look at defects in the previous chip. Chip defects should be fixed, even if there are firmware workarounds for them. A correctly operating block is much better than a firmware workaround from a long-term maintenance and support point of view.

Not only does this apply to coding defects but also to design defects. In other words, can the design be changed to improve the hardware/firmware operation? If so, then consider implementing that change into the next generation of the block.

Sometimes there is an attitude that can be summarized as, "If firmware has a workaround, then we are not going to change the chip." That is a simplistic view. It assumes that all firmware workarounds have little risk or cost. But, on the other hand, it does have to be weighed against the risk of making the block design change "just to make it work nicer."

When planning for the next-generation chip, the high-level chip architects may not be aware of problems in existing blocks. They may note that the block is working in the current chip, and therefore it can be leveraged untouched into the new chip. Even if the block defects were brought to their attention, they might say that since firmware workarounds exist and are already in place, there is still no need to change the block. However, there is a risk of quality and a lack of features implicit with firmware workarounds.

The following are several reasons why firmware workarounds are not ideal in the long run.

- Some workaround function only because the block will be used in specific modes and conditions, which may be fine for the current product. But if the block were going to be used outside of those conditions in any future product, then the firmware workaround will not work.

- Some workarounds are fairly complex and require a deep knowledge of the firmware and block to understand it. After time passes, firmware engineers forget details and move on to other positions, leaving the workaround prone to having new errors introduced.

- Some workarounds can never guarantee 100% reliability.

- Firmware workarounds will never be as fast and responsive to events in the hardware.

- Hardware engineers making future changes and enhancements to the block may not know the defect or the basis under which the workaround functions. Making changes may cause problems.

On the other side of the complexity and risk of firmware workarounds is the complexity and risk of making the fix in the block. The complexity and risk on both sides should be weighed. If the firmware workaround is complex and the fix in the block is easy, then the block should be fixed. Conversely, if the firmware workaround is easy but fixing the block is risky, then the firmware workaround should be kept.

Firmware and hardware engineers should go over the block defects and firmware workarounds together to understand the risks and make decisions on what to fix and what not to fix. For those that do get fixed, be sure to notify appropriate firmware engineers so they can make necessary changes and take out any firmware workarounds.

All known defects should be documented. This serves to help remind hardware engineers the nature of the defect when they are ready to fix the block. It also serves to remind firmware engineers of the details as they support the firmware workarounds.

📖 **Tales from the Trenches**

After completing the mono video device driver for the Unity mono video block, I analyzed the code and discovered that more than 10% of the lines in the device driver were for workarounds. Because of the time required to first understand each and every problem and then come up with functional workarounds, I estimated that about half of my time developing the device driver was spent in dealing with the defects in the block. That is significant considering that the device driver took several months to develop.

I worked closely with the hardware engineer to fix all those defects in the next-generation chip. When the chip came back from the fab, I had the new device driver up and running in 3 days.

☑ **Best Practice**

4.4.3 Review the list of defects to select those that should be fixed on the next version of the chip.

4.4.3. Test Plan to Look for Defects

Typically a block can be used in many different ways. When preparing the test plan for a block, find out how firmware engineers intend to use the block and write the block tests accordingly. This may be difficult at first if firmware has not written a device driver for this block yet. But if previous versions of the block and device driver exist, it is easier to see how firmware uses the block.

Usage by firmware not only includes what bits are set in what registers and in what order the registers are programmed, but an overall flow of when, how often, and how much it is used. The block tests should maintain the same values, order, and steps that firmware uses where possible.

📖 **Tales from the Trenches**

Tale 1: A block was designed to process several chunks of memory, one chained after another. However, because simulation is slow, only one block was simulated and chaining was not tested. There was a defect in the chaining operation that was not caught by a test.

Tale 2: A block operation worked fine when tested in the simulator but not on real hardware. A study of both the device driver and the test case showed that both were writing the same values to the same registers. However, it was discovered that the device driver was programming the registers in a different order than the test case and a problem was exposed. The device driver had to use its order, so a firmware workaround was necessary.

> ☑   **Best Practice**
>
> 4.4.4 Develop and review hardware/firmware interface test plans with the firmware team to ensure that test cases for the block reflect actual firmware usage.

4.5. Analysis

While planning and architecting a new chip, several aspects must be analyzed to avoid problems later on.

4.5.1. Shared Pins

In order to maximize the usefulness of the chip among several products, it is desired to put as many blocks on the chip as possible, including blocks that require pins. However, that could create a chip that requires too many pins for the targeted package size. Increasing the package size is costly and undesired.

The package size can be kept smaller by having blocks share pins. Of course it cannot be done without paying attention to and watching out for usage conflict issues. Two different blocks cannot use the same pins at the same time so attention needs to be made as to when each block will need to use the shared pins. Here is a list of possible shared uses of pins.

- Block A uses the set of pins in Product Group A, while Block B uses the pins in Product Set B. This requires that Blocks A and B are mutually exclusive, that both will never be needed at the same time. If it is possible that a Product Set C could require both Blocks A and B, then the pins should not be shared.

- Block A is used in certain configurations of the product while Block B is used in other configurations of the same product. An example would be an I/O card slot that can either take a memory card or an I/O card. Block A is used if a memory card is installed and Block B if an I/O card is installed. And it is not possible to have both installed that would require both Blocks A and B to operate at the same time on the shared pins.

- Block A uses the pins only during bootup to configure other components in the system or to determine board or system it is installed on. Once that is done, Block A releases the pins and allows Block B to use them for normal operation.

- Block A uses the set of pins only when the chip is put in a special test mode during chip turn on. Then Block B is used during normal operation. However, there may be a conflict if the test mode is needed to troubleshoot a problem in normal operation.

This is an excellent area where hardware engineers should collaborate with the firmware engineers since they will also be aware of potential conflicts for shared pins.

☑ **Best Practice**

4.5.1 Avoid functional conflicts of shared pins by assigning them to separate pins if it is possible that they will be needed at the same time.

4.5.2. Buffer Management

The challenge with buffers in chips is to determine the right tradeoff between larger buffers with rich management control to improve system performance vs. smaller buffers with limited management control to reduce silicon space. Just as computers seem to never have enough hard disk space, so likewise on-chip buffer space never seems to be big enough.

Determining the right size of the buffers requires an analysis of the various use cases. A chip with a single UART could easily have its eight-byte buffer increased to 128 bytes with very little impact to silicon. Plus 128 bytes will greatly reduce the frequency of interrupts to firmware. But doubling DMA buffers from 128 to 256 bytes, especially considering there are several instantiations of DMA controllers in the chip, will take up too much silicon space. Not all DMA controllers need the same buffer size. Low-traffic DMA controllers can get away with less, such as 32 bytes. High-traffic controllers may need more, such as 512 bytes.

Besides buffer sizes, the amount of management control functions should be analyzed. A variety of interrupts based on buffer full, overflow, empty, timeouts, and other events provide flexibility to firmware. Being able to inspect buffer contents, find out how full the buffer is, and read its control registers will help troubleshoot many hardware/firmware integration problems.

☑ **Best Practice**

4.5.2 Analyze the design of each I/O block to ensure that it provides the proper buffer management support for status, control, interrupts, errors, and debug.

4.5.3. Hardware/Firmware Interactions

Some hardware/firmware interactions can be rather complex. Complexity is not good because it tends to be prone to bugs and hard to maintain. Asking firmware engineers what they consider to be complex interaction and what they suggest to improve it will help keep complex interactions minimized.

Table 4.2: Loading Two Tables

Address	Byte	Table A	Table B
0x00	0xA1	0xA	0x1
0x01	0xB2	0xB	0x2
0x02	0xC3	0xC	0x3
0x03	0xD4	0xD	0x4
0x04	0x?5	?	0x5
0x05	0x?6	?	0x6
0x06	0x?7	?	0x7
0x07	0x?8	?	0x8

To illustrate this discussion further, I will use as an example a case where multiple tables need to be loaded by firmware into the block. Each entry in the table is four-bit wide. Table A has four entries and Table B has eight entries. To make firmware more efficient, both tables are loaded at the same time by writing a byte with the lower four bits going to Table B and the upper four bits going into Table A. Table 4.2 illustrated the byte written for each address and how it will map into the two tables.

Table A should end up with 0xA, B, C, and D while Table B should end up with 0x1, 2, 3, 4, 5, 6, 7, and 8. However, for this example, Table A only looked at the lower two address bits, ignoring the third address bits. What happens then, is that when a byte is written to addresses 0x04-0x07, Table A will put the upper four bits into its address locations 0x00-0x03. So, after writing all eight bytes, Table A will end up with ?, ?, ?, and ?. This is an address aliasing problem.

If this were the way it was designed in the chip, then firmware would have to work around this problem. One solution, though messy, is to grab the upper four bits of the first four locations and put it in place of the upper four bits from any location. Listing 4.1 part X shows C code for a for()-loop that will do that.

Listing 4.1: Part X, complicated way to load the table. Part Y, a simpler way.

```
// Part X: Hard way to make sure Table A gets the right stuff.
for (idx=0; idx<8; idx++)
    writeReg (base+idx, (table[idx]&0x0F) | (table[idx&0x3]&0xF0));

// Part Y: Easy way to make sure Table A gets the right stuff.
for (idx=7; idx>=0; idx--)
    writeReg (base+idx, table[idx]);
```

But that requires excessive data manipulation. A simpler approach would be to load the table backward, causing Table A to end up with the right stuff. This is illustrated in Listing 4.1 part Y.

Both of these are possible firmware workarounds but, unless the firmware engineer knows of the problem and works around it, bugs could be introduced. This hardware/firmware interaction is more complex than it needs to be.

Here are two possible solutions to solve this in hardware. One is to have the two tables in different address ranges, such as moving Table A to the address range from 0x10 to 0x13 and using the lower four bits. This allows firmware to keep the two tables separate but it does require additional writes to the block, which would have an impact on large tables. The other option is to change the hardware to have the smaller table ignore writes that are outside of its range. This would allow firmware to safely load up both tables with one pass.

📖 **Tales from the Trenches**

This example actually occurred, except that there were four tables, each of different bit sizes, within a 32-bit word, and the biggest table had 2048 entries. I discovered the problem when I loaded up the tables and then read it back to see if it worked. It did not. The smaller tables were corrupted. After consulting with the hardware engineer, he discovered it was an address aliasing problem. He had the idea to work around it by having the device driver load the tables backward.

Although this specific example is not commonly used, the lesson here is to be aware of potential complex hardware/firmware interactions and consult with firmware engineers when in doubt.

☑ **Best Practice**

4.5.3 Keep interactions between the firmware and the block as simple as possible.

4.5.4. Analyzing Third-Party IP

Part of the planning for a new chip is determining if and which third-party IP should be used in the chip. Besides the strictly hardware-related check items, such as what internal bus or what silicon process type it is designed for, there are firmware-related items that should be taken into consideration. Here are a few.

- Have device drivers been written for that block's IP already? If not, there is a risk that there are still undiscovered defects that will appear when firmware tries to use it.

- If device drivers have already been written, are they available for the target processor and OS that it will go in to? If not, will source code be made available to support your own team in writing them?

- Does the IP vendor have a strong technical support team to assist in firmware issues? Is there access to the original designers of the block IP to assist the firmware team on difficult integration issues?

- Are the style and layout of registers and bits in the block's IP similar to other blocks going into that chip? Is the style and format of interrupts also similar? If not, it could add complexity and confusion as the various device drivers work together.

☑   **Best Practice**

4.5.4 Evaluate prior silicon history, the existence of device drivers, and strong technical support when purchasing IP from third-party vendors.

4.6. Postmortem

In *The Life of Reason*, George Santayana wrote, "Those who do not remember the past are condemned to repeat it." When planning the next chip, look to previous versions of the chip for defects to be fixed, changes to be made, and features to be enhanced and added. Don't allow defects, like an occasional bus contention problem, to propagate across several versions of the chip without getting fixed.

☑   **Best Practice**

4.6.1 Review the postmortem notes from the previous chip during the specification phase of the new chip and apply appropriate changes to fix defects and add design enhancements.

After the product has been released to customers, bring the hardware and firmware engineers together in the same room for a postmortem, a discussion of the results of the design and implementation of the chip. This is for both good and bad things. By having both teams in the same room, they will help each other remember problems and details of events of the prior months. Here are some possible topics to discuss.

- What went well about the overall program and about each block? What did not?

- What defects are there in the chip that should be fixed in the next generation?

- How was the documentation? How can it be improved?

- How did the process go?

- Were the regular meetings useful? How could they be better?

- Were there problems with communications among engineers? How can it be improved?

- How did the hardware/firmware testing go? What testing holes were discovered? Were they fixed?

- Any other problems?

- What do you want to see happen again? What changes in process or design would you like to see made?

It should be stated at the beginning of the meeting that the comments are to be factual. It is not a time to berate or belittle anybody or their work. The comments should be brief and without jumping into detailed solutions to solve the problems. After the postmortem meeting, write up the notes and send it out to all for review. Then refer to them when undertaking follow-on chip designs.

☑ **Best Practice**

4.6.2 Conduct a postmortem review of the chip soon after product release.

4.7. Summary

The focus of this chapter was on the planning and specification activities that occur in preparation to start on a new chip.

When using an industry standard, implement it exactly to the standard. Seek to develop, use, and maintain a common version of the block IP. As changes are made in the design of the block, strive to make it as compatible as possible to the previous version. Study defects, look for them, eliminate them, and document them if not fixed. By following these and other concepts in this chapter in the planning of the new chip, subsequent development and integration efforts will be greatly improved.

4.7.1. Supporting Principles

The concepts of this chapter support the principles of hardware/firmware interface design as follows:

1. **Set and Adhere to Standards:** When using an industry standard, use it with exactness.

2. **Balance the Load:** Look for firmware workarounds used for previous chips and fix those defects in future chips to eliminate the workarounds.

3. **Design for Compatibility:** Strive to make future versions of the block fall higher within the compatibility range.

The next chapter comprises a discussion on documentation, the importance of it, the types of documents, and its content.

CHAPTER 5

Documentation

Proper documentation is the most important tool for collaborative development between hardware and firmware engineers. Firmware engineers need it to write device drivers for the blocks. Hardware engineers need it to convey their designs to others. Both sides use it as they develop their respective components. Quality documentation is essential for hardware and firmware engineers to do their jobs.

Lack of good documentation was the number-one complaint among the firmware engineers whom I interviewed for this book. The documentation is the primary source of information for firmware engineers as they develop and debug their code, but it tends to be inaccurate and incomplete. A few of the engineers interviewed told me that wrong documentation is worse than no documentation. No documentation basically means that firmware engineers cannot work. But with wrong documentation, they are working in the wrong direction with the wrong information, wasting time.

When hardware engineers get their chips back from fabrication and start testing them, they already know their blocks, and know what they are supposed to do. They have access to the source code, which reminds them of the locations of bits and registers and how the block is supposed to work. For portions that do not work as expected, they can refer to the source code to solve the problems. They might refer to their documentation, but are not dependent on it. This makes it difficult for them to validate the documentation for accuracy and completeness.

Without accurate and complete documentation, firmware engineers have difficulty doing their job. They generally do not have access to the chip's source file to refer to, and even if they did, they may not know how to read those files. Depending on the organization of the teams, firmware engineers may or may not have access to the hardware engineers. Documentation, therefore, is the best source of information for the chip, and must be as accurate and complete as possible.

In this chapter, I will discuss document management, reviews, and content. But first, I will discuss and define types of documents that I will be referring to.

5.1. Types

Each company has its own standards, conventions, styles, and procedures for documentation. They are called by different names, have different sets of contents, and have different procedures for archival and security. Specifying all aspects of documentation creation, management, and distribution is beyond the scope of this book. There are aspects of documentation that pertain to the hardware/firmware interface and those are discussed here.

Because of the variety of documentation types, styles, names, and organizations, I will define terms that I use in this book. Translate those names to fit your particular organization. And likewise, translate the best practices to fit your organization.

5.1.1. Level and Types of Documentation

These are the types of documents referred to in this book:

- **Chip level:** These documents discuss the chip as a whole, specifying which blocks are included, how the block are connected, and other chip-level details.

   Chip high-level specification: This document is relatively short and contains a high-level description of the chip and its purpose in the embedded product. It discusses which blocks are in the chip and how those blocks are set up or modified for that chip. This document is given to firmware engineers at the beginning of the chip design phase to allow them to review and comment on the architecture of the chip.

   Chip-level documentation: This document contains specifics that are at the chip level, not at the block level, such as chip-level interrupt and other global registers.

- **Block level:** These documents discuss each block within a chip. Ideally, these describe the block regardless of which chip it is instantiated in.

   Block-level documentation: This is the primary document that firmware engineers use. Unless otherwise specified, all discussions in this book about documentation refer to this one. It contains everything firmware engineers need to know to develop their components. Some companies call it "external reference specification" and others call it a "programmer's guide."

   Block unsupported specification: This contains unsupported information that may be useful when troubleshooting, diagnosing, and working around issues in the chips. It could include a list of test and debug registers, some state machine diagrams, and other possibly useful information. See Section 5.1.3, Supported vs. Unsupported Documentation, for more details.

Block test plan: This contains the test plan for testing the block. This is reviewed by firmware engineers to ensure that the test plan tests the block in terms of how the firmware will use the block. Firmware engineers review this once or twice during the life cycle of the block.

Block design specification: This contains any details that hardware engineers need for the design and implementation of the block. Generally, firmware engineers do not need access to this documentation. But if there is a difficult defect that firmware engineers are trying to diagnose and work around, they may need to look at this.

5.1.2. Chip-Level vs. Block-Level Documentation

Blocks are designed to be reused—to be instantiated in different chips. This encourages the design of the block to be independent of which chip it is instantiated in. The same should apply to the documentation; it should have very little, if any, chip-specific information.

When a block is instantiated within a chip, there will be chip-specific details about the block. That information should be in both the chip-level documentation and the block-level documentation. The chip-level documentation contains specific details about each block in the chip, and the block-level documentation contains specifics details of how it is instantiated in each chip. Except for the chip-specific details, the block-level documentation remains unchanged when the identical block is instantiated in a different chip. Figure 5.1 illustrates how chip-level documentation covers several blocks for one chip, while block-level documentation covers several chips for one block.

As illustrated, the JPEG compressor block exists in all chips. The parallel port block only exists up to the potato chip. USB 1.0 started in the chocolate chip and moved to 2.0 in the

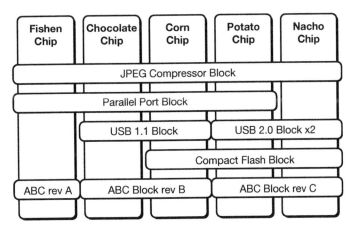

Figure 5.1: Blocks in use across several chips.

potato chip. And the compact flash block started in the corn chip. The ABC block is shown to be in all the chips, although there are three different versions.

The chips in Figure 5.1 could be sequential generations of the same chip over time, or they could be different families of chips being produced at the same time. For example, a high-end chip might have a parallel port block among others, while a low-end chip being designed at the same time might not.

Ideally, a block is implemented exactly the same way across all chips. Once firmware engineers have written the device driver, it will work on all chips that contain that block. However, that is not the case in the real world. Block designs change as they evolve, as they are enhanced, and as errors are discovered and corrected. But by documenting the revisions and in which chips they are used, confusion is minimized.

The chip-level documentation contains the chip-specific information about each block in the chip. The following list contains examples of some of those items:

1. List which blocks are instantiated in the chip, including blocks with multiple instantiations.

2. Global registers such as interrupts, power control, reset control, GPIO, and so on.

3. The base address of the chip.

4. For each instantiation of each block:

    •   Version of the block instantiated

    •   The address offset from the chip base address

    •   How the interrupt line (or lines) from the block are mapped into the chip-level interrupt module

    •   Priority levels on the internal bus

    •   The settings of customizable parameters used in the instantiation, such as buffer sizes and number of channels

    •   Mapping in the global power, reset, and other applicable registers that control this block

Table 5.1 illustrates an example table in the chip-level documentation that contains chip-specific information about each block in the chip.

Table 5.1: Example of Chip-Specific Implementation Details for Blocks in the Nacho Chip

Block	Rev	Base Address	Interrupt	Other Notes
JPEG Compressor	B	0xFEED0000	0x00000001	Look-ahead buffers are set up for 8 tiles.
USB 2.0 Copy 1	D	0xFEED4000	0x00000004	Support for USB OTG is not supported in this instantiation.
USB 2.0 Copy 2	D	0xFEED5000	0x00000008	Support for USB OTG is supported in this instantiation.
Compact Flash	B	0xFEED8000	0x00000010	No changes.
ABC	C	0xFEEDF00D	0x00000040	Only two of the five I/O lines were implemented. The auto feeder feature was added.

> ☑ **Best Practice**
>
> 5.1.1 Include in the chip documentation the specific details about each instantiated block including address offset, mapping of interrupt lines into global interrupt registers, and customizable parameter settings.

Most of the rest of the discussion in this chapter has to do with the block-level documentation. Since the block can be instantiated in multiple chips, the block-level documentation should be applicable for all chips, with just a section that contains chip-specific information. Section 5.4.3, History, will discuss more on putting chip-specific information in the block-level documentation.

5.1.3. Supported vs. Unsupported Documentation

The block documentation contains everything that firmware engineers need to know or may need to know to develop their device drivers. Companies who develop chips or IP to be sold to end customers distribute this document to those customers and third-party developers for their respective firmware teams to use to develop their versions of the device driver.

The block unsupported specification contains details are unsupported in that their behavior, locations, and existence are not guaranteed to remain the same in future versions of the chip. Therefore, device drivers should not depend on this functionality, and is only to be used to deal with issues. This document is intended for use only by the in-house firmware team.

Table 5.2: Differences between In-House Usage and Customer/Third-Party Usage

	Blocks for In-house Use Only	Blocks for Customer/Third-Party Use
Type of chip	Custom ASIC, SoC, and FPGA IP.	Standard ASSP, SoC, and FPGA IP.
Target product	To be used in company's own product.	To be sold to other companies for them to put in their products.
Firmware teams	One team located within the company (or contracted or outsourced).	Many other teams located in end-customer companies or third-party developer companies.
Number of platforms	Limited to just the one (or very few) processor and OS that the company is using in their product family. One device driver for each block is sufficient.	Used with a variety of processors and OSs. Each processor/OS combination will likely need its own device driver for each block.
Target products	Just for the company's own product family.	Used across several end-customers' own product families.
Distribution	Has both documents, the block documentation and the unsupported specification.	Has only the block documentation.

For chips that are to be sold to customers and third-party developers, only the block documentation is given to them, not the block unsupported specification. The company developing that chip may have its own in-house team to generate the first device driver and to verify functionality. Once they verify the chip, they can then sell it. If that in-house team discovers a defect in the chip that requires firmware to use a test and debug hook to work around the issue, then they send a notice to third-party developers with specific instructions on how to use it but with a warning to not depend on it for the next version of the chip. Only enough information is given to put in the workaround, not the whole unsupported specification document.

Table 5.2 compares and contrasts the differences between the in-house teams with access to both the block documentation and the unsupported specification, and the customer/third-party teams that only have access to the block documentation.

☑   **Best Practice**

5.1.2 Distribute the block documentation to all applicable firmware teams, whether located in-house or with end customers and third-party developers.

☑   **Best Practice**

5.1.3 Distribute the block unsupported specification only to in-house firmware teams.

Registers and bits listed in the block unsupported documentation exist in the register and bit space covered in the block documentation. In some cases it may be possible for firmware engineers to write device drivers that inadvertently access those registers and bits.

Firmware engineers generally assume that they can safely write either ones or zeros to bit positions listed as "unused." And they may write their code to take advantage of that assumption. If one of those unused positions is really an enable bit for some unsupported features, then it is not desirable that firmware inadvertently turn it on.

To avoid this situation, bit positions that have unsupported functionality must be so noted in the block documentation to alert firmware engineers to keep those positions set properly. It should not explain the purpose of those bits but simply something to the effect, "Use of this bit is unsupported and must be kept set to zero to avoid undesirable behavior," or "This bit is unsupported and may return a 1 when read, which should be ignored."

This note is needed for all unsupported bits that exist in supported registers, that is, registers that firmware needs to access for normal operation. It is generally unlikely that unsupported registers will be inadvertently accessed by normal-operating firmware, and therefore do not need to be mentioned with a warning in the block documentation, thus helping to keep hidden the existence and locations of unsupported registers.

☑ **Best Practice**

5.1.4 Document in the block documentation the unsupported bits in supported registers with a note to say that they are unsupported and must use zeros when writing and be ignored when reading.

5.2. Document Management

Several things must be done to manage and develop documents properly. This section will discuss a few of them.

5.2.1. Document Standards

Develop a standard in the format of the documentation, not only within the one block, but across all blocks in the chip and across all chips the organization develops. Standards apply to all aspects of the documentation, such as which sections it contains, the format of register maps, and reference and tutorials.

Firmware engineers have to write, support, and maintain device drivers across several blocks and chips. Consistency in the format makes it much easier for firmware engineers to get the needed information out of the document, which leads to fewer errors in the firmware.

☑ **Best Practice**

5.2.1 Develop documentation standards in content and format to be used across the whole block, across all the blocks in the chip, and across all chips produced by the organization.

5.2.2. When to Write

The block documentation should be written before implementing the block, at the beginning of the design phase and before writing code to implement the block. It forces hardware engineers to think about the interface and usage model of the block. And it gives firmware engineers a chance to review the design before it is committed.

If co-development is going to be done where firmware engineers can start writing the device driver and testing it before the chip is in silicon form, then the document has to be ready early and it has to be accurate.

☑ **Best Practice**

5.2.2 Write the block documentation at the beginning of the design phase of the block.

Unfortunately, writing the block documentation is not simply a one-time event. What is finally implemented is not exactly what was originally specified in the first version of the documentation. Changes are made due to many reasons.

- Design is an iterative process. Problems with the original intent will cause a change in design. More problems cause more iteration until a workable design is in place.

- Better ways of implementation will cause more iteration in the design.

- When implementing the design in RTL, the hardware engineer does not refer to the documentation, causing some variation in the implementation.

- As the block is exercised in the simulator, problems may be found, resulting in more iteration.

- The original objectives for the block may change, requiring the block to change.

- Co-development activities with firmware could uncover more problems requiring more changes.

- The chips being used during development are FPGAs or other PLDs, allowing for frequent and quick changes in the design.

In order to keep the documentation current with the changes, engineers must make a point to keep the documentation updated as they're making changes to the design. If they don't make the change in the document as they are making the change in the design, they may forget that they made a change in the design or forget the exact details of the change. It requires extra work to keep the document updated during the development but it will pay off later.

☑ **Best Practice**

5.2.3 Update the documentation regularly as the design of the block changes.

Once the design of the block is frozen, engineers should make one final pass through the documentation to ensure that all the details have been updated properly. The engineers should do this as soon as possible while the details are still fresh in their minds.

☑ **Best Practice**

5.2.4 Review the documentation soon after the design is frozen to ensure accuracy and completeness and that it contains all design changes.

5.2.3. Accuracy

Most firmware engineers have had experiences with inaccurate documentation. If something does not make sense, it must be a documentation problem. If something in the block does not behave as expected, it must be a documentation problem. At least that is generally what they assume.

For custom chips, such as ASICs that stay in-house, the readership is small since there are few firmware engineers that use the chip. For standard products, such as ASSPs, where there are many potential customers, more rigor must be put in to writing the documentation and verifying its accuracy. If this is not done, there will be many disgruntled customers.

Since new blocks for a chip are generally leveraged from previous versions of that block or from other blocks that are similar, the documentation for the new block should also be leveraged from the block that it comes from. This helps reduce errors that can occur by typing the same thing twice.

☑ **Best Practice**

5.2.5 Use the documentation of a leveraged block as the baseline documentation for the new block.

Using a leveraged documentation is a great start but it is not perfect, especially as registers and bits are added, deleted, and moved around. Care must be taken to scrutinize the documentation to find details that need to be changed. The following are common documentation errors to watch out for.

- **Wrong addresses:** This typically happens on leveraged blocks. New features are added and some features deleted. Their corresponding registers are inserted and deleted, which occasionally causes some other registers to be shifted around. When dealing with similar functionality from other blocks, the writer often cuts and pastes the parts from the other block's documentation and forgets to adjust the addresses within the new block.

- **Wrong bit positions:** Likewise with bits being added, deleted, and shifted within a register. The writer needs to make sure all the changes make it into the documentation.

- **Wrong bit sense:** The documentation says the bit needs to be a one or a zero when it should be the other way around. This can happen when negative logic is involved, or when a new bit is added to disable something when bits usually enable something.

- **Old functions still listed:** A block was leveraged to a new chip and some functionality was removed. Or, a block was only partially implemented in a chip. The documentation needs to be updated to remove those functions.

- **New functions not listed:** A block was implemented in a chip with some new functions added. The documentation needs to be updated to add those new functions.

- **Missing information:** The documentation did not contain enough information needed to allow the firmware engineers to use the block properly.

☑ **Best Practice**

5.2.6 Correct common documentation errors such as wrong register address, wrong bit position, old functions still listed, new functions not listed, and missing information.

Conveying information from hardware engineers to firmware engineers is a very manual process. Hardware engineers write the documentation and then hand that to firmware engineers who then have to interpret it to write the firmware. Part of improving accuracy is to use unambiguous names.

When assigning names to registers, bits, and functions, watch out for obscurity and ambiguity. Look for alternate meanings of names that could be interpreted differently by some firmware engineers. Try to avoid names that mean something different in a different context.

Very clear descriptions of registers, bits, and functions help reduce ambiguity, especially with terms that can have several different interpretations.

For example, the term "reset" can have different meanings, especially when other words are added in front, such as a cold reset vs. warm reset, soft reset vs. hard reset, and synchronous vs. asynchronous reset. Describe in detail what each one means and how they differ.

☑ **Best Practice**

5.2.7 Reduce obscurity and ambiguity of registers, bits, and functions by using clear names and descriptions.

5.3. Reviews

Firmware and hardware engineers conduct a "computerized review" of their code simply by compiling or synthesizing their code and then running test suites. If the compilation/synthesis or a test suite fails, there is a problem in the code. However, there is no "computerized review" available to verify accurate syntax, details, and completeness with regard to documentation. Thus, an important aspect of writing documentation is to have it reviewed.

Since this book focuses on improving collaboration between hardware and firmware engineers, this next section will discuss when reviews should occur and the responsibilities of firmware engineers with regards to reviewing the hardware documents written by hardware engineers.

5.3.1. When to Review

Firmware engineers have a better chance to positively influence the design of hardware when they are participating early in the design while the design is being worked on.

As stated earlier, the documentation should be done at the beginning of the design phase. After the document is written, it should be distributed to appropriate firmware engineers for review.

☑   **Best Practice**

5.3.1 Distribute the documentation to firmware engineers for the initial review after it is written at the beginning of the design phase.

Feedback from the initial review is likely to result in changes to the documentation. After feedback from all the reviewers has been incorporated into the document, it should be distributed again for a subsequent review to allow reviewers to comment on the changes made.

Throughout the life cycle of the block, other changes will be necessary.

- As the block is coded, it may become evident that changes in the design are necessary.

- As firmware engineers develop the firmware, they may discover missing or unclear sections that need to be clarified, or may have a need to change the design.

When changes in the documentation are significant, it should be re-distributed to firmware engineers for subsequent reviews.

☑   **Best Practice**

5.3.2 Distribute the documentation to firmware engineers for subsequent reviews as the documentation changes due to updates, corrections, or design changes throughout the life cycle of the block.

5.3.2. Tracking Documentation Changes

During the life of the documentation, changes will be made based on reviewers' comments as the block design changes, when more details are inserted, and when corrections are made. Reviewers (mainly firmware engineers but could include others) then need to read the new version of the documentation and be familiar with the changes.

However, reviewers are busy (or lazy) and do not have the time (or patience) to read through every version of the document. Any help that can be given to indicate where changes were made since the last version will help reviewers quickly find and understand the changes. There are several ways of doing this:

- **Change tracking tool:** Turn on the change tracking tool in the word processor. This will automatically record where changes are made and allow reviewers to quickly jump to those locations in the documentation. If desired, minor editing changes such as a change in font and minor word changes could be eliminated, leaving behind more pertinent changes to be reviewed.

- **Electronic document compare:** Use a word processor or other such tool to compare the new with the older version of the document. This will generate a list of differences and provide a way to quickly find where changes were made. This one is useful in case you forgot to turn on the change tracking tool before you started editing. It is also useful to compare the current document with any one of the several versions back.

- **Manual highlighting:** If the changes are few, use the word processor to manually highlight changes with a different color.

- **Return reviewers' comments:** After incorporating the comments from all reviewers, return to them their respective comments so they can quickly remind themselves what their comments were. This allows them to jump to the sections they commented on and see what changes were made. Their comments may have been handwritten on paper, on a marked up copy of the document, sent in an email, or edited straight into the document with the change tracking tool enabled.

The changes marked should only indicate the differences between the current and previous version of the documentation, not of prior versions. Once a version has been released for review, remove all markings before starting to make changes for the next version.

☑ **Best Practice**

5.3.3 Explicitly notate all changes in the documentation between current and previous versions distributed for reviews.

The changes discussed here are only between the current and previous versions of the documentation. A history of document changes helps keep track of changes across multiple versions and is discussed later in Section 5.4.3, History.

5.3.3. *Firmware Engineers' Responsibilities Regarding Reviews*

Since documentation is an important communication tool that hardware engineers use to convey necessary information to firmware engineers, it is important that firmware engineers review the documentation to make sure the communication is clear. This section is addressed to firmware engineers.

When you (the firmware engineers) read a document for review, try to understand what the block is doing. Think about how you would access and control the block. Does it have everything you need? Do you understand everything that is discussed? This requires detailed reading and is not easily skimmed over.

As you are reading it, write down any comments you have. If there is anything that you do not understand and have to ask the hardware engineer questions, that is something that is not clear in the document and needs to be corrected. If you see any errors or inconsistencies, note them. Look for and note any issues regarding the design, functionality, and capabilities of the block.

If you know some necessary detail that is not in the document, insert that detail. By the time the chip is ready for firmware, you may be off on a different project and somebody else would have to write the device driver for the block. Getting all the necessary details in the document will help whoever will be writing the device driver.

If you are reviewing an electronic copy that is markable, make changes and add comments to the document so that the changes and comments are highlighted and easy to find by the author. If using a paper copy, use a red pen or other color that will stand out to make it easy for the author to find changes and comments.

These documents are essentially the specifications of what the block will be and will do. There are so many details about a block that neither the firmware engineer nor hardware engineer will remember every detail. Not only does the document remind firmware engineers of necessary details, it also reminds hardware engineers of what they had agreed upon. It is as if the document becomes a contract between hardware and firmware engineers.

☑   **Best Practice**

5.3.4 Firmware: Review the block's documentation and provide feedback to the hardware
  engineers regarding issues on the design, functionality, and documentation.

When you get a document from hardware engineers to review, review it within a timely fashion, such as within a few days or a week. This will mean setting aside the current work you are focusing on. But it will be time well spent by catching and correcting problems early on.

The initial review of the document may take some time to read through. Subsequent reviews will not take as much time, especially if changes are highlighted. Even if, after reviewing a document, you have no comments, issues, or changes, still notify the authors that you reviewed the documentation and found no issues to report. This closes the loop with the authors, allowing them to finish up.

☑ **Best Practice**

5.3.5 Firmware: Review the block's documentation and respond to the hardware engineers in a timely fashion.

5.4. Content

As has been mentioned, the block documentation is the primary means by which firmware engineers learn the necessary details to know how to write the device driver to carry out the necessary tasks in the block. The rest of this chapter will go over many of the content elements that need to be covered in the documentation.

5.4.1. General Content

In general, the content that needs to be in the document includes the following:

- A detailed description of the block and each task

- Why and when each task should be used

- All registers and bits required to set up the block for each task

- The order in which registers should be written, if important

- Any restrictions that limit the valid conditions or values used

---

☑ **Best Practice**

5.4.1 Include detailed descriptions of the block that firmware engineers need or might need to know, such as details of its tasks, its registers and bits, and its limitations.

One way to help decide what to include in the documentation is to imagine taking ownership of the block, not knowing anything about it. Think about what you would need to know. In addition to the content mentioned above, think of other items that should be included in the document.

Aside from the documentation being necessary for firmware engineers, it will be useful for hardware engineers several months later. A few engineers have commented how the documentation they wrote helped them recall some of the details of the block months later.

Insert aspects that may seem obvious. What is obvious to you may not be obvious to firmware engineers, may not be obvious to you several months later, and may not be obvious to the next hardware engineer taking ownership of the block. Even the nomenclature and the terms used may need to be defined. The more clearly you document and define, the less likely there will be misinterpretation of the documentation.

☑ **Best Practice**

5.4.2 Include sufficient and clear information in the block documentation to allow others to take ownership of the block.

5.4.2. Sample Document Template

Appendix B is a sample template of block documentation. The example block being described is a bicycle controller to be used in an embedded, electrical-assisted bicycle. This block is completely made up. Any resemblance to any existing embedded bicycle controller is purely coincidental. This is not intended to be a complete and functional bicycle controller but rather is designed primarily to illustrate various points in this book. This template is also available online (publisher's website, elsevierdirect.com/companions/9781856176057; author's website, garystringham.com/hwfwbook).

Section B.1 of the template provides a brief introduction of the block.

Section B.1.1 in the template gives an overview. Section B.1.1.1 gives a system overview of the block's role in conjunction with other blocks on the chip and with other components in the system. Section B.1.1.2 presents an overview of the components within the block.

Before firmware engineers can understand the specifics of how the block works, they need to know the overall picture. Not having a high-level description can be compared to seeing a box full of nuts, bolts, springs, levers, and other parts and not being able to recognize that it is supposed to be a toaster. But by first stepping back and looking at a high-level description of the toaster as a whole, and understanding how it toasts bread, then it is easier to understand how to assemble the components to make a toaster that works.

The overview helps firmware engineers see and understand the big picture of how that block should operate, allowing them to understand the detailed registers and bits and how they should be used.

This overview section by itself is an ideal first document to give to firmware engineers for review, allowing them to get an overall picture before dealing with the register and bit details. Giving them this overview of the system as a whole may help uncover potential problems that could be corrected before the design progresses too far.

> ☑ **Best Practice**
>
> 5.4.3 Include in the documentation a top-down description of the block that describes its theory of operation, its function in the system, and its parts.

5.4.3. History

Section B.1.2 contains the history of the document (B.1.2.1), of the block (B.1.2.2), and of the chips in which the block was instantiated (B.1.2.3).

The document history (section B.1.2.1) captures changes made to the document, no matter if the design of the block changed or not. The document history only keeps track of document changes for the current version of the block, not previous versions of the block put in other chips.

Table 5.3 is an example of changes to the document for each release of the document. The marked changes discussed in Section 5.3.2, Tracking Documentation Changes, indicates changes only between the current and previously released version. Table 5.3 and template Table B1, summarize those changes for each of the released versions during the development of this version of the block.

Note that the list is in reverse chronological order with the newest version listed on top. This allows readers that have already read the document to more easily learn of the latest changes.

> ☑ **Best Practice**
>
> 5.4.4 Include in the block's documentation a document version history, indicating the various documentation releases and the changes made for each release.

Table 5.3: Example Table of Changes to a Document

Rev	Date	Changes	Who
3.3	13 May 08	Added section 4.3.6, which provides a tutorial of how to operate the block in double-rate mode. Changed the font styles in the examples. Made other minor editorial changes.	Bill E. Reeder
3.2	17 Mar 08	Modified sections 5.3–5.5 to reflect new registers added for bidirectional support.	Bob R. Wright
3.1	21 Dec 07	Incorporated comments throughout the document from all reviewers.	Bob R. Wright
3.0	23 Nov 07	Initial version of the document for version C of the block.	Bob R. Wright

The block history (section B.1.2.2 of the template) keeps track of changes to the block from one major version to another. Or in other words, what is different between the versions that were cast in silicon. This does not keep track of changes made to the design during the development phase, only how the design at the current stage in the development is different from the previous design cast in silicon.

This keeps track of only changes that affect or could affect firmware. Features added or deleted are noted, such as "added support for bidirectional mode." Defects fixed are also noted in case the firmware had to work around them. Detailed changes of the RTL files would be kept with the respective RTL files, such as "added three registers, two counters, four wires, a state machine, and some combinatorial logic to support bidirectional mode."

This keeps track of the version of the block, no matter what chips it is instantiated in. If version X has a feature, then all chips that instantiated version X will have that feature.

Table 5.4 and Table B2 are examples of how block versions are documented.

Again note how the chips are listed in reverse chronological order. The newest version is listed on top. This allows readers that are already familiar with the block to more easily learn of the latest changes.

☑   **Best Practice**

5.4.5 Include in the block's documentation a block version history, indicating changes made and defects fixed.

Ideally, the block documentation has no information about the chips the block is instantiated in. However, for logistical reasons, it may make sense to include brief chip information (Table B3 in the template) so that only the block documentation needs to be distributed to third-party device driver developers.

It could also be a useful place to document how this block was instantiated across several chips. Going to this one location is better than rounding up all the chip-level documentation of all the chips that the block was instantiated in. The problem is that information is now

Table 5.4: Example Table of Block Versions

Version	Changes
C	Added support for bidirectional mode. The auto-feeder feature was added. The internal buffer was increased from 2 kilobytes to 2 terabytes.
B	A heartbeat monitor was added along with a quadruple bypass to generate more pulses to the block head.
A	Original version.

Table 5.5: Example Chip-Specific Implementation for ABC Block

Chip	Rev	Base Address	Interrupt	Other Notes
Nacho	C	0xFEEDF00D	0x00000040	Only two of the five I/O lines were implemented.
Potato	C	0xB015E000	0x00000008	No changes.
Corn	B	0xB015E000	0x00000008	No changes.
Chocolate	B	0xB015E000	0x00000020	No changes.
Fishen	A	0x1DA40000	0x00000100	The second channel was not implemented.

duplicated in two places. A list of all blocks in a chip is listed in each chip-level document, as illustrated by Table 5.1 referring to the Nacho Chip column in Figure 5.1. A list of all chips the block is instantiated in is listed in each block-level document, as illustrated here by Table 5.5, referring to the ABC Block row in Figure 5.1. So care must be taken to ensure the data is correct in both locations if this approach is used.

☑ **Best Practice**

5.4.6 Include in the block's documentation a chip-specific history, indicating instantiation details for each chip, such as base address, interrupt mask, and supported I/O pins.

5.4.4. *Features and Assumptions*

Section B.1.3 in the template describes what the block will and will not do. Section B.1.3.1 lists the features that the block supports, or in other words, it is a list of its capabilities. Section B.1.3.2 lists features that the block does not support. These would be features that might be reasonable to assume that a block of this functionality might support but, in this design, it does not.

☑ **Best Practice**

5.4.7 Document the features that this block does and does not support.

The line between hardware and firmware can sometimes vary, with functionality in some designs being done in hardware and in other designs being done in firmware. The hardware engineers make assumptions as to what functionality the firmware will provide. Those assumptions should be listed so that firmware engineers are aware of it and are okay with it. Section B.1.3.3 contains those assumptions.

> ☑   **Best Practice**
>
> 5.4.8 Document the assumptions made of what firmware will do for this block.

Section B.1.4 is a list of other documentation that is relevant to the block and may be useful to the reader for more information. Possible documents in this list include the following:

- High-level documents that describe the system and its theory of operations

- Internal design specifications for this block

- Block specifications of other blocks that this block has to work with

- Specifications of other system components (e.g., displays, electromechanical devices, and plug-in devices)

- Documents detailing any standards that this block is abiding by

> ☑   **Best Practice**
>
> 5.4.9 Include a list of other documents to reference that may provide useful or necessary information for this block.

5.4.5. Reference and Tutorial

The document should have both a reference section and a tutorial section, which are sections B.2 and B.3, respectively, in the template.

The reference section has a list of all registers in the block, typically in address order. It describes each register and the bits and/or bit fields in that register. The tutorial section shows the steps of how to use those registers and bits to carry out a task.

Many technical documents are written as a reference, with detailed descriptions about each part. For example, the man pages for UNIX (and Linux and other variants) describe in great detail all the command-line commands in alphabetical order but do not describe very well how to use them together to carry out a task. On the other hand, books on writing UNIX shell scripts are written in tutorial style, explaining how to do various tasks, using command-line commands as necessary to accomplish the tasks.

> ☑   **Best Practice**
>
> 5.4.10 Provide both a reference section and a tutorial section in the block documentation.

Starting from Section 5.5, Registers, to the end of the chapter, the discussion goes into details of what the reference section should contain. This next little bit wraps up the rest of the content of the block documentation. This next part discusses the tutorial section, section B.3 in the template.

The tutorial section illustrates how to carry out a task. It shows what registers to write to and in what order. It typically gives examples.

■ Example

To perform the basic task:

- Write 0x123 in the ABC Control Register.

- Load the address in the Start Address Register.

- Set the Start bit (0x1) in the Start Register.

- Wait for the Task Complete Interrupt (0x4).

- Clear the Task Complete Interrupt by writing 0x4 to the Interrupt Status Register.

- Read the result from the Data Register.   ■

From this basic example, firmware engineers can figure out how to use the steps for similar variations. The steps in the variations would basically be identical but different values might be written in the control register, putting the block in different modes.

Other tasks that require different steps also belong in the tutorial section, such has how to abort the operation, how to handle errors, and how to resume normal operation. In this example, the abort procedure is described.

■ Example

To abort the operation:

- Set the Abort bit (0x8000) in the ABC Control Register.

- Wait for, then clear, the Abort Done Interrupt (0x20) in the Interrupt Register.

- Write 0x0 in the Count Register to empty the buffer.

- The block is now ready for a new task.   ■

> ☑   **Best Practice**
>
> 5.4.11 In the tutorial section, describe the steps necessary to carry out each type of task.

Note how the specific name of each bit and register is mentioned. These are the names of the respective bits and registers as outlined in the reference section. This ensures that the example is clear to the reader.

> ☑   **Best Practice**
>
> 5.4.12 Identify bit fields discussed in the tutorial section by register and bit-field name.

5.4.6. Glossary and Errata

Section B.4 of the template is a glossary of terms that may be unfamiliar or ambiguous to the reader. Remember that the primary readers of the block documentation are the firmware engineers. They use a different set of terms and vocabulary, so put in the glossary terms that may be common for you but not for them.

> ☑   **Best Practice**
>
> 5.4.13 Define terms that may be unfamiliar in a glossary section.

The block documentation specifies what the block is supposed to do. But defects do end up in silicon. Some modes may not work, some condition must be met, some action must take place first, or some values returned will be incorrect.

Ideally, chip defects are detected and fixed before the chip is made into silicon. Firmware engineers do not need to know about defects that are caught and corrected beforehand. But they do need to know about defects that are in silicon. Those defects are listed in an errata section in the block documentation (section B.5 in the sample template).

Some of those defects may have been known before the chip was cast into silicon but was deemed too risky to fix. Some defects may be discovered after the chip is back from fabrication while the hardware team is trying to turn it on. And other defects might not be discovered until late in the development cycle when the product is going through strenuous system testing.

No matter when or where those defects appear, they need to be put in the errata section when discovered.

Defects are chip-specific. Defects found in one chip will (should) be fixed in the next chip. The errata section will identify which chip contains which defects. This example shows a few defects.

■ Example

Nacho Chip:

- The block is supposed to be able to handle packet sizes of up to 255 bytes. But there is a defect at 255. So the max packet size that will work is 254. To work around the problem, break the packet up into two packets.

- The link mode is broken and cannot be used.

Chocolate Chip:

- The abort does not work properly if the last byte is 0x00. To work around this, hit the abort bit twice.

☑   **Best Practice**

5.4.14 Include an errata section, which describes where and how the block does not work as specified. Keep this updated, especially with defects found by firmware engineers.

5.5. Registers

The rest of this chapter on documentation is directed towards the reference section of the block documentation, or in other words, the registers and bits. This section is not just a matter of listing all registers and bits, but it must also include important little details which are often left out. These details are required to make this section complete, accurate, and useful for firmware engineers as they do their jobs.

In the document template, this is section B.2. Examples of the points discussed in the rest of this chapter are illustrated in no particular order in the template's section B.2.

5.5.1. Document Registers

List all firmware-accessible registers that exist in the block, even if it is unlikely that firmware engineers will need them. The time will come when they will need to access one or more of them to troubleshoot problems. Separate all registers into two groups, normal-use registers and test/debug registers.

Normal-use registers are those required to be accessed by the device driver in order for it to properly carry out its tasks and handle exception conditions. These registers should be thoroughly documented.

Test and debug registers are ones that would primarily be used by hardware engineers to test their block and to see internal conditions of the block. Since these registers are not expected to be used by firmware, the documentation requirements are not so stringent. The documentation can be brief explanations of what the registers do. If firmware engineers are trying to solve a problem, they can browse through this section and if something looks helpful, they can ask the hardware engineers for further details.

Depending on where the chip will be used, test and debug registers might be documented in the block unsupported documentation, as discussed earlier in Section 5.1.1, Level and Types of Documentation. If the test and debug registers are kept in the main block documentation, then it should be listed after all the normal-use register.

☑   **Best Practice**

5.5.1 Document all registers in the block, even test/debug registers.

5.5.2. Register Design Tools

A problem with documentation is its susceptibility to being inaccurate and out-of-date with the actual block. Registers and bits are modified in hardware but the documents are not updated. Documents are updated but firmware is not changed. Or typos are introduced along the way. Failure to catch these problems typically results in hours wasted on debugging that could and should have been avoided.

Design teams have attempted to solve this problem by using scripts to extract register information from hardware Verilog and VHDL files and converting them into firmware C header files. Others have extracted data from FrameMaker, XML, and CSV files and generated C and Verilog/VHDL files from those. These home-grown tools are limited in the information that they extract, they do not produce documentation, and they create a tool maintenance burden on the design team.

A few companies have produced tools to address that issue. This is a new niche market and there is no consensus on the name of that market or its tools. But I will use the name, "register design tools."

The key feature of these register design tools is the ability to keep pertinent hardware, firmware, testing, and documentation files in sync. They can also generate system modeling files.

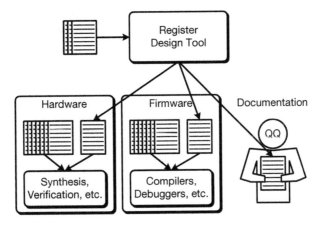

Figure 5.2: Register design tools generate hardware, firmware, and document files.

Register and bit specifications, including addresses and descriptions, are written in a strict format using an editor or a GUI front end. The register design tools then process the input files to generate a variety of hardware, firmware, verification, modeling, and documentation files. The generated hardware files are synthesized with other hardware design files and the generated firmware files are compiled with other firmware files. The documentation files are made available to technical publications and appropriate development engineers. The diagram in Figure 5.2 illustrates how the one set of register design files are processed through the register design tool to generate appropriate hardware, firmware, and document files.

When a change is needed, the input files are modified as appropriate and the tool regenerates all the hardware, firmware, and documentation files for re-synthesis, re-compile, and re-distribution. This avoids the arduous and error-prone task of manually updating all those files.

These tools are not meant to be used to develop all of the hardware or firmware design files. They at least produce include files that specify bit and register mappings. Each brand is different as to how much their tools can do.

I'll give an example of how these tools can be used. Listing 5.1 is a simple listing of an example input file, `monkey.rdt` (using a made-up suffix, .rdt) to the register design tool.

The register design tool processes `monkey.rdt` and generates `monkey.vh`, `monkey.h`, and `monkey.rtf`. Listing 5.2 shows two hardware files, the .vh as generated by the tool and the .v file as generated by hand.

Listing 5.3 shows two firmware files, the .h as generated by the tool and the .c as generated by hand.

Listing 5.1: Listing of the monkey input file for the register design tool.

```
// monkey.rdt
define register monkey_reg
    {
    address: 0x14
    description: This is the monkey register that does something.
    define bit some_bit
        {
        mask: 0x02
        type: readonly
        description: This bit is true when the state machine is busy.
        }
    define bit some_other_bit
        . . .
    . . .
    }
define register monkey_other_reg
    . . .
```

Listing 5.2: The hardware files for the monkey register.

```
// monkey.vh
// Generated by the Register Design Tool
reg [31:0] monkey_reg;
monkey_reg[1] = some_bit;

// monkey.v
`include "monkey.vh"
if(condition_a & condition_b) begin
    some_bit <= 1'b0;
end
```

Listing 5.3: The firmware files for the monkey register.

```
// monkey.h
// Generated by the Register Design Tool
#define MONKEY_REG_ADDR 0x14
#define SOME_BIT_MASK 0x02

/* monkey.c */
#include "monkey.h"
statusBit = readReg (MONKEY_REG_ADDR) & SOME_BIT_MASK;
```

The Monkey Block

This section describes the registers in the Monkey Block.

monkey_reg 0x14: This is the monkey register that does something.

This register contains the following bits:

- some_bit 0x02 Read-only: This bit is true when the state machine is busy.

- some_other_bit ...

Figure 5.3: The documentation file for the monkey block.

And Figure 5.3 shows how the documentation file might appear in a word processor.

If, for some reason, we need to move some_bit from 0x02 to 0x08, then `monkey.rdt` is modified accordingly, the file is re-processed by the register design tool to regenerate the .vh, .h, and .rtf. Then the hardware files are re-synthesized, the firmware files are re-compiled, and the document files re-distributed.

Most of these tools have ways of customizing the output files generated. This permits the user to control the contents and format of the generated files. This enables the use of these tools to generate files for use in co-simulators and virtual prototypes.

Although register design tools can capture and generate block documentation (among the other files), they cannot be used to generate all of the documentation necessary for a block. The block documentation generated fits only in the reference section (section B.2 of the document template). It contains only register and bit details, not overviews or tutorials. Even within the reference section, there are some bits and registers that will require more details and explanations than the register design tools can handle. The generated documentation will need to be hand-edited and put in with the rest of the block documentation. If the register design files are modified and the document file regenerated, care must be taken to make sure the same hand-edits are done. Though they do have limitations, register design tools are worth looking into.

As stated earlier, this market niche is new and there is no standard name by which it is called. So I will name specific brands and companies that are in this niche to help you find those tools. But recognize that by time you read this book, some of these companies may have been purchased, some may have closed their doors, and some new companies may have started. The following list contains register design tools that I am currently aware of:

- **1Team®-Genesis Registers** by Atrenta (atrenta.com/solutions/products/1team_genesis-registers.htm)

- **Bitwise™** by Duolog Technologies Ltd. (duolog.com/products/bitwise-register-management)

- **Blueprint™** by Denali Software (denali.com/en/products/blueprint.jsp)

- **csrCompiler™** by Semifore, Inc. (semifore.com/products)

- **IDesignSpec™** by Agnisys Inc. (agnisys.us/product/idesignspec.aspx)

- **SpectaReg™** by PDTi (spectareg.com)

☑ **Best Practice**

5.5.2 Use automated register design tools to generate register and bit documentation from block design files.

These tools have the added benefit in that they encourage interdisciplinary interactions between hardware and firmware engineers by improving communication between them, and allowing firmware engineers a chance to review the designs sooner in document format. This collaboration leads to better product development.

5.5.3. Table of Registers

At the beginning of the reference section is a table (Table B4 in the template) listing all the registers in the block. This provides a quick glance over the registers. It is listed in address order, the same order that they are listed in detail (section B.2.2 in the template).

The table has at least two columns, the address offset and the name of the register, as shown in Table 5.6. If desired, other columns can be included such as the page number where the detailed explanation resides.

If the block has many registers, it may also be beneficial to include another table with the registers listed in alphabetical order. This makes it easier to look up a register by name and then look at either address or page number to go find more details. (See Table B5.)

☑ **Best Practice**

5.5.3 Include table of registers in address order. Optionally include one in alphabetical order of the register names.

Table 5.6: Example Table of Registers

Address Offset	Register Name	Page
0x00000000	ID Version	10
0x00000004	Control	10
0x00000008	Interrupt Status	11
. . .		

5.5.4. *Register Details and Description*

The table of registers, as discussed in the previous section, simply lists the register name, address, and maybe other details. Following that table is a more detailed description of all the registers. The registers are listed in the detail section in address order.

For each of the registers, document the name of the register, a name that is a brief description of the register.

Along with the name, document the register's address offset relative to the base address of the block. In some systems, the chip may have a known base address so it would be possible to list the register's actual address here; but this is the block documentation, not the system documentation. This block documentation should be usable when the block is in a different chip with a different offset from the chip base address, or the chip may be put into a different system, causing the chip's base address to be different. Specifying register addresses as an offset from the block's base address allows firmware engineers to write the device driver in a more portable fashion to be used in different systems.

The following diagram is an example of a blank register map that will be used several times. This one documents a 32-bit register. It will be filled in as various points are discussed. This example register map shows that the register name is, "ABC Configuration Register," and that the register address offset from the block base is 0x0020.

			ABC Configuration Register – 0x0020					
	31 30 29 28	27 26 25 24	23 22 21 20	19 18 17 16	15 14 13 12	11 10 9 8	7 6 5 4	3 2 1 0

> ☑ **Best Practice**
>
> 5.5.4 Document the register name and its address offset.

Document any interactions that exist between registers. For example, if register A is used only if bit B in register C is turned on, document it. If register D must be written to before writing to register E, document it.

> 📖 **Tales from the Trenches**
>
> I was trying to get a sub-block of the Unity mono video block to work in a specific mode as outlined in the documentation. After several attempts to get it working, I went to the hardware engineer for help. (See the conversation between him and me in Section 3.3.1, Formal Organizational Structure.) After some discussion, I learned that the sub-block was

retrieving some information from a register that was not part of the sub-block, but was elsewhere in the block. My device driver had not written to that other register yet, so the sub-block was getting and using garbage data. The documentation for the sub-block did not indicate the usage of that other register so I did not know to write to it first. I corrected the device driver and successfully operated that sub-block in that mode.

☑   **Best Practice**

5.5.5 Document all interactions between registers.

For registers that contain numbers, document what the minimum and maximum values of those numbers are. Just because a bit field in a register uses six bits, it does not mean that the maximum value is 63. It could be 50. Specify what happens if firmware tries to write something outside of those boundaries.

If the register is a count of something, is it a one- or a zero-based count? (Does a value of n mean n or n+1 items?) What are the units of the count? System clock ticks? Milliseconds? Data transferred?

☑   **Best Practice**

5.5.6 Document the units of numbers in the registers, their minimum and maximum values, and the response for illegal values written to those registers.

Registers that contain address and count values are used to handle large chunks of data. As the block is processing the data, the block will change the address and count values. Usually, firmware simply writes those values to the registers then launches the task without needing to read those registers. But what will be returned if firmware does try to read from those registers while the block is processing the data? Will it be the address and byte count as originally written? Will it be the current address and byte count of where the block is currently processing data?

In this and all other cases where firmware writes values to registers that the block will change and modify, document what will be returned if firmware were to read those registers before the block's task starts processing, while the task is executing, and after the task is done.

> ☑ **Best Practice**
>
> 5.5.7 Document what will be returned when reading address and count registers, whether original values written by firmware, the changing values while the block is processing, or the end values after processing.

These last two best practices are illustrated in the template for the trip log buffer address and byte count registers, sections B.2.2.12 and B.2.2.13.

5.6. Bits

The previous sections discussed registers. In this section, I drill down deeper to discuss bits.

5.6.1. Register Map Format

This register map is shown in a horizontal format. This is done to make it easier to translate between hex values and bits in the register. The 32 bits are grouped by fours to facilitate alignment with hex digits. Decoding 0x0000001D for the register shown here indicates that the A and C bits are set and that the D field is set to 0x3. Likewise, a desire to set the B bit can be easily translated to get 0x00000002.

	ABC Configuration Register – 0x0020							
Bits	31 30 29 28	27 26 25 24	23 22 21 20	19 18 17 16	15 14 13 12	11 10 9 8	7 6 5 4	3 2 1 0
							D D D C	B A

While firmware can easily do the manipulation for masking and shifting of bits, humans often have to do the translation mentally, such as decoding an 8-digit hex number put out by the debugger.

Try doing the same back and forth translation with the following vertical table format. Suppose the debugger reads 0x0000002E from this register. Use the table to determine which bits are set.

Name	Bits	Description
Abort	[0]	Set this bit to abort the current task.
Bypass	[1]	Set this to put the block in bypass mode.
Combine	[2]	Set this to combine outputs.
Data width	[5:3]	Specify the number of bytes in a word.

The answer is that D is set to 0x5, B and C are set, and A is cleared.

☑ **Best Practice**

5.6.1 Display the register map in a horizontal format in the block's documentation.

5.6.2. Bit Positions, Types, and Defaults

Put the LSB (least significant bit) on the right side of the (horizontal) register map and the MSB (most significant bit) on the left side. This allows for easier writing of the hex values.

Number the first bit in the register to be 0, not 1. Also, make bit 0 be the LSB. In most cases, registers in chips do start with bit 0 and it is the LSB. But there are chips that are different. From a firmware programming point of view, having bit 0 be the LSB has a side benefit. Listing 5.4 is a line of C code that shows how to access bits 5 and 12. As can be seen, the numbers 5 and 12 are used directly in the line of code.

If either bit 5 or 12 are set, then the validCondition variable will be non-zero. Having the LSB be bit 0 helps reduce errors when writing firmware based on the documentation.

In addition, with bit 0 always being LSB, it is known that bits 5 and 12 can be written as 0x20 and 0x1000, no matter if it is an 8-bit, 16-bit, 32-bit, or whatever-bit register. (Obviously, bit 12 would not exist in an 8-bit register.) If bit 0 were the MSB, then the register size needs to be known, adding some complications.

With the LSB as bit 0, the bit number for the MSB is dependent on the register size. For an 8-bit register, it is bit 7. For a 16-bit register, it is bit 15. And so on. For the examples in this book, I am using 32-bit registers, so bit numbers ranges from 0 (LSB) to 31 (MSB).

In this register map, both the LSB and bit 0 are on the right side. All bit positions are numbered in the second row. In the third row, a dash is used to indicate an unused position. Since I am starting new with this register, all bits are initially unused.

In the first column of the third row, "R/W" indicates that it is a read/write register, that firmware can both read and write the register. For read-only and write-only registers, "Read" or "Write" (or RO or WO) would be used. For registers that have more than one type, insert another row. For example, the third row could indicate bits that are read/write bits while the fourth row indicates read-only bits. See section B.2.2.14 in the template for an example.

Listing 5.4: Using bit numbers to get at bit positions.

```
validCondition = registerConfig & ((0x1 << 5) | (0x1 << 12));
```

	MSB			ABC Configuration Register – 0x0020			LSB
Bits	31 30 29 28	27 26 25 24	23 22 21 20	19 18 17 16	15 14 13 12	11 10 9 8	7 6 5 4	3 2 1 0
R/W	- - - -	- - - -	- - - -	- - - -	- - - -	- - - -	- - - -	- - - -

☑ **Best Practice**

5.6.2 Put the LSB on the right side of the register map.

☑ **Best Practice**

5.6.3 Number the bits starting with the LSB as bit 0.

☑ **Best Practice**

5.6.4 Indicate the type of each bit—read-only, write-only, read/write—in the register map.

The register map needs one other piece of information, the power-on defaults. Firmware engineers need to know what the defaults are to determine if the device driver needs to do something at bootup.

In some cases, the power-on default of a bit is unknown. An example is a bit that indicates the level of an input pin on the chip. Since it is unknown what will be connected to that pin and how it will drive the pin at power on, its default value is unknown. Use an X in that position (or some other character to indicate unknown).

In this configuration register example, the D field defaults to 0x1 and the rest of the bits default to 0. In the template, the Instantiation register, section B.2.2.2, has several unknowns because it depends on how the block is instantiated.

	MSB			ABC Configuration Register – 0x0020			LSB
Bits	31 30 29 28	27 26 25 24	23 22 21 20	19 18 17 16	15 14 13 12	11 10 9 8	7 6 5 4	3 2 1 0
R/W	- - - -	- - - -	- - - -	- - - -	- - - -	- - - -	- D D D	C - B A
Reset	0 0 0 0	0 0 0 0	0 0 0 0	0 0 0 0	0 0 0 0	0 0 0 0	0 0 0 1	0 0 0 0

☑ **Best Practice**

5.6.5 Document the power-on defaults for each bit in the register map.

5.6.3. Bit Descriptions

Below the register map is a detailed description of each bit, as indicated by each bit's or bits' one-character mnemonic. List the bit descriptions in position order, starting with LSB.

	MSB						LSB
				ABC Configuration Register – 0x0020			
Bits	31 30 29 28	27 26 25 24	23 22 21 20	19 18 17 16	15 14 13 12	11 10 9 8	7 6 5 4	3 2 1 0
R/W	- - - -	- - - -	- - - -	- - - -	- - - -	- - - -	- D D D	C - B A
Reset	0 0 0 0	0 0 0 0	0 0 0 0	0 0 0 0	0 0 0 0	0 0 0 0	0 0 0 1	0 0 0 0

A: **Abort**—Set this bit to abort the current task.

B: **Bypass**—Set this to put the block in bypass mode.

C: **Combine**—Set this bit to combine outputs.

D: **Data width**—Specify the number of bytes in a word. Valid values are as follows: 0x1=1 byte (default), 0x2=2, 0x3=4, and 0x4=8 bytes.

☑ **Best Practice**

5.6.6 Provide a detailed description for each bit under its register map.

☑ **Best Practice**

5.6.7 Sort the bit descriptions under the register map from the LSB down to the MSB.

5.6.4. Abort Impact

Firmware engineers need to know how an abort will affect bits. Many bits are generally understood in how they behave in an abort. For example, Interrupt Status and Enable bits are not changed by an abort (except, of course, the abort-done interrupt). There is no need to enumerate all of those bits as unaffected by an abort.

Bits that are modified by an abort, and bits that the reader might wonder whether they are modified by an abort, should be documented regarding whether they are or not.

☑ **Best Practice**

5.6.8 Document how each bit is affected—or not—by an abort.

5.6.5. *Test and Debug Bits*

Test and debug registers are kept in a separate document, the unsupported documentation, as discussed at the beginning of this chapter. This allows, among other things, to withhold that information from third-party developers and customers.

However, some test and debug bits might reside in normal registers and therefore should have some mention in the normal block documentation. But that mention can be in vague terms, simply listed as notes or warnings, such as in the following examples:

- This bit is used for testing purposes only and will at times return a 1 but should be ignored.

- This bit is used for testing purposes and must always have a 0 written to it. Writing a 1 causes undefined behavior in the block.

This vague description is used in the block documentation. But these bits will be documented in detail in the unsupported documentation, although because they are not design for normal use, the documentation requirements are not so stringent. The unsupported documentation will be made available to firmware engineers, if needed, to use them to help diagnose and work around chip design flaws.

☑ **Best Practice**

5.6.9 Explicitly indicate each bit that is reserved for test and debug purposes.

☑ **Best Practice**

5.6.10 For documents distributed to third-party developers, mark test and debug bits as bits that should be ignored and always contain zeros, but do not describe what they do.

Because test and debug bits are not designed for normal usage, their purpose and position can easily be changed with each revision. Where test and debug bits are documented, whether in the block documentation or the unsupported documentation, a warning should be included that their location and behavior may change on subsequent revisions, and so they should not be relied upon.

☑ **Best Practice**

5.6.11 Provide the warning in the document that the use of test and debug hooks is unsupported and may change in the next version of the block.

Section B.2.2.14 in the template illustrates these best practices in a debug register.

5.7. Interrupts

Interrupts come in a wide variety of styles and flavors and firmware engineers know that. Therefore, a lot of details about behavior of the interrupt in the block must be documented.

5.7.1. Edge- vs. Level-Triggered

Interrupt modules responding to interrupt lines are either edge-triggered or level-triggered. Firmware engineers need to know what type of interrupt it is because the firmware has to be written differently, depending on the type. For example, in level-triggered interrupts, firmware must service the interrupting device before it can "ack" (acknowledge) the interrupt to avoid being re-interrupted for the same interrupt. But in edge-triggered interrupts, firmware should ack the interrupt first before servicing the device to avoid missing a new edge.

> ☑ **Best Practice**
>
> 5.7.1 Document each interrupt as edge- or level-triggered.

Interrupt source signals that are external to the chip are visible or known to the engineers. As with many logic signals, interrupt source signals can also be active high or active low. The question when dealing with an interrupt module is if it will trigger with positive or negative logic. For level-triggered interrupts, will it trigger when the level is high or low? For edge-triggered interrupts, will it trigger on a rising edge (low-to-high transition) or a falling edge (high-to-low transition)? Whatever it is, it needs to be documented.

In some cases, an active low signal from an external device is inverted when brought into the chip. When the external signal is low, a read from a register will show a 1 in that bit. Make those nuances clear in the documentation.

> ☑ **Best Practice**
>
> 5.7.2 Document if the interrupt is triggered on the rising or falling edge for edge-triggered interrupts or the high or low level for level-triggered interrupts.

The interrupt source signal feeding into the interrupt module can be either a short pulse or it can stay active until cleared by some means. If it feeds into an edge-triggered interrupt, the interrupt can be acked whether or not the interrupt source signal is still active. But if it feeds into a level-triggered interrupt, firmware must first somehow clear the interrupt source signal before it can ack the interrupt. Document how firmware is supposed to clear the interrupt source for level-triggered interrupts. Document if it is just a short pulse that will go away, if it is as simple as clearing a bit in some register in the block, or if it requires sending a command to some external device to clear its condition.

☑ **Best Practice**

5.7.3 Describe when and how to deassert the interrupt source to level-triggered interrupts.

5.7.2. Enabling and Acknowledging Interrupts

For some blocks the register to control whether or not an interrupt is allowed to propagate up to the processor is called "Enable," while in other blocks, the register is called "Mask."

The term "Mask" is unclear to the reader. Does it prevent or allow an interrupt to propagate? Some blocks use a 1 to provide a mask which is OR'd with interrupts, allowing it to propagate (a more common use of an interrupt mask). Other blocks use a 1 to mask off an interrupt, not allowing it to propagate (an uncommon use but it does exist). Since the term is unclear, firmware engineers have to read the document very carefully to determine whether a 1 or a 0 is needed to allow an interrupt to propagate. (This assumes that the document contains that information and is accurate.)

A better term to use is "Enable," which makes it clear to firmware engineers that a 1 allows the interrupt to propagate.

☑ **Best Practice**

5.7.4 Assign the name, "Enable," to the register that controls which interrupts will propagate.

Put in the documentation how to clear an interrupt condition. This may mean writing a zero to a bit position with a one in all other bits (an uncommon method but it does exist) or by writing a one to a bit with a zero in all other bits (the more common method).

☑ **Best Practice**

5.7.5 Indicate the bit value—1 or 0—required to ack each interrupt.

5.7.3. Interrupts Not Quite Done

In some cases, a "done" interrupt might occur even though the task is not quite done. One example is a state machine where one state posts the done interrupt but the state machine has not yet returned to the idle state. Typically, though, it will get there in one or two clock cycles and that is not a problem for firmware.

Another example is data that is written out to a memory buffer. When the block sends its last data out to memory, it may also post a done interrupt at the same time. However, in some systems, it might take time for the data to get to memory, depending on bus architecture, memory controller, traffic, and DMA priorities. Under the right conditions, it is possible for firmware to respond to the interrupt and read the memory before the data actually gets there. System constraints may not allow the option to fix it so that the interrupt only comes after the data is actually written in memory. In that case, document that this situation may occur so that firmware engineers can implement firmware safeguards.

☑ **Best Practice**

5.7.6 Indicate which interrupts might occur before the task is completed.

5.7.4. Interrupts Repeating without Intervention

Some types of interrupts will only occur once after firmware launches a task. Once the interrupt occurs, it will not occur again until firmware launches the task again. An example is a DMA transfer that will generate one interrupt when done and that's it, until firmware initiates another transfer.

Other types of interrupts will occur repeatedly without any firmware intervention in between. An example is data arriving from an I/O port. Data will keep arriving whether firmware does anything or not. Firmware engineers need to know which interrupts could occur without firmware intervention.

For these types of interrupts, firmware engineers need to know how fast these interrupts could occur so that they can write code accordingly.

They also need to know what will happen if a subsequent interrupt occurs before firmware services the previous. It may be that nothing happens. It may increment a counter to inform firmware that another one has occurred. Data may be lost and overwritten if firmware doesn't retrieve the previous one fast enough. It may generate a different interrupt, such as an overflow interrupt.

☑ **Best Practice**

5.7.7 Document which interrupts can be generated multiple times without being handled.

☑ **Best Practice**

5.7.8 Document how quickly an unhandled interrupt could occur again.

☑ **Best Practice**

5.7.9 Document what would happen if an unhandled interrupt occurred a second time before firmware serviced the first one (e.g., data loss, an error interrupt).

5.8. Time

The concept of time for hardware is different than firmware. Hardware can keep track of clock cycles and can do so independent of whatever else is going on in the chip or elsewhere in the system. Firmware is running on a processor that is typically running at a different clock frequency than the chip where the block is located. But even then, firmware does not have a way of monitoring the passage of time, especially since it can be swapped out when another firmware task needs to run for an unknown period of time.

5.8.1. Ranges of Time

When firmware has to handle delays in time by hardware, firmware engineers need to know what to expect.

Firmware launches a task in the block by setting a queue bit. But the block may or may not start on that task immediately. In the documentation for the block, include a note to indicate how long it will take for the block to start executing the task. It could be similar to one of the following examples:

- When the queue bit is set, the block will start the task immediately.

- When the queue bit is set, the block will start immediately if the port is free. If the port is not free, the block will wait until it is free, and then start.

- When the queue bit is set, the block will start the task the next time the external ready signal is true.

Though not specifically stated, the minimum time for each of these is 0. The maximum and typical time for the first one is also 0. The maximum for the second may be known if the engineer knows that a port is only tied up at most X seconds for a packet transfer. The third is waiting on an external signal, so the maximum time could be forever. Typical times would be somewhere in between.

☑ **Best Practice**

5.8.1 Document the minimum, maximum, and typical times for the block to start the task after its queue bit is set.

Once the task in the block is executing, firmware engineers need to know how long it will take to complete. Document the minimum, maximum, and typical times of how long the block will take to complete the task. If specifics cannot be given, then give generalities. The first example is very specific.

- When the queue bit is set, the block starts immediately and takes 128 clock cycles to complete the task.

- The block takes approximately 1500 clock cycles per 1 Kbyte of data.

- The time the block takes to complete this task depends on the speed of the handshaking with the external device.

- If the block is already idle when the abort bit is set, the abort done interrupt will occur immediately. If the block is active, then an abort will typically take at least 10 clock cycles. However, if the outgoing data pipe is stalled waiting for the receiver to take the data, the block will take up to 20,480 clock cycles before it will timeout and throw away the data.

For the last example above, firmware engineers know that in most cases, the abort done interrupt will occur in less than 15 clock cycles; therefore, the firmware can be designed to loop a few times to see if it will occur then. But if not, then it will take the time to enable the interrupt, suspend that task, let another task run, wait for the interrupt, service the interrupt, and resume the task.

☑ **Best Practice**

5.8.2 Document the minimum, maximum, and typical times for the block to complete the task, process the abort, or generate other time-delayed events.

Besides dealing with time delays of hardware tasks initiated by firmware, hardware events could generate successive interrupts without firmware intervention, such as incoming I/O data. Firmware may need to respond to the interrupt within a certain time period in order to avoid data overruns. Document how quickly those events could occur. An example follows.

■ Example

Basic data packets with no payload can come as frequently as every 45 microseconds. Extended data packets with 16 bytes of payload can come as frequently as every 105 microseconds.   ■

☑   **Best Practice**

5.8.3 Document the minimum and typical times that successive identical hardware events could occur.

In addition to stating minimum, maximum, and typical, the examples above also indicate what would cause the variations in timing, such as current state of the block, amount of data, and external conditions. Be sure to document those, too.

☑   **Best Practice**

5.8.4 Document the conditions and states that affect the variations of minimum, maximum, and typical times for each operation.

5.8.2. Unit of Time

A delay is specified in terms of some unit of time. The unit of time may be in terms of seconds or it may be in terms of some other regularly occurring event, such as a chip clock cycle.

Suppose that on a chip running at 100 MHz, an event will occur in 10 ms, which is 1 million clock cycles of the chip. If the next generation chip went from 100 MHz to 133 MHz, will that event still take 10 ms or will it now take 7.5 ms? It depends on what that delay is for.

If it takes 1 million clock cycles to process the data, then it will still take 1 million clock cycles on the faster chip, so the new time will be 7.5 ms. And in this case, the time should be specified in units of clock cycles. It will always take 1 million clock cycles to complete,

Table 5.7: Time Measured in Units of Seconds vs. Units of Clock Cycles

	Time in Units of Seconds	Time in Units of Clock Cycles
Chip running at 100 MHz	10 ms (1,000,000 clocks)	1,000,000 clocks (10 ms)
Chip running at 133 MHz	10 ms (1,330,000 clocks)	1,000,000 clocks (7.5 ms)

no matter how fast the clock is running on the chip. For the 133 MHz chip, it will take only 7.5 ms.

But if the block must wait 10 ms because of some protocol specification, then it has to still wait 10 ms in the new chip in the new chip, no matter how fast the clock is. For the 133 MHz chip, it must count 1.33 million clock cycles to maintain a 10 ms delay. Table 5.7 illustrates this distinction.

This distinction is important when porting firmware from one product generation to the next. The next generation is likely to have a different processor and/or chip, with either or both running at a different frequency. The same unit of time must be preserved in the port, whether it is in units of seconds or clock cycles.

Firmware is generally set up to deal with time in units of seconds. As firmware is ported from one processor/chip set to another, adjustments are made in the support code to keep seconds accurate. This makes it easy for firmware to delay in units of seconds and have it portable across products.

On the other hand, it is not easy for firmware to handle time in units of clock cycles. Other techniques are required to ensure proper delay in the new product, such as tuning the firmware (not reliable) or have hardware provide support in the form of counters and interrupts.

The documentation should state very clearly the units of time. For example, "This event will occur in 10 ms." Or, "This event will occur in 1 million chip clock cycles, which at 100 MHz will take 10 ms."

☑ **Best Practice**

5.8.5 Document the duration of an operation in its primary unit of time, such as seconds or clock cycles.

5.9. Errors

A college professor taught that 20% of our code is used to handle the normal operation; the other 80% is for error handling. I have found that generally to be true.

Not only is most of the hardware and firmware design used for error handling, but most of the engineers' time is spent on dealing with errors. It is not only with errors in the engineers' own design that causes them to spend that time, but errors elsewhere in the system that their design catches or that break their design.

Unfortunately, in many cases very little time and effort are put into handling and documenting errors, resulting in much wasted time when errors do occur. This section will discuss types of information to put in the documentation to help reduce the time to diagnose and resolve errors.

5.9.1. Two Types of Errors

From the perspective of firmware engineers writing a device driver for a block, errors that the block detects generally fall into one of two buckets: errors due to problems within the device driver and errors due to problems elsewhere in the system.

Errors by the block's device driver are due to something that the device driver did wrong in the setup and operation of the block. This would include errors such as the following:

- Loading an out-of-range value in a register

- Setting configuration bits in an invalid mode or combination

- Loading an invalid address pointer to data in memory

- Not performing steps in the right sequence

Errors due to problems elsewhere in the system are not the fault of the device driver but must be handled by the device driver when detected by the block. Some of these types of errors include the following:

- A delay in the arrival of an event

- Missing, invalid, or corrupt data in the data stream

- Error in the operation within the block or within adjacent blocks

Errors due to problems in the device driver are generally easy to fix by correcting the device driver before releasing the product. But errors detected by the block that are due to problems elsewhere in the system must be handled by the device driver. And that error-handling code must be included in the released product.

During the development of the product, when an error is detected but not yet diagnosed, engineers have to spend time trying to figure out what happened. They do not yet know if it is a problem in the device driver that can be fixed, or if it is an error that the device driver needs to handle. The more information engineers have at their disposal, the quicker they can diagnose and resolve the errors. In Section 7.4.1, Error Information, I discuss how the hardware can be designed to help provide information when errors occur. Here I will discuss information that should be in the documentation.

5.9.2. Copious Information about the Errors

I have seen documentation that simply says something to the effect, "The XYZ error bit is set when an XYZ error occurs." That is all it says. It does not give any more information about the error. What is the XYZ error, how did it occur, and how can it be avoided?

Provide copious information, as much as is practical and possible. Some little tidbit within that abundance of information might be a clue for what went wrong.

Include fairly detailed information on the normal operation of the block. When firmware engineers understand what normal operation is, it is much easier to recognize and understand abnormal operation. Identify what types of error conditions the block checks for when starting or executing normal operations.

☑ **Best Practice**

5.9.1 Document the details of normal operation and what error checks are performed.

Generally, when the block detects an error condition, it reports that error to firmware by sending it a message via interrupts or in a status register. Be sure to document all error messages that the block could send to firmware.

☑ **Best Practice**

5.9.2 Document all error messages that the block could generate.

Document the reason or reasons why each error occurred. Some errors may have more than one reason. Document them all.

Write it in terms that the firmware engineer can understand. "The XYZ error occurs when the internal LMN signal drops before going idle. The LMN signal indicates the presence of data in the buffer. The buffer may run out of data before the block goes idle because the incoming DMA was stalled or because the byte count used in the DMA was too small."

📖 **Tales from the Trenches**

The Unity mono video block had a decompressor that would occasionally generate a decompression error. There was just 1 bit which indicated that error, so all that was known was that there was an error in the decompressor. Why did it occur? Was it a bad setup by my device driver? An invalid value in a register? An unexpected size? Not enough data? Not enough memory? Corrupted data? Or what? Since no other information was given, my device driver could not take further action aside from reporting that it occurred. Nor was there additional information in the documentation to help understand possible causes as to why they occurred.

During the development of the product, we were getting several occurrences of this error. We had to use debuggers and other clues to determine the root cause. At one count, we had identified six different root causes that resulted in that one error bit being set. Had the documentation described the details as to why that error was generated, we could have spent less time diagnosing the problems.

☑ **Best Practice**

5.9.3 Document in detail all the conditions that could cause each error message.

5.9.3. State of the Block after an Error

Errors can occur any time so it might not be clear if something happened or not. When an error is detected, does the block immediately stop? Or does it keep processing? If it kept processing, did it assume some valid mode or could it be processing garbage?

As an example, an I/O block might keep processing data that is flowing through even though one of them had a bad parity or other error. Or, for more severe errors, such as too many retries, the block would shut down and not process any more data.

☑ **Best Practice**

5.9.4 Indicate whether an operation stops or continues in response to a given error.

What state was the block was left in? Did the block reset itself or did it stay put in the bad state? Did it continue and terminate normally and is back to the idle state?

☑ **Best Practice**

5.9.5 Describe the state of the block after an error occurs.

What is the state of the data? Was the data left unchanged? Is the data corrupted? Is it partially transmitted or received? Is it known to be good, is it known to be bad, or is it unknown if it is good or bad?

☑ **Best Practice**

5.9.6 Document the state of data—valid or invalid—after the error.

5.9.4. Firmware Steps to Recover

When an error does occur, it needs to be handled. In some cases, normal operation can resume afterwards, but in other cases it cannot. Again, the firmware engineer needs to know how to handle each error bit.

This list describes possible actions that firmware might do to recover from errors detected by the block:

- **Ignore it:** This could be for minor problem with which firmware does not need to take any action. If firmware does not need to take any action on this, then firmware engineers could disable that interrupt or mask off that bit.

- **Log it:** Some errors need no action unless they happen too frequently. By logging it, a history is kept so that engineers can monitor its frequency.

- **Abort the block:** Some state machines are left in an error or other state. Firmware would need to abort the block to get everything back to a known state.

- **Perform a sequence of steps:** Depending on the nature of the recovery process, a series of steps might be required to get the block back to normal operation mode.

- **Power cycle the device:** The block gets into a state that firmware cannot get it out of. Or it may be that the block interfaces with external blocks, chips, or hardware that is in a bad state. A power cycle may be required to get all the subsystems back to normal mode.

☑ **Best Practice**

5.9.7 Describe how to recover from each error condition.

5.10. Information

Include any other information that firmware engineers may need to know in order to develop their device drivers and to diagnose problems that will arise. The following are a few such types of information to include.

5.10.1. Illegal Configuration

Include what would happen if firmware did something wrong, such as program some configuration registers in an invalid mode. For example, what would happen if both bits B and G were set when the block was told to start? What would the block do?

- Did it go ahead or did it not do anything?

- Did it assume a mode (e.g., bit B overrides bit G)?

- Did it go ahead but the results are unpredictable?

- Could something be clobbered?

- Would an error bit be set?

☑ **Best Practice**

5.10.1 Describe how the block responds when configured to an invalid mode.

5.10.2. State Machines

Blocks use state machines to control order, sequence, and timing of events and tasks within the block. Conditions where state machines cause different behaviors of the block in its interaction with firmware should be documented. Example questions that need to be answered include the following:

- Will a write to a register while the block is busy cause corruption?

- Will a write during certain states generate an error?

- Under what conditions will the block generate an error?

- Does the current state affect whether the block will respond to firmware request immediately, later, or never?

- While the state machine is busy with one firmware request, will a second request cause the first to be aborted, be held until the first is done, or be ignored?

- If firmware issues two requests at the same time, will one override the other, are they both executed at the same time by two different state machines, or will an error be generated?

- What is the protocol sequence of signals lines on an I/O bus?

Answers to these questions should be documented. Depending on their nature, they could be answered in paragraph form. But sometimes, it is more precise and detailed to include a state machine diagram in the documentation.

State machine diagrams are customarily documented in the block design documents, which describe the internal workings of the block and are used by hardware engineers. These internal design documents are generally not accessible by firmware engineers. But for those state machines that do impact firmware interaction, place those diagrams in the block-level documentation that firmware engineers use.

☑   **Best Practice**

5.10.2 Document state machines that firmware engineers might need to know about.

5.10.3. How to Abort

If an abort is not as simple as setting 1 bit, then document the procedure. This is needed to avoid extraneous errors and other problems. It may be something like this:

1. Abort Module A

2. Abort Module B

3. Wait for the Module B Abort Done interrupt

4. Abort Module B again

5. Wait for the Module B Abort Done interrupt again

6. Abort Module C

☑ **Best Practice**

5.10.3 Document the steps required to cleanly abort a block.

5.11. Summary

As I stated at the beginning of this chapter, documentation is a very necessary part of helping firmware engineers develop firmware for the block. There are several reasons why documentation is beneficial. Documentation helps:

- New firmware engineers quickly get acquainted with the block.

- Firmware engineers remind themselves of little details.

- Firmware engineers familiar with multiple versions of the block keep straight the differences between the versions.

- Hardware engineers remind themselves later how they intended to implement the design.

- Both hardware and firmware engineers remember what they had agreed on for design aspects of the block.

- Keep firmware engineers from interrupting hardware engineers too often.

- Backup engineers cover primary engineers when they are out or have moved on to other job positions.

📖 **Tales from the Trenches**

The Unity mono video block was fairly complex and the documentation did not contain sufficient details on its nuances. I had to consult with the hardware engineer frequently to understand the block. This meant that I had undocumented information in my head that was required to write the device driver. Since no one else could have quickly stepped in to take over, I had to change my vacation plans to get the device driver functional before a deadline.

After that incident, I worked closely with the hardware engineers to reduce the complexities of the block and to improve the documentation for the next-generation chip.

In this chapter I have discussed the importance of having complete and accurate documentation for the block. I covered several aspects of what the content should be, such as high-level descriptions, reference and tutorials, registers, interactions, and state machines. I discussed writing the document early in the design cycle for the block so that firmware engineers can review it and make comments. I also stressed the importance of keeping the document updated as the block is being implemented.

To help document variations of blocks across time and chips, I discussed the concept of a block documentation that contains what the block does regardless of what chip it is in; then chip-specific implementation, which details how that block is implemented in that chip; and an errata section which documents errors discovered and how to work around them. I also discussed a few different types of tables that contain a history of document changes, block changes, and chip details. I discussed how those tables contained a history of several versions to help those familiar with some but not all of the past.

5.11.1. Supporting Principles

The concepts of this chapter support the principles of hardware/firmware interface design as follows:

1. **Collaborate on the Design:** Documentation is the most important collaborative tool. It conveys information from hardware engineers necessary for firmware engineers to write their device drivers.

2. **Set and Adhere to Standards:** Follow the same standard for all documentation in terms of format and content to ensure that it contains all the necessary information.

3. **Plan Ahead:** Write the documentation at the beginning of the project to allow review and changes before the hardware design has progressed too far.

The next chapter will discuss the superblock concept, a block that contains a superset of functionality at any subset that the block will need.

CHAPTER 6

Superblock

A "superset" contains everything that a "subset" contains and maybe more. If there are two or more "subsets," a "superset" contains everything those "subsets" contain and maybe more.

A superblock is a block that has a superset of functions and capabilities needed for that domain, even if only a subset will be used in a given product. The primary advantage is the ability to reuse the same hardware and firmware design files. Reusing the same files across current and future chips and products reduces defects and development time, allowing the products to get to market sooner.

However, there are cost implications in terms of silicon space, package size, and test and verification efforts. The advantages and disadvantages need to be weighed so that the right tradeoffs can be made. The disadvantages are primarily in the upfront effort required to implement a superblock and the incremental silicon space required. But in the long run, it will pay for itself.

In this chapter I will give reasons why a block should be a superblock and reasons why not. I will discuss how a superblock can minimize impact on firmware, how it can be scalable to remove large unused portions, and how to plan for future uses.

6.1. Benefits of a Superblock

Blocks are often designed to handle variations of related tasks. Different products may need different subsets of those variations. A superblock that can handle all variations can be used for any product, no matter which subset that product chooses to use.

Table 6.1 shows an example feature list (A through E) for an RS-232 UART block that needs to be used in both product X and product Y. It shows that product X needs features A, B, and C and product Y needs features A, B, and D. Neither product X nor Y needs feature E.

DOI: 10.1016/B978-1-85617-605-7.00008-3.

Table 6.1: RS-232 Features Needed for Products X and Y

Feature	Description	Product X	Product Y
A	Speeds up to 115,200 baud rate	Yes	Yes
B	Hardware handshaking	Yes	Yes
C	256-byte buffer	Yes	
D	Auto speed sensing		Yes
E	Automatic software handshaking		

Should there be one chip with features A, B, and C for product X, and one with features A, B, and D for product Y? Or should one chip be made with features A–D? What about feature E? Should it be included? The answer depends on many factors such as application, size, cost, schedule, turmoil, and priority, which engineers need to take into consideration.

The next several sections will cover reasons for and against a block that supports all features, A-E, and will discuss how it impacts the block's supporting entourage.

6.1.1. The Block's Entourage

A block used in a chip is not designed, developed, debugged, and deployed in isolation. It is accompanied by many support steps, each with its own set of files and infrastructure uniquely developed for this one block. For instance:

- Modeling and stimulus files are required to support this block in virtual prototype and simulation platforms.

- Test and verification files are required to support functional, formal, manufacturing, and system level verification of this block.

- Device driver files are required to support this block in various processor, OS, and product platforms.

Making a change in the block could impact the block's supporting entourage for the above areas. A change in the block requires ensuring that associated changes are made in its entourage, and that the correct change is made in the entourage without introducing defects.

6.1.2. Reasons for Having Unused Logic

The following are several reasons for including block features, even though no plans exist to use them.

Same as the Previous Generation

If the block existed in a previous generation of the chip, then using the same block allows for a quicker implementation (i.e., less development resources) of the block in the new chip. The block has been used before; it has been tested and is known to work. The block and its entourage are known to work.

Leaving out a feature (such as feature E above) when the feature existed in an earlier version requires making changes in the files of the block and its entourage, exposing a risk of introducing defects in all those areas.

Changes do need to be made. Defects need to be fixed and new features need to be added. But leaving in existing features, including those that are not planned to be used, will reduce the risk and the amount of work required to bring the block into the new chip and making necessary changes in its entourage.

Consolidated Features

Making a block in a chip that includes only the features that the target product needs precludes the chip from being used in products that need other features.

In the above RS-232 block example, making two chips, one for product X with A, B, and C, and one for product Y with A, B, and D, incurs the time and costs for two different chips to be fabricated. In addition, two sets of supporting entourage needs to be developed and maintained. In contrast, consolidating all features, A, B, C, and D, into one chip provides a chip for both products X and Y while only incurring fab costs for one chip and one entourage. Figure 6.1 illustrates the separate blocks vs. a superblock.

Other reasons may force products X and Y to have separate chips, such as a different mix of other blocks on the chip. But if this block (RS-232 in this example) were a superblock

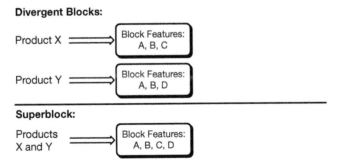

Figure 6.1: Two separate and different blocks with their own subset of features vs. one superblock with all features available, allowing any subset to be used.

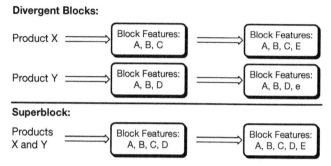

Figure 6.2: Enhancing multiple separate blocks creates multiple divergent lines, while enhancing one superblock provides support for all features on a single line.

that was instantiated in both chips, the supporting entourage will be almost identical. The same verification suites can be run. The same device driver can be used.

Now suppose that for the next-generation chip, both products X and Y need feature E. In the separate-block case, their respective teams have to add feature E in their respective block design files. In addition, their respective supporting entourage needs to be appropriately enhanced. The problem is that feature E is not likely to be implemented the same way in the two blocks. Figure 6.2 shows that "E" is implemented for product X while "e" is implemented for product Y. Same feature, but with enough differences that they are not identical. The locations of the new bits in new registers may be different. Or they might have different bugs.

By consolidating all the features into a superblock, only one supporting entourage, with its files and infrastructure, needs to be enhanced to support feature E. Figure 6.2 shows the divergent blocks and the superblock when feature E is added.

Reducing Defects

When divergent block lines exist, defects found in one line may not necessarily get fixed in the other line. In the above divergent-line example of Figure 6.2, suppose that the engineers supporting the block for product X discover and fix a defect in feature B. Depending on the communication lines in the organization, the engineers supporting the block for product Y might never be notified of the defect and it will stay in the block. If this trend continues, the two divergent lines of this block will continue to diverge. Defects fixed in one line may be difficult to fix and ensure thorough testing in the other line.

In the superblock line, a defect found and fixed in B will be fixed once and tested once, and both products X and Y will get the fix.

Usable for Future Products

Typically, blocks and chips are designed with one or more products in mind with features included to support those products. Invariably new future products come along that want to use existing chips. If an existing chip has the features that the new products need, then it can be used. The more features that the chip supports, the more likely it will be usable in future products that have yet to be planned. This has the obvious advantage of increasing the life of the chip and avoiding the time and expense of designing, testing, and fabricating a new chip with its supporting entourage.

Continuing with the same example, suppose a new product is defined, product Z, that requires features A, C, and D. In the divergent-block case, neither the block for product X nor Y will work. So a new block must be designed and is illustrated in the divergent-block section of Figure 6.3. The illustration shows the block for product Z being leveraged from the block for product X. Feature B was removed, features A and C are already in the block, and now feature D has to be added. But this feature D is unlikely to be the same as the one in the product Y block. So a little "d" is used to illustrate that it is the same feature but slightly different.

In contrast, the superblock supporting A, B, C, D, and E can be used as is for product Z, even though features B and E are not planned to be used.

If products X and Y have separate chips because of differences in other content on the chip, and if this superblock is instantiated on both chips, product Z has the option to use either product X's chip or product Y's chip, allowing product Z to have access to features A, C, and D as needed.

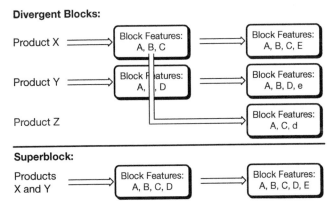

Figure 6.3: Creating a separate chip for product Z when the superblock would do.

If the engineering team for product X needs their own chip, it may be difficult to justify spending extra time and money to use the superblock. Some future potential product Z is not their concern, so why incur extra cost to product X's program?

Scrutinizing the cost savings of one product without taking into account the impact on other products is a narrowly focused, short-term view. By looking at the big picture, it is easier to see that if different decisions were made, a better financial picture appears, even though the one product has to spend a little more.

What is very hard to measure is overall cost across several products, not just in terms of pennies saved on one chip for one product, but in terms of greater revenue generated across all products. While some of the concepts in this book add cost to chips themselves, implementing them will save costs elsewhere in terms of fewer respins, quicker time to market, and increased life of the chip in other products. The following are tough questions to answer because there are too many unknowns.

Is it worth adding a few cents to the cost of a product:

- If it reaches the market 3 months sooner?

- If it reduces the costs of another product?

- If it allows creating a new product without making a new ASIC?

- If it reduces the organization's operating costs by 10% or 25%?

Besides ASICs, maintaining and using a superblock on FPGAs is also beneficial, especially as FPGA designs evolve rapidly and deploy frequently during development. Ensuring that one set of block design files are used for all iterations of an FPGA design ensures that all FPGA versions have the latest features and bug fixes. This also helps make sure the correct version of the device drivers is paired with the correct version of the FPGA.

By following the concepts of the book, there will be fewer delays, fewer respins of the chips, and less need to design new variations of chips. While it will be difficult know how much each of the implemented best practice saved in future costs, identifying just one that averted the cost and delay of one respin will prove that adding all of them was worth it.

Accommodate Late Product Changes

Chips and blocks are designed for products to meet their specific feature requirements. In reality, requirements change. Blocks in the chip that are superblocks are more likely to be able to accommodate those changes.

Using the above example, suppose that late in the development of Product X, it is decided that it should now also use feature D. If that block were a superblock, then it would be fairly easy to add that feature into Product X.

📖 **Tales from the Trenches**

Late in the development of a LaserJet printer, the laser horizontal sync detector was changed, for technical reasons, to quit sending horizontal sync pulses earlier than before. Video blocks in other ASICs had logic to detect when the pulses quit and generate an interrupt but the video block in this ASIC did not. It took me several experiments of various algorithms over a 3-week period to try to find a viable firmware workaround. I determined one of them to be the best, even though under "rare" conditions, it would cut the print speed in half. I implemented the workaround and we started shipping the product.

However, one particular customer bought several of these LaserJet printers for printing under specific conditions. Those conditions caused this "rare" performance penalty to occur all the time, impacting the print speed of all the printers they purchased. They were not happy. I had to spend another 2 weeks to design, develop, and test a new algorithm to fix the customer's problem. I changed the workaround to monitor the internal raster data buffer address. As long as it was changing, I knew the pulses were occurring and consuming raster data. But if it quit changing, I knew the pulses had quit and I could stop that operation and prepare for the next printer page. We sent the new firmware to the customer, their printers were upgraded, and they were happy.

Had the block on the chip been a superblock, containing the pulse cessation detection logic, I could have accommodated the behavior change within an hour. Instead, it took 5 weeks of my time, some warranty dollars, and impacted HP's reputation.

6.1.3. *Reasons* against *Having Unused Logic*

The above arguments are in favor of leaving in unused portions of a block when instantiated on the chip. Following are arguments in favor of taking it out. All the pros and cons must be evaluated for each case.

Requires Time to Add Them In

It takes time, resources, and expense to add in features if they are not already implemented and if there are no plans to use them. It takes time to code it and to test it. It takes time to develop the supporting entourage. If a feature is not implemented yet and it is not needed yet, do not add it in yet. But by being aware that it might be needed in the future, design decisions can be made that will ease the addition later if and when it is needed.

For blocks that adhere to an industry standard (RS-232, USB, JPEG, etc.), the complete standard (or a standard subset) needs to be implemented. Much of the supporting entourage (virtual prototype models, test vectors, device drivers, etc.) is available off the shelf and it expects the whole block to be implemented. For more discussion about industry standards, see Section 4.1.2, Implementing the Standard.

Requires Too Much Silicon Space

The high-volume commodity market is very cost-sensitive. Huge amounts of efforts are spent to eek out every fraction of a penny from the cost of the product. That translates into making the chip as small as possible. It is difficult to make a business case to add a few pennies to the cost of the product "just in case there might be a defect" or "just to keep the block as is for the next-generation chip."

If the planned unused portion is big, it does not make much sense to leave it in. But if it is small, it should be left in. All this requires engineering judgment:

- How much space is there?

- What is the potential future benefit if the unused portion is left in?

- What is the risk in the future if it is taken out?

- What is the risk of introducing defects when taking it out?

- What is the priority compared to other unused portions?

Later, in Section 6.4, Parameterization, is a discussion on ways to make a block scalable, to allow portions to be removed to save silicon space. It can be done in such a manner to minimize the impact on the block and device drivers, to keep out defects, and to allow scalable support in future chips.

Consumes Too Much Static Power

Logic left on the silicon, though never used, still consumes power in its static state. At 65 nm and below, it is a significant problem.

Porting Effort Required

When designs are ported from one platform to another, such as from FPGA to ASIC, it may be cost-prohibitive to port the portions that will be unused. Some of the supporting entourage is pertinent to one platform but not the other, so porting unused logic will require associated entourage changes.

Obsolescence

For logic that will never be used again, removing it will eliminate required maintenance support. Deciding when to take it out requires a careful assessment of future plans. It is not enough to say that no new products will use it because there could be cases where the chip is needed to give old products new life.

Obsolete logic is logic that can be taken out of the design and will never have to be put back in. If there is a possibility that some future application might need that logic, then the logic is not quite obsolete.

> 📖 **Tales from the Trenches**
>
> A proprietary interface used in our LaserJet printers changed which required a new block. But with printers from several product lines being developed at a time, it was going to take a while before all product lines switched over to the new interface. We had both the old and new interface blocks in a few chips, allowing the chips to be used for either interface during the transition. Eventually, no printers used the old interface and it was safely removed from the chip.

- - - ✄ - - - - - - ✄ - - -

I've discussed the pros and cons of designing and maintaining a block as a superblock. In general, blocks should be maintained as superblocks. The cons do not indicate that a block should not be a superblock, but it indicates when a portion of a block's design should not fall under the superblock concept. While there may be some portions that should not follow the superblock model, most portions should and this chapter contains ways to maximize the superblock content while providing flexibility in instantiation options.

6.2. Consolidation

I've discussed why the superblock model should be used. I will now discuss how to do it.

6.2.1. Make a Superblock

To make a superblock, look for and understand the requirements put on the block by all products using that block. Consolidate all those requirements and design the superblock to fit those requirements.

Use one set of design files for this block. This same set is used in all instantiations among the different chips that need this block. Slightly modifying one or more files to meet requirements for a chip starts down a path of diverging product lines.

> ☑ **Best Practice**
>
> 6.1.1 Design each block as a superblock—using a single set of design files—to provide the superset of all features needed by all chips instantiating the block.

Look where this block was instantiated in existing chips. Figure out what was different and why it was necessary. Then consolidate those features to make the superset so that the superblock can replace the block in those other chips, if necessary.

There may be cases where two different versions have some differences in their implementation. One version might enable a mode by setting bit 3 in a register where another version uses bit 5 in that register. Pick one (using good engineering judgment) for the superblock to use.

📖   **Tales from the Trenches**

Two different versions of a block were being used on two different ASICs, one for mid-range and high-end LaserJet printers and the other for low-end LaserJet printers. The two versions had several differences because they had diverged several versions prior and were managed by two ASIC teams, each of which had added features and made changes for their own needs.

A new ASIC was being designed to be used for both the low-end and mid-range printers. However, neither version of this block had all the required features. After analyzing both, the engineers decided to use the low-end version and add in necessary features. Since the low-end version was quite different than the mid-range version, I had to write a new device driver to support the low-end version on the mid-range printers.

However, the version in the new ASIC still did not support all the features that the mid-range version did. Meanwhile, the mid-range version was still being used in high-end and other mid-range printers.

Over the course of the next two generations of chips, by submitting change requests to the hardware team, I was able to have them enhance the mid-range version to become a superblock by adding in the features that the low-end version had. When a new low-end ASIC was being designed, the superblock in the mid-range version became the version of choice because it had all the necessary features required by low-end, mid-range, and high-end LaserJet printers. That one version for all helped reduce device driver and other support requirements.

Consolidating all versions of a block is ideal but it may take two or three generations to get there.

☑   **Best Practice**

6.1.2 Consolidate all versions of the same block from different chips into a superblock with all capabilities to be used in future chips.

Once all the versions have been consolidated to a single set of design files, this set must be used from that point forward. Whenever the block is used in a chip, it needs to be instantiated from the one set of design files of that superblock. Don't make duplicate copies of the set and use them; otherwise it is prone that the copies start diverging again.

☑ **Best Practice**

6.1.3 Use the same set of superblock design files to instantiate the block one or more times in all chips.

6.2.2. Make a Supermodule

A chip consists of one or more blocks. A block consists of one or more modules. Some modules carry out common functions and are used more than once, whether in just one block or across many blocks. An example is a DMA controller. One block may need two DMA controllers, one to read data in from memory and one to write it out to memory. Other blocks may need four, such as a color printer that needs to read in data for all four planes for a color page.

Making a common module a supermodule takes advantage of the same benefits of a superblock. One set of files can be instantiated multiple times where needed. Enhancements and defect fixes will be propagated to all future instantiations.

☑ **Best Practice**

6.1.4 Design each module (e.g., DMA, interrupts) as a supermodule with the superset of the features needed by all blocks instantiating the module.

6.2.3. Evolutionary Design

Designs evolve as they iterate from one generation to the next—changes are made, new features are added, defects are fixed, and old sections are taken out. Making these changes to the superblock's set of design files will ensure that the superblock is current with the latest design. Often designs are temporarily branched out on their own to during development and testing to make sure it works. But it should merge back to the main code before being shipped in a product.

Each new generation of a block often adds new features to support new requirements for the next generation of products. New features are added in to the superblock so that they become part of the superblock, working well with the rest of the block.

> ☑ **Best Practice**
>
> 6.1.5 Add new features to the common superblock rather than creating separate design branches of the block.

Part of crafting a superblock is to leave in the unused parts that may or may not be needed in the future. As was discussed in detail earlier in Section 6.1.3, Reasons against Having Unused Logic, cost and space constraints may not permit leaving in unused parts. But if the space and risk is low enough, leave it in and it will be there if plans change.

> 📖 **Tales from the Trenches**
>
> An SoC for LaserJet printers was designed to be used only on portrait-fed printers. (Paper is fed in portrait orientation with raster line buffers capable of handling U.S. letter paper at 8.5 in wide and international A4 paper at 210 mm wide.) It was stated up front that the SoC would only be used for portrait printers and it was approved by management. The chip was made and used as stated.
>
> However, months later, management wanted to expand the use of that SoC into landscape-fed printers. (Feeding paper in landscape mode with U.S. letter at 11 in wide and international A4 paper at 297 mm wide.) Since the SoC was designed to handle paper only 8.5 in/210 mm wide, it was unknown if the raster line buffers inside the SoC could handle the wider 11-in/297-mm paper. After some analysis by several hardware and firmware engineers, it was determined that the chip could be used in the expanded role.
>
> The reason that this was possible was because the blocks in that SoC were superblocks used in chips for previous landscape printers and the hardware engineers had not reduced the size of the buffers. Designing a new SoC for landscape-fed printers was not necessary; the superblocks thus saved much time and money.

> ☑ **Best Practice**
>
> 6.1.6 Retain all known low-overhead functionality in a superblock, even if current requirements do not call for it.

When a feature in a block is being modified and upgraded, depending on the nature of the changes and the silicon space available, it may be possible to leave the old functionality in the chip. The old and the new may be completely separate blocks. Or it may be a new mode that is slightly different than the old. Leaving in the old when adding the new allows the possibility of using either as needed, or to use the old legacy version if there are defects in the new. After the new has been proven to work, then the old can be removed.

Some have commented that this duplication of hardware (old and new) is risky. However, leaving the old alone reduces turmoil to the design. The old is already mature, known to work, and has support in the entourage. Turmoil will be induced just by adding the new. Taking out the old will induce more turmoil. Turmoil must also be induced in the supporting entourage to take out support for the old. And if the new logic has defects, the old will no longer be there as a backup plan. So, if possible and if there is space, leave the old logic in the chip.

☑   **Best Practice**

6.1.7 Leave in old functionality, if possible, until its replacement functionality has been proven.

Note:

Later in this chapter I will discuss how to leave the old functionality in the design files, and then use parameterization to take it out for a given instantiation.

6.2.4. Add Future Features

In the software world, there is a line of thinking that says that when designing for a new product, only the one target product should be taken into account. No functionality should be added for any possible future products or to make the software more flexible. Additional design features should be added "tomorrow" (see Beck, 1999). One of the reasons software can get away with that type of thinking is because they can and are able to change software rapidly by simply recompiling and re-executing. But hardware does not have that luxury. Waiting until tomorrow means missing the opportunity to be on this chip. The next opportunity will cost millions of dollars and come several months later. Now is the time to consider adding new designs and features.

To help develop new technology, experimental portions could be added to the block with no intentions of using it in actual products. This provides a useful test bed in the lab for complicated logic that is not easily simulated or tested in a simulator, virtual prototype, or FPGA prototype platform. Lessons learned from the experiments can be applied in the next generation chip when the logic is ready for actual use.

A big concern for adding in experimental logic is the risk it imposes on the rest of the block. If the experimental portion breaks something in the rest of the block, that becomes a very expensive experiment. Experimental logic cannot be added to the chip at the expense of pushing out other features or increasing the cost of the chip and the products that will use it.

However, if the risk is low, if there is room, and if a successful experiment has the potential for a big payoff, then adding it in could be considered.

Beside experimental designs, there may be opportunities to add logic that will make the chip more useful for more products. It is not uncommon to have a chip used for more than its original product targets. New product designs try to use existing chips before incurring the time and cost to design, develop, simulate, verify, and fab a new chip. Even if only some of the blocks in the chip were used in the new product, it is cheaper than making a new one.

📖   **Tales from the Trenches**

HP engaged the services of a third-party company to develop an I/O chip (with USB, parallel, RS-232, PCIe, etc.) for LaserJet printers. The company produced one chip which HP tested but found problems. A few months later after a respin, a new chip came but it had problems too. And the third version did as well.

Fortunately for HP, an old HP ASIC had the right set of blocks and could be used in this application, even though it was more expensive and had other unneeded blocks. So HP canceled the project with the third-party company, switched to their old chip, and got the product to the market on time.

When designing a new chip, if there are some extra pins or silicon space, add things that could help make the chip last longer. For instance:

- Add more pins to the GPIO port.

- Put back in some of the removed portions.

- Add more debug support.

- Increase on-chip RAM buffers to increase performance.

- Increase the clock to provide more performance for future, faster products.

If the extras added to the chip allow the chip to be used in just one unplanned product, then the time and expense of adding those extras will have paid for itself. The time and money that would have been spent to design a new chip for that product would have been avoided.

Of course, all this needs to be tempered with the realities of costs and schedules. If extras can be added with little effort, risk, and cost, then it should be done.

☑   **Best Practice**

6.1.8 Include low-impact, low-risk features in the design of the chip that could be used in future products or aid future development.

6.2.5. Superblock Version Number

For changes to the design of the superblock that firmware can see, such as new features and defect fixes, increment the version number in the block's version register. But do not change the version number when instantiated in different chips. This allows firmware to use the version number to accommodate different versions of the block, no matter which chips the blocks are instantiated in. See Section 8.4.2, Block ID and Version for more discussions about the block version register.

☑ **Best Practice**

6.1.9 Increment the block version register whenever the superblock design changes, but not when the same superblock is instantiated in multiple chips.

6.3. I/O Signals

Through I/O signals, blocks interface with other blocks, chips, other components on the board, other boards, and other products. Primary access is through data and address signals that allow firmware and memory to interact with the block. Other I/O access is for standard or proprietary interfaces or for discrete signals.

Following the superblock concept means that all I/O signals that a block can use must be included in the superblock design. However, pins on a package are very expensive and there will be cases where there is no justification to incur the cost of more pins and potentially a larger package just to connect I/O signals that will never be used. So the superblock must be designed to have its optional signal lines left unused in desired instantiations.

I will again use the RS-232 UART as an example. The RS-232 protocol has at a minimum the Rx and Tx lines. But it also has optional lines, the hardware handshaking signals. Some implementations have the hardware handshaking lines and others do not. The superblock UART will have support for hardware handshaking lines. But it may be that in a given instantiation, it is not desired to tie up several pins for those hardware handshaking lines. Thus, they will not be connected through.

Adapting the superblock for that instantiation should be done outside of the block's boundaries. It is not necessary to go inside the block to make accommodations for non-use of I/O pins. In the case of output signals, simply leave them disconnected at the block boundary. Input signals at the block boundary cannot be left dangling, but need to be tied high or low. Whether the signal needs to be tied high or low depends on the function of the signal and the desired result. In the case of a UART, the incoming hardware handshaking lines should be tied so that it appears to the device driver that the interface is connected and ready to communicate. If, however, the Rx and Tx signals are not connected, then the incoming signals should be tied to indicate that the interface is not connected and not ready to communicate. (I don't know why a UART would be instantiated if the Rx and Tx lines won't be connected, but at least you get my point.)

Unused logic when leaving output signals disconnected and tying input signals high or low will be optimized out by the synthesis tools.

Figure 6.4 illustrates this concept by showing a superblock with three output signals and five input signals. Only one of the output signals is connected to a pin; the other two are left unconnected. Only two of the input signals are connected to pins. One of the three unused input signals is tied high and the other two are tied low.

☑   **Best Practice**

6.2.1 Deactivate unused output signals from a block by leaving the signal unconnected at the block boundary, rather than changing the internals of the block.

☑   **Best Practice**

6.2.2 Activate (deactivate) unused input signals to a block by tying the signal to its enabled (disabled) state at the block boundary, rather than changing the internals of the block.

The advantage of this method is that the device driver does not need to change for this instantiation. It appears to the device driver that the superblock still supports three output signals and five input signals. However, in some cases, the device driver will need to know which signals are connected and which are unused. The device driver may expect something

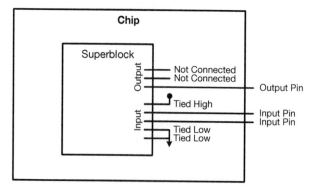

Figure 6.4: Unused output pins disconnected and unused input pins tied high or low.

to happen if it asserts some output signal and will have a failure if nothing happens because it is left disconnected. The documentation for this superblock needs to describe all the signals but may need to indicate which ones are used in each instantiation.

☑ **Best Practice**

6.2.3 Clearly document which I/O signals are active for each instantiation of the block.

6.4. Parameterization

Silicon space is a concern with superblocks. Sticking with the superblock concept costs too much silicon space if large portions of large blocks have to be implemented even though they are unused. Being able to take out large, unused portions is necessary for the superblock concept to be viable.

6.4.1. Reducing the Silicon Space

Parameterization can be used to configure the superblock's IP to exclude large sub-blocks or portions during instantiations. Examples of large sub-blocks include the following:

- **RAM:** Some blocks need large RAM buffers to operate on data. The size of the buffer can be used to control the trade-off between costs and performance.

- **Features:** Some blocks have large sub-blocks needed to perform specific optional features. If that feature is not needed in that chip, it can be excluded.

- **Duplicates:** Some blocks add more performance by adding parallel logic. For example, more PCI Express channels allow for more throughput.

- **Supermodules:** Supermodules that are instantiated multiple times throughout the chip can be configured as appropriately for each instance. For example, DMA controllers require memory for its FIFO buffers. Some applications will have high bandwidth requirements so bigger FIFO buffers are needed. Even though the silicon space for each DMA controller and its FIFO buffer is small, it adds up with all of the instances of DMA controllers on the chip.

☑ **Best Practice**

6.3.1 Parameterize superblock configuration (e.g., buffer size, number of channels) as needed to allow the same block to be used one or more times in multiple chips.

Not every change and difference needs to be parameterized. Not every optional portion needs to be excludable via parameterization—only those that will have the biggest impact on silicon space. The main reason for a superblock is to have all features available in all chips. The primary reason for parameterization is to reduce silicon space if there is not room for the whole superblock. Using parameterization to remove parts of the superblock will pay for itself later when needing to add that part back in on a future chip. Parameterization keeps defects down and enables better code leverage and reuse. This has the same benefit to firmware, also reducing defects and improving leverage and reuse.

☑ **Best Practice**

6.3.2 Use parameterization only where it will significantly impact the silicon space used.

Look for the biggest gains in silicon space that can be achieved with less effort. If one block takes up 25% of the silicon space and the block is not going to be used, then it is an obvious choice to remove, especially if it is easy to remove an entire block.

If a block has a large portion that is optional, that is a potential candidate to exclude via parameterization.

However, if a superblock is small relative to silicon space, it is not worth it to use parameterization, even if half of it is optional and can be removed. For example, it is not worth excluding portions of a 7000-gate UART when only one or two UARTS will be instantiated on silicon that can hold 10 million gates.

☑ **Best Practice**

6.3.3 Review each large superblock for large optional sub-blocks to include or exclude using parameterization.

6.4.2. Minimizing Parameterization Risks

It requires extra time for engineers to add parameterization ability for a superblock—not only extra time to implement it, but extra tests to ensure it works properly with various combinations and permutations of the parameters. And this includes the supporting entourage such as the virtual prototype models and the device drivers.

For a block that has a short life span and is not likely to be used in future chips, it is not worth the effort. But for blocks with a longer life expectancy, parameterization will help. As the superblock is modified for a next generation, changes needed at that time could become parameterized. New features that are added can use a parameter to keep it removable in the future if the new feature does not work.

Old features that need to be removed could be done so by making a parameter that will exclude that feature, effectively removing it. This allows temporary removal of obsolete parts that can be put back in if the new does not work or if the old is not quite yet obsolete.

☑   **Best Practice**

6.3.4 Use parameterization to include new features and exclude old features as the superblock evolves, allowing the same source files to produce instantiations of both current and previous block versions as needed.

Not every imaginable portion of the superblock should be made excludable via parameterization. Careful study is required to make sure that the portions excluded are done so without introducing defects to the fixed portions or to the included optional portions. Good design practices subdivide the overall design into smaller modules with clean interfaces. It is at those clean interfaces where accommodations can be made to safely include or exclude sub-blocks.

Figure 6.5 illustrates complex and error-prone boundaries for removable portions compared to simple and clean boundaries.

☑   **Best Practice**

6.3.5 Ensure that optional sub-blocks of a superblock have clean boundaries to the rest of the block.

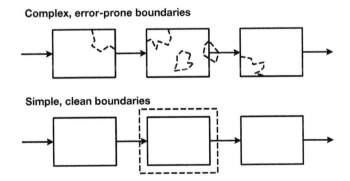

Figure 6.5: Comparison between complex and simple boundaries of removable portions.

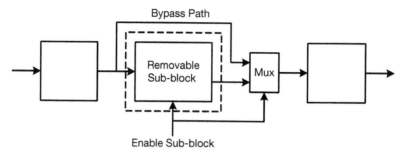

Figure 6.6: A bypass path around the removable sub-block.

If the removable sub-block is part of a pipeline, a way to make it easy to take out is to implement a separate bypass path around the removable portion. That bypass path can be used, even if that portion is instantiated but not enabled at the moment. When the removable portion is excluded via parameterization, the bypass path is already in place and known to function. Since the excluded portion cannot be enabled, the bypass will always be enabled.

Figure 6.6 illustrates the bypass path around the removable sub-block. A mux on the downstream side selects whether data should come from the removable sub-block or from the bypass path. When the removable portion is excluded, the mux select is tied to select the bypass path all the time.

☑   **Best Practice**

6.3.6 Provide a fixed bypass path around the optional portion of a pipeline.

6.4.3. Parameterization Information for Firmware

Just as a superblock contains the superset of block features, its corresponding device driver is a super device driver, able to use and access all features built into the superblock. However, parameterization allows the superblock to be configured differently for each instantiation as desired. The super device driver needs to configure itself at runtime based on how the superblock was instantiated. It needs to know how big the buffer sizes are in order to use them fully without overrunning them. It needs to know which optional sub-blocks are excluded so that it won't try to use them. It needs to know how many channels were instantiated so that it can maximize their usage.

> **Note:**
>
> In Section 5.5.2, Register Design Tools, I talked about using those tools to create the firmware header files. For a superblock that is being instantiated with some of the optional portions left out, those tools need to put out just the instantiated subset in the hardware files, but should put out the full superset for the firmware files to enable the one super device driver to support all instantiation variations.

Some superblocks may be instantiated more than once on a chip. This requires the super device driver to create separate instantiations of itself in order to configure each super device driver instantiation to correspond with each respective superblock instantiation.

To help the super device driver know about the superblock's instantiation, the superblock provides a read-only instantiation register. Bits in that register indicate what optional sub-blocks, features, modes, and so on, are included or excluded. It could indicate configuration values such as buffer sizes and number of channels. The following is an example instantiation register that could be in a UART superblock.

	MSB							UART Instantiation Register—0x0004																								LSB
Bits	31	30	29	28	27	26	25	24	23	22	21	20	19	18	17	16	15	14	13	12	11	10	9	8	7	6	5	4	3	2	1	0
RO	-	-	-	-	-	-	-	-	-	-	-	-	-	-	-	-	-	-	B	B	B	B	B	B	-	-	-	-	-	A	S	H
Reset	0	0	0	0	0	0	0	0	0	0	0	0	0	0	0	0	0	0	X	X	X	X	X	X	0	0	0	0	0	X	X	X

H: **Hardware handshaking**—This bit is set if the hardware handshaking lines are connected to pins.

S: **Software handshaking**—This bit is set if the automatic software handshaking sub-block is included.

A: **Auto speed sensing**—This bit is set if the automatic speed-sensing logic is included.

B: **Buffer size**—This indicates how big the Rx and Tx buffers are in units of 8 bytes. Minimum value is 0x1=8 bytes. Maximum value is 0x20=256 bytes.

> **Note:**
>
> The reset values cannot be documented here because it depends on how each UART was instantiated.

> **Note:**
>
> I said earlier that a UART, with so few gates, may not be worth using parameters to create different configurations. If that is the case, then the whole superblock would be instantiated. But if it will be put on a small chip, then parameterization may be necessary.

> ☑   **Best Practice**
>
> 6.3.7 Store all parameter values for each instantiation in one or more firmware-readable instantiation registers.

As the superblock evolves, more configurable parameters may be added. One example is an existing feature that may become optional in order to save silicon space. Since the feature already exists, the super device driver knows how to handle it. But if it becomes optional, and therefore excludible, then the super device driver needs to be able to accommodate its potential exclusion. Making that feature optional requires adding a new parameter for instantiation and requires a new bit in the instantiation register.

Because this requires a change in the super device driver, the superblock's version number needs to be incremented to indicate a different superblock version, allowing the super device driver to know about the feature that is now optional.

> ☑   **Best Practice**
>
> 6.3.8 Increment the block version register as new parameters are added to the superblock.

Using the superblock's version and instantiation registers, the super device driver has all the necessary information it needs to know about the block it is dealing with. Since the instantiation register conveys how the superblock was parameterized, the superblock's version number should not be changed for each combination of parameterization used.

> ☑   **Best Practice**
>
> 6.3.9 Do not change the block version register for different instantiations of the same version of the superblock.

6.4.4. Optional vs. Fixed Registers and Bits

When an optional sub-block is excluded via parameterization, the associated registers for the excluded sub-block should also be excluded. In other words, the registers should behave as if they did not exist. Writes by firmware to excluded optional registers are ignored and reads from those registers return zeros. This gives firmware the flexibility to continue to read and write to those addresses without consequence. Reads from an excluded status register will return all zeros, signifying that nothing is active, pending, working, or enabled. Since no bits are set, firmware will not take action to handle anything.

☑   **Best Practice**

6.3.10 Design optional registers to ignore writes and return zeros when the associated optional sub-block is excluded.

Excluded optional bits located in fixed registers should likewise ignore writes and return zeros for reads. Other bits, either fixed bits or included optional bits, in those fixed registers remain operational.

☑   **Best Practice**

6.3.11 Design optional bits in fixed registers to ignore writes and return zeros when the optional bits' associated optional sub-block is excluded.

Fixed registers and bits should remain in the same address and bit locations no matter which optional registers and bits are included or excluded. This allows the super device driver to read and write to those same locations no matter what parameterization settings were used. Otherwise, the super device driver would have to do some complicated mapping based on the settings in the instantiation register to figure out where bits and registers are located.

Some commercial IP vendors advertise as a benefit that when the IP is configured for an instantiation, the bits that are selected for inclusion will be automatically packed together in the register such that no holes will exist in between bits. That is a bad idea. It kills the super device driver because it does not know where the bits are. Separate (non-super) device drivers must be hand-configured for each instantiation based on how the bit packing was done for that specific parameterization setting.

All fixed and optional bits and registers must be assigned to some location and not change. Location of excluded optional bits and registers must be left empty and unused.

☑   **Best Practice**

6.3.12 Design fixed and optional registers and bits to remain at the same position even when some optional registers and bits are excluded.

6.5. Summary

I discussed many concepts in regard to turning a block into a superblock. Ideally, the block on the chip will be able to carry out any one of the related tasks for the block. The ideal superblock can be put into any chip and used on any product even though only a portion of the superblock will be used on that product.

I described how a block has a supporting entourage of test and verification suites, virtual prototype models, and device driver and firmware support. Making just one version of a block means that only one version of its entourage needs to be developed and maintained.

Defect fixes and new features added to the superblock are tested once but available for all future instantiations.

However, not every block can be a fully implemented superblock due to silicon space, pin count, and cost constraints. So I discussed how to handle unused I/O signals with disconnects or by tying high or low and letting synthesis take out unused logic. I discussed how to implement portions of the block using parameterization. I discussed how portions can be taken out for some chips and added back in for other chips while minimizing the turmoil in the device drivers.

The importance of planning ahead was discussed. By looking ahead and seeing the general direction that is being taken, design decisions can be made to save time and money later on. Not every suggested future feature should be implemented, but being aware of them now will guide decisions to make them more easily implemented later.

6.5.1. Supporting Principles

The concepts of this chapter support the principles of hardware/firmware interface design as follows:

1. **Design for Compatibility:** A superblock helps ensure compatibility from one chip to the next, even if they are instantiated with different options.

2. **Anticipate the Impacts:** A superblock provides a positive impact because a stable and tested block will be more widely used instead of constantly making changes to accommodate the needs of the current chip being designed.

3. **Plan Ahead:** Making a superblock that will work across several families of chips and products requires looking ahead and seeing what future products will be coming.

The next chapter, Design, will cover several aspects in the design of the chip and how it can benefit firmware, allowing for smoother hardware/firmware integration into a final product.

Reference

Beck, Kent. *extreme programming eXplained: embrace change*. Reading, MA: Addison-Wesley, 2000.

CHAPTER 7

Design

In an embedded system, hardware and firmware each have their respective jobs to do but must work together as a system. Coordination must occur between hardware and firmware, especially to keep both working optimally. However, if the system is not balanced, performance could be impacted if firmware is waiting for hardware to finish something or if hardware is waiting for firmware to say what to do next.

Firmware has to wait for hardware to complete a task. In the meantime, firmware often busies itself with other tasks. But if hardware does not generate any kind of task completion signal, firmware is often left guessing and accommodating a worse-case scenario. On the other hand, if firmware is too busy to respond to interrupts from hardware, hardware is left idling and possibly could miss external events it needs to handle.

Timing is not the only aspect, but efficiency across the hardware/firmware interface is a factor, too. Inefficient designs are prone to defects that need to be detected and resolved.

In this chapter I will discuss several design aspects that will help hardware and firmware work more efficiently to increase performance and reduce unnecessary waiting.

7.1. Event Notification

When some event occurs in the block that firmware needs to respond to, firmware needs to be notified. Events in the block result from block tasks that were launched. Launches can be divided into two categories: external launches and firmware launches.

Events from external launches come as a result of something from outside the block launching a block task, such as an incoming data packet or a signal from another block. They come asynchronously; neither the block nor its device driver can anticipate when it will come. The block is set up to watch for it and generate an interrupt for the device driver to handle it.

Events from firmware launches come as a result of firmware having launched some task in the block, such as process some data or send out a packet. Often the hardware engineers designing the block have a good idea as to how long the task will take. However, that information may not be very useful for firmware. For example, if it is known that a block task will take 2000 clock cycles, how can firmware use that information? Firmware engineers do not know what that means for a number of reasons:

- The CPU and the chip are not necessarily running at the same frequency.

- Firmware engineers typically do not know how many CPU clock cycles a section of code takes (unless they are writing in assembly).

- A CPU with a multiple core or that reorders instructions makes it difficult to calculate.

- When idle, a CPU could shut itself down, which stops its own clocks.

- Other system interrupts will stop the current firmware thread from executing temporarily, and the thread will not know that it occurred.

- The CPU may be busy working on some other firmware task.

- I/O reads and writes from the CPU to the chip typically take a few extra clock cycles.

- The CPU can buffer up I/O reads and writes, so others may be in front.

- Different CPUs have different read/write characteristics.

So how should firmware know when the task is done? Firmware can only know how much time passes by reading some counter in the CPU or chip. But firmware is not so concerned with how much time has passed; it is more concerned about when some event has occurred. Different methods have been used, each with their own advantages and disadvantages. Events from external launches always generate an interrupt. But if firmware just launched a task with a very short time, generating an interrupt right back to firmware might not be optimal.

Firmware finds out that it can proceed with the next step using one of these four methods:

- No indication.

- Timed delay.

- Status bit.

- Interrupt.

7.1.1. No Indication

The block does not have a way to notify firmware that the task is complete. This is often used when the task completion is immediate; or, in other words, synchronous with firmware's access of the block, such as changing configuration settings or an instantaneous abort. This is okay because firmware can safely and immediately write something else to the block.

However, when designs evolve and tasks that used to be instantaneous are delayed or take time to complete, there is the risk that firmware could access the block again before it is ready.

It is not good design to not indicate to firmware that a task has completed or that an event has occurred that is not synchronous to firmware's access to the block. Firmware is left guessing when it can take the next step and is prone to guess wrong. In the best case, firmware will know immediately that it guessed wrong and can wait a little longer. But in the worst case, firmware will not know immediately that it guessed wrong, and its premature access will have caused problems elsewhere in the system, resulting in a very difficult defect to diagnose.

Make sure that firmware will be able to know about every event that will occur asynchronously to its access to the block.

☑ **Best Practice**

7.1.1 Always provide an indicator to firmware of any event or condition that firmware needs to know about.

7.1.2. Timed Delay

A timed delay is when firmware needs to wait for a specific amount of time before it can take the next step.

The method that firmware uses to wait must be portable across generations, types, and speed of chips and CPUs. Specifying delays in units of clock cycles is difficult for firmware and not very portable. As mentioned above, telling firmware to wait 2000 clock cycles is difficult.

Specifying delays in units of seconds is portable and firmware generally knows how to handle that on any given platform. Delays measured in seconds are generally implemented using one of three implementations: OS timer, CPU busy loop, or hardware timer.

OS Timer

Most OS platforms provide some type of timer delay facility that will invoke a task after a specified number of ticks. Most systems have a tick size of 1 ms, 10 ms, 100 ms, or other value within that range. The OS timer works well for long delays: seconds, minutes, hours, and so on.

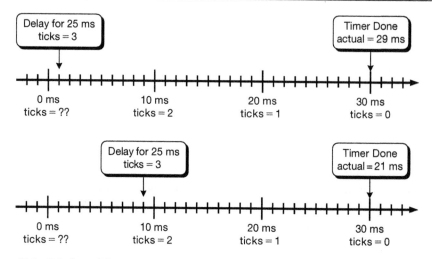

Figure 7.1: OS time-delay request can occur anywhere within the 10-ms tick window.

Short delays, that require just a few ticks, are prone to problems. If the OS tick were 10 ms, then asking for a 25-ms delay requires analysis. If that is a minimum of 25 ms, then 3 ticks are needed and it will generate a 30-ms delay. If 25 ms is a maximum, then 2 ticks are needed which will generate a delay of 20 ms.

Using 3 ticks to get 30 ms when a 25-ms delay is wanted incurs a penalty of an extra 5 ms, or a delay time of an extra 20%. However, this assumes that when a 25-ms delay is requested, it is launched at the beginning of the next 10-ms tick window. But firmware does not operate that way. The task that wants a 25-ms delay could launch that delay anywhere within the 10-ms window.

Figure 7.1 illustrates how a timer delay for 3 ticks can result in a delay anywhere from 20 to 30 ms; therefore, a minimum 25-ms delay cannot be guaranteed with a 3-tick delay. So 4 ticks must be requested, which will result in a delay greater than 30 ms and less than or equal to 40 ms.

The OS timer cannot handle delays less than 1 tick. To induce delays of a shorter amount of time, the CPU busy loop or a hardware timer must be employed.

CPU Busy Loop

A CPU busy loop involves spinning in a loop, reading a hardware or CPU counter incrementing at a known speed until the desired time has elapsed. But spinning in a busy loop ties up the CPU too long, preventing lower-priority tasks from executing. The spinning task is doing nothing useful besides waiting.

Though the spinning loop is undesirable, it may be necessary if a short delay is needed and no hardware timer support is available.

📖 **Tales from the Trenches**

A team member needed a delay of at least 1 ms for an I^2C device driver. The OS timer tick was at 10 ms, and there was no hardware timer available. However, she did not want to use a CPU busy loop. Instead, she used the OS timer with 1 tick, inducing a delay up to 10 ms, which was 9 ms longer than needed. But it avoided the CPU busy loop.

However, 1 tick would only guarantee a delay anywhere between 0 and 10 ms. Depending on when the timer was installed, there was a 10% chance that the delay would be less than 1 ms. So she had to set the timer tick to 2 to guarantee a minimum of 1 ms in all cases.

If a hardware timer is available, the CPU busy loop should not be used.

Hardware Timer

A high-resolution hardware timer, such as general-purpose timers, will generate an interrupt to firmware after the programmed delay. This provides better precision than the OS timer and does not require tying up the CPU with a busy loop.

As a rule of thumb, the hardware timer should have a resolution of at least 1 µs and should have enough bits to count up to 10 times the OS tick. If the OS tick were 10 ms, then the hardware timer should be able to count up to 100 ms. This allows some overlap between the hardware timer and OS timer. This permits firmware to use the precision of the hardware timer for delays less than 10 times the OS tick.

In the above example of OS timers, to guarantee a minimum of 25 ms, firmware must install an OS timer request for 4 ticks, which would yield a delay from 30 to 40 ms. But with a hardware timer with a 1 µs resolution, the delay would be at most 25.002 ms.

☑ **Best Practice**

7.1.2 Provide support in the chip—such as a general-purpose timer—that will generate an interrupt after short delays (less than 100 ms).

7.1.3. Status Bit

The OS timer facility is best suited for long delays. For shorter delays, rather than using a hardware timer, a better option is to have the block indicate when firmware can take the next step.

This allows the block to generate it sooner or later, depending on the task at hand, and it takes the burden off of firmware to launch, manage, and respond to other timers.

📖   **Tales from the Trenches**

On the Unity mono video block, firmware was required to wait for a minimum (but short) amount of time after a reset before writing to any of the registers. There was no status or interrupt bit to indicate that the minimum time had been met. I ran experiments and discovered that going six times through a busy loop was enough to induce a long enough delay before writing to the registers.

About 3 years later, the device driver was ported to a different CPU that ran through the loop faster. This caused the device driver to write to those registers too soon. But there were no indications of errors, except that the printer was behaving incorrectly. I was not working on that project at the time; two other engineers spent months trying to solve it and could not so they asked for my help. After 2 weeks of looking at the problem, I remembered that obscure little timing constraint. The solution was simple; I bumped up the loop count to 30. Had there been a status or interrupt bit to indicate ready, months of engineering resources would have been saved.

The block can indicate task completion in one of two ways, status bit and interrupt. This section talks about status bits.

A status bit is simply a bit in some register that indicates that the event has occurred. It could be an active bit that is cleared when the task is done. Or it could be a ready bit that is set when the block is ready for the next task. Firmware has to read the bit to see what state it is in. If firmware has to wait for the bit to change, it spins in a polling loop, reading the bit over and over until it changes. Listing 7.1 shows a typical polling loop.

Obviously, it is not good design to have an infinite loop in firmware. A max counter should be employed and that is illustrated later in Listing 7.2.

Having firmware poll for the bit to change is best suited if the delay is short.

Listing 7.1: A polling loop used to watch and wait for a bit to get set.

```
// Poll until the 0x10 bit is set
while (1)                // Loop forever
    {
    status = *regStatus; // Read the hardware
    if (status & 0x10)   // If bit is set,
        break;           // then exit the loop
    }
```

☑ **Best Practice**

7.1.3 Use a status bit to indicate completion of tasks guaranteed to complete within an efficient polling period.

If the bit will change within a fcw passes of the loop, it is more efficient for the device driver to poll than to have the firmware system handle the overhead and interrupt as shown here:

- The device driver launches a task in the block in the chip. The device driver then becomes blocked waiting for the interrupt.

- Since that device driver becomes blocked, it is swapped out and another firmware process is swapped in.

- An interrupt occurs and current process is swapped out.

- The main firmware interrupt handler wakes up, reads the interrupt register, decodes where the interrupt came from, then calls the device driver's interrupt handler.

- The device driver's interrupt handler wakes up, reads the block's interrupt register, sets a flag for itself, and exits.

- The device driver now becomes unblocked and can move on.

If the delay is long, then firmware should not tie up the CPU by polling but should incur the overhead and use interrupts.

7.1.4. Interrupts

In general, interrupts are the best way to notify firmware of events because it allows firmware to stay busy doing other tasks and then know immediately when the event occurs.

☑ **Best Practice**

7.1.4 Use an interrupt to indicate completion of tasks not guaranteed to complete within an efficient polling period.

What is an efficient polling period that would determine if a status bit or an interrupt should be used? That is a difficult question because it depends on the hardware and firmware platform. If the task takes 10 clock cycles to complete, a status bit is likely the choice. If it takes 1000, then an interrupt is likely better. What about 100? Where is the boundary?

It is further complicated by events that can sometimes occur quickly and sometimes take a long time, depending on the task. A good example is the abort task. If the block is already idle, abort will likely finish within one or two clock cycles. But if the block is busy and has huge buffers to clean up, it can take a while.

Rather than trying to decide, just wire it to an interrupt channel. Firmware can decide later if it should enable that interrupt channel or just use the channel's interrupt pending bit in the polling loop. Not only does it allow later tuning of where that boundary is, but it also accommodates variability in delays.

☑   **Best Practice**

7.1.5 Use an interrupt channel to indicate completion of tasks that sometimes complete within an efficient polling period.

In Chapter 9, Interrupts, I discuss my preferred style of interrupts. A brief description of that style is needed here for this discussion:

- A bit in the Interrupt Pending register contains a 1 when that interrupt is pending.

- Firmware acks the interrupt by writing a 1 to that bit in that same register.

- A bit in the Interrupt Enable register control whether or not a pending interrupt in the corresponding bit in the Interrupt Status register will be allowed to propagate to the CPU.

- If the interrupt is disabled in the Interrupt Enable register when the interrupt source asserts, the corresponding bit in the Interrupt Pending register will be set to 1, showing an interrupt pending, but it will not be allowed to propagate to the CPU.

- Reading the Interrupt Pending register will show that the interrupt is pending even though it is disabled in the Interrupt Enable register.

- Enabling an already-pending interrupt will cause the interrupt to propagate to the CPU.

This behavior for the interrupt module provides a benefit to this status bit vs. interrupt dilemma. A task's completion signal is wired to a channel in the interrupt module to generate an interrupt to firmware. Normal usage is that the interrupt is enabled and firmware wakes up when the interrupt occurs, thus handling the interrupt case. But firmware has the option to not enable the interrupt and then poll on the bit in the Interrupt Pending register and wait for it to assert. Once asserted, the polling loop drops out, acks the interrupt, and moves on.

If the delay is variable, then firmware can leave the interrupt disabled and poll a few loops. If the bit is not set yet, then enable the interrupt and block waiting for the interrupt to occur. Listing 7.2 illustrates how firmware can poll and then switch to interrupt mode.

Listing 7.2: Look to see if task completes quickly. If not, then wait for an interrupt.

```
/* Launch the XYZ task and wait for completion */
*regIntrEnable &= ~XYZ_INTR_BIT;      /* Disable XYZ intr */
*regQueue = XYZ_TASK_BIT;             /* Start the XYZ task */
for (loop=0; loop<MAX_LOOP; loop++)   /* Loop up to MAX_LOOP times */
    {
    pending = *regIntrPending;        /* Read pending register */
    if (pending & XYZ_INTR_BIT)       /* If XYZ intr is pending, */
        break;                        /* then exit the loop */
    }
if (loop == MAX_LOOP)                 /* Intr has not occurred yet */
    {
    *regIntrEnable |= XYZ_INTR_BIT;   /* Enable XYZ's interrupt */
    blocking_wait (XYZ_INTR_FLAG);    /* Wait for XYZ intr */
    }
else                                  /* XYZ intr has occurred */
    {
    *regIntrPending = XYZ_INTR_BIT;   /* Ack the interrupt */
    }
/* Continue with next step */
```

Even if short delayed events would never need the interrupt style, but just the status-bit style, using the interrupt module for those short delayed events will provide consistency in implementation with long delayed events. In addition, some firmware engineers may decide, for consistency reasons, to implement all delayed events, both short and long, as interrupts, even though some would be more efficient polling the status bit. To allow firmware maximum flexibility, especially in a variety of future platforms, wire all delayed events, both short and long, to channels in the interrupt module for firmware to use.

☑ **Best Practice**

7.1.6 Use the interrupt module to provide both the status bit polling functionality and the interrupt functionality.

7.2. Performance

A success factor of embedded systems products is its performance. Is it fast enough to meet the customer's requirements and expectations? But is it cheap enough that the customer will buy it? Putting a V-8 engine on a lawn mower will definitely provide sufficient performance; however, it will be too expensive for the consumer. Performance must be weighed against cost.

The previous section discussed tradeoffs between polling a status bit and waiting for an interrupt. Interrupts allow firmware to work on something else until the event occurs, and then be notified immediately when it does occur. But judicious use of interrupts is required to avoid bogging down the system with interrupts occurring too frequently.

Likewise, other aspects of the hardware/firmware interaction require judicious designs to ensure optimal performance. This section discusses a few techniques to maximize the performance at the hardware/firmware interface without incurring too much cost in the platform.

7.2.1. Increasing the Buffer

Increasing the buffer size for I/O data allows more data to be transferred with fewer interrupts. But the question is: how big should the buffers be? It depends on the application. Table 7.1 contains some guidelines.

Table 7.1: Guidelines on Buffer Sizes

System Attribute	Guideline
Data packet size and burst size	The buffer should be big enough to hold all the bytes of a multi-byte packet or burst of bytes. The hardware block should be able to handle all bytes in a packet without requiring mid-packet intervention from the device driver.
Quantity of data	For large quantities of data with high-speed I/O, increasing the buffer size reduces the frequency and overhead of device driver interrupts. If the device driver is taking too much time to handle the data, increasing the buffer size can improve performance.
Operating system	If there is no OS or a very basic one, then a larger buffer size in hardware can help reduce firmware complexity. Conversely, firmware with proper OS support is more likely to have separate device drivers, each with its own threads and memory buffers that can efficiently handle I/O traffic with smaller hardware buffers.
Space on chip	If space availability on the die is constrained, the size of the buffer may be limited, requiring firmware to take a bigger load.
Synchronicity of data	If the protocol is such that more data cannot be received without first sending some sort of synchronization data, then the buffer needs to be only as big as the largest expected batch of synchronous data. If the data are asynchronous, the buffer should be sized bigger to accommodate multiple batches that may arrive before the device driver has a chance to respond.
Buffer location	Memory for smaller buffer sizes can be accommodated on the chip itself but it is fixed in size. For large and flexible buffer sizes, consider adding a DMA to access external memory.

These and other system requirements may compete against each other in driving the buffer sizes and will require striking a proper balance.

Increasing the buffer size does require more space on the chip, which must be taken into consideration. The overall silicon space of the buffer as a percentage of the whole chip is a factor. Doubling the size of the buffer from 8 bytes to 16 bytes has a small impact on the chip. But doubling the size of the buffer from 8 Kbytes to 16 Kbytes will impact the space requirements on the chip.

☑   **Best Practice**

7.2.1 Size receive and transmit buffers appropriately for efficient communication between hardware and firmware.

7.2.2. Working Ahead

It may not be just a matter of making the buffer size bigger. Once the buffer fills up, firmware has to deal with it. But firmware will do so whenever it is allowed, given its priority compared to other tasks that need to run. After the block fills up one buffer, must the block wait around until firmware empties that buffer? Or is there another buffer that the block can start filling up?

If the block can work ahead, it can keep busy. The size and number of buffers dictate how far ahead the block can work.

The same applies in the other direction. If firmware can queue up a bunch of work for the block, firmware can forget about it for a little while.

DMA controllers can help by providing chaining capabilities, allowing immediate continuation from one chunk of memory to the next.

☑   **Best Practice**

7.2.2 Provide data buffering, queuing, and chaining to maximize data throughput.

Buffers and chaining allow for continuous processing of data from one chunk to the next assuming that associated settings in configuration registers stay the same. However, if configuration settings need to change between chunks, the block needs to finish with one chunk and stop, and then allow firmware to change the settings and start the next chunk. Stopping between chunks and requiring firmware interaction will not work if the system requires moving from one chunk to the next in a timely fashion.

An example of this type of system is a LaserJet printer where the raster image for one page is maintained in several chunks. Once the mechanical gear train starts moving paper and scanning the laser, it cannot stop. So the block has to move from one chunk to the next within 50 ns. Firmware cannot step in, set up, and start up the next chunk during that time.

The solution to this is to double-buffer the necessary configuration registers, or basically have two sets of registers, the working set, and the hold set. When hardware is working on one chunk with its configuration settings, firmware can load up the hold register set with the settings for the next chunk. When hardware is done with the one chunk, it can then transfer settings from the hold set to the working set and continue with no delay. When the block transfers from one chunk to the next, it interrupts firmware, notifying it that the hold register set is empty and can be filled with the settings for the next chunk.

☑   **Best Practice**

7.2.3 Provide double-buffered registers so that firmware can queue the next task while the block is still running the current task.

7.2.3. Tuning

When a system is being designed, a lot of study is put into optimizing performance vs. power consumption. Educated guesses are used to figure out bus priorities, memory bandwidth, and clock speed. Simulations are used to refine those numbers. But even after a thorough study, numbers may not be right because of incorrect assumptions or unanticipated use cases. This causes problems for fabricated chips if those numbers are hard-coded and need to change.

Some performance aspects in the chip can be designed to allow firmware to tune those numbers if the default values need to be changed. This could include being able to adjust bus priorities, DMA transfer sizes, clock speeds of different buses or blocks.

In some cases dynamic changes in the tuning numbers may be desired to alter the behavior based on conditions. Many battery-powered products do this by switching between being optimized for battery life or for performance.

☑   **Best Practice**

7.2.4 Make the chip tunable so that firmware can adjust performance characteristics such as bus priorities and clock speeds.

7.2.4. Margins

Consumers always want the new model of the electronic devices to be faster than the previous model. To satisfy that demand, it is not uncommon for existing chips to be looked at for producing faster products. However, it is difficult to know if there will be enough bandwidth. Existing products are known to work okay, but how much performance leeway is there? Is it running at 60% or 95%? If it is 95%, then it cannot go much faster.

If the chip were designed with a 10 or 20% performance margin, it will increase its chance of being usable in the next faster product, thus saving several months and millions of dollars of designing a new chip just to make it slightly faster.

☑   **Best Practice**

7.2.5 Maximize performance margins to increase the potential for chip reuse in faster products.

7.3. Power-On

Power-on initialization requires extra consideration because different hardware and firmware components are turning on in different states and initializing at different rates.

7.3.1. Power-On Interaction

Hardware typically comes out of power-on reset very quickly. Firmware typically does not. Firmware takes a long time to boot; it tests memory, installs the OS, installs the device drivers, and launches the applications. Each device driver and each application has to be launched serially. Each one starts, initializes its data structures, and opens any connection ports to other firmware components.

It is not until the device drivers are installed (one at a time) that firmware starts to communicate with hardware. Each device driver initializes their respective block by configuring registers and enabling interrupts.

Before one firmware component can interact with another firmware component, both need to be up and running before they can start talking to each other. This requires some agreement or protocol between the two. Typically if one block needs to interact with another block, they wait until their respective device drivers are up and running to coordinate the interaction. If, however, blocks need to interact at power-on, they must be able to do so without firmware assistance. Any results (such as success, failure, status) from that power-on interaction can be reflected in registers that their respective device drivers can read when they start up.

☑   **Best Practice**

7.3.1 Design the block such that it does not require firmware interaction immediately at power-on.

If the two blocks are on different chips on different devices, it is very likely that power will not be applied to both devices at the same time. An example is a printer that is already on when the computer turns on. The blocks handling the power-on protocol for the interface must be able to handle that power-on protocol, even if it already had had its power applied for some time.

Besides going through the power-on protocol when the remote block powers up even though the local block has had power for some time, the local block must safely handle the case when it powers up when the remote block is off. With the remote block off, then any incoming signals from that remote block must be assumed unstable and incorrect. The local block must gracefully handle that case. It should also convey that condition to the device driver when it starts up.

📖   **Tales from the Trenches**

An engine interface block in an ASIC on the printer formatter board communicates with a print engine via a proprietary protocol that includes a power-on handshaking sequence. Most of the time, both the formatter and the engine are on the same power supply. But during early development in the lab, they are often on separate power supplies. When turned on at different times, the power-on handshaking sequence would fail and the block would cease further communications.

When the engine interface device driver boots, it reads the status and discovers the communication error. Fortunately, the proprietary protocol contains a communication reset capability that the device driver invokes, allowing both sides to try again to get in sync.

☑   **Best Practice**

7.3.2 Design each block such that is still works at power-on even if its collaborative blocks are not ready yet.

7.3.2. Power-On State of I/O Lines

The power-on state of I/O lines must be in a safe or off state to avoid problems and danger until firmware can boot up and start safely coordinating the various activities.

The final usage of GPIO lines is typically undefined when the chip is designed; it is unknown if they will be used as input or output. In order to avoid contention with multiple devices on the lines, the GPIO lines should default to input. Once firmware is up and running, it can change appropriate pins to output as needed.

☑ **Best Practice**

7.3.3 Default GPIO pins to input.

Besides GPIO lines, any other lines controlling external motors, switches, and so on should wake up in the off and safe state. It then waits until firmware is up and running enough to put everything in the desired state.

7.3.3. Block-Level Power Control

As devices become more sophisticated, as batteries and power sources become smaller, and as government regulations become more stringent, power is an ever-increasing issue. There are many efforts in the industry to make faster and denser chips run with less power.

One area is the ability to power down individual blocks. This may be done by actually removing power or by stopping the block's system clock. Powering down individual blocks is desired when the system is in a power save or quiescent mode, or if the block will not be used at all in this system, or if the block is not being used at the moment. When firmware determines that conditions exist to do so, it can remove power from the block.

☑ **Best Practice**

7.3.4 Provide firmware-accessible power controls for each block.

When power is reapplied to a block, it will go through its power-on sequence, even though the rest of the chip and any of its collaborative blocks will have already been alive and operating. This requires the blocks and firmware to handle "re-power-on" cases.

7.4. Communication and Control

Efficient hardware/firmware interface requires access to necessary information and flexibility in operation control. This section discusses some of those aspects.

7.4.1. Error Information

Section 5.9.2, Copious Information about Errors, discusses how ample information about error situations, causes, and results should be provided to help diagnose and resolve errors conditions.

In addition to copious information in the documentation, copious information should also be provided by the block when the error occurs. This includes current values of addresses, counters, external and internal signals, and state machines. Present as much relevant and even marginally relevant information to firmware as possible; it is unknown what little tidbit of information will give a clue into the problem. Copious information allows the device driver to make intelligent decisions in its error handling procedure.

📖   **Tales from the Trenches**

In the engine interface block controlling a proprietary communication protocol with the print engine, a state machine controls the protocol and watches for various error conditions during the communication. When an error is detected, it transitions to the error state to generate an error interrupt, and then returns to idle. Firmware is interrupted and told that than an error occurred. But there was no indication of what the error was.

We enhanced the block and added some extra status bits to an existing register to indicate which state detected the error. Then when an error occurs, firmware queries the status bit for the additional information, providing useful error data.

☑   **Best Practice**

7.4.1 When an error occurs, provide copious status information to firmware, including internal and external signal levels, state machine states, and counter values.

7.4.2. DMA Features

A distinct advantage of hardware is the ability to do things in parallel. A DMA controller is transferring data in and out of memory. It can perform some basic tasks on that data without impacting the data throughput.

One that has proved useful is a byte swapping ability. This can help in a few different ways:

- The block can work with big- or little-endian processors.

- It can facilitate data exchanges between blocks or processors of different endianess.

- It can handle data downloaded to the device in either endianess.

- Minimize the amount of time firmware has to spend on byte swapping, a very tedious firmware task.

- It could workaround endianess problems within the chip.

📖 **Tales from the Trenches**

The incoming DMA of a block was incorrectly wired to the bus with the wrong byte order. Since that DMA had a byte-swapping feature, firmware was able to configure it to swap it back before the data went on into the block. This feature averted an expensive chip respin.

☑ **Best Practice**

7.4.2 Include a byte-swapping capability in the DMA controller module instantiated throughout the chip.

A common problem with embedded systems is memory stomps and corrupted data. Building a CRC and/or a checksum generator inside the DMA can provide a data signature that provides a sanity check on the data. Comparing the signature to data when written to memory by one block to the signature of the data when read by another block will catch memory data corruption while in memory.

Since data corruption problems are typically not noted until the end of the pipeline, looking at the DMA controller CRC and/or checksum signatures at the various steps within the pipeline may give clues to corruption problems. Note that the signature may not be the same throughout the data pipeline. A block processing the data is likely to be modifying the data. So the DMA controller signature when the block reads the data may be different than the signature when it writes the data.

Adding the CRC and/or checksum generator in the DMA controller module that is instantiated throughout the chip will ensure that the same algorithm is used in all locations.

☑   **Best Practice**

7.4.3 Include a CRC and/or a checksum generator in the DMA controller module instantiated throughout the chip.

7.4.3. Sharing I/O Pins

Given that pins on a package are expensive, it is not uncommon for more than one block to share pins. Output signals from more than one block to the same output pin must be muxed since only one block can be allowed to drive the pin.

Input pins that fan to more than one block should also be switched such that only one block will get the actual signals. This will prevent inadvertent interrupts and responses from blocks that are supposedly not active. The input signals not currently configured to be connected to the pin still needs to be configured to an appropriate asserted or deasserted level, such as deasserted to indicate that the block is not ready for transmission.

Figure 7.2 illustrates this pin sharing between three blocks: A, B, and C. Block A is currently selected to be connected to the pins. The signal coming out of block A is routed through the mux to the output pin. The output signals of blocks B and C are not connected and therefore ignored. The incoming signal is routed through the mux to block A. The input signal of block B is tied high while not connected to the pin and the input signal of block C is tied low.

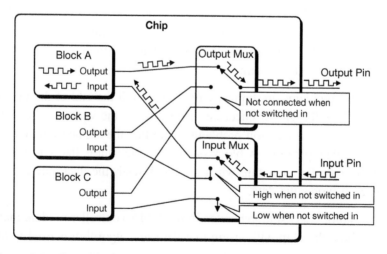

Figure 7.2: Three blocks using the same I/O pins, but only one at a time.

☑ **Best Practice**

7.4.4 For each chip output pin connected to multiple blocks on the chip, multiplex the block output lines to select which block controls the signal on the chip output pin at any given time.

☑ **Best Practice**

7.4.5 For each chip input pin connected to multiple blocks on the chip, multiplex the input line to select which block (or blocks) receives the signal at any given time.

7.4.4. Hiding Implementation Details

The main emphasis of this book is with regard to what hardware looks like to firmware. To firmware, a register is a storage location that holds bits. But it makes no difference to firmware how that register is implemented, whether the flip-flop is a JK-, SR-, T-, or D-type flip-flop. No matter which type is used, it looks the same to firmware. Firmware can write to it and firmware can read from it.

This permits hardware engineers the flexibility to implement the designs as desired, especially since the technologies and resources available vary widely on the varieties of chip platforms available. The fundamental building blocks and available resources for circuits are different among the various FPGA and ASIC technologies.

I will use as an example countup and countdown counters. Both have their uses with respect to their real-world application. Table 7.2 illustrates their uses.

A countdown counter can be implemented with a countup counter. Counting from 20 (0x14) down to 0 can be treated as counting from -20 (0xEC) up to 0. Translating 20 (0x14) to -20 (0xEC) is easily done by taking the two's complement. Reading 0xF7 (-9) from the

Table 7.2: Uses of Countup vs. Countdown Counters

Countup Counters	Countdown Counters
Bytes received	Bytes left to transmit
Time elapsed	Time remaining
Address counter	Waveform generator
Event counter	Watchdog timer
Stopwatch	Timer delay

counter and taking a two's complement yields 0x09 (9) will let firmware know where the count is at.

Hardware engineers might prefer to use countup counters because they may be readily available on the FPGA they are using. Other factors, such as bit width, flip-flop type, fan-in, LUTs, and XOR gates affect whether a countup or countdown counter is preferable.

Firmware should not have to care about the details of the implementation. If a countdown counter was implemented with a countup counter, it is possible for firmware to handle it by taking a two's complement of the value before writing to the register. However, firmware engineers must then remember to take a two's complement anywhere in the code that writes to that register. In addition, a two's complement must be taken anywhere in the firmware code for any reads from that counter register. Other companion registers often accompany a counter register, such as a reload register containing a value that is used to load the counter upon some event. Firmware engineers must also take a two's complement anytime the companion register is written to or read from. This exposes firmware to errors if two's complement is applied where it should not be, or is not applied where it should be.

This is further complicated if the block was implemented as a countup on an FPGA but as a countdown on an ASIC. Then the device driver will have to add the ability to first determine the implementation used and then switch everywhere applicable depending on the implementation. Again, another potential source of bugs.

Firmware should not be required to accommodate a hardware-specific implementation because it leaves exposed an incorrect firmware/hardware pairing. Hardware should accommodate the hardware-specific implementation because the accommodations will always correctly pair with the implementation. Therefore, the block should contain the two's complement translator, thus hiding implementation detail from firmware. In other words, hardware should provide a black box to firmware, removing the need for firmware to know how it was implemented inside.

Figure 7.3 illustrates how one two's complement translator can be implemented in the chip to provide that translation for any countup counter in the chip being used as a countdown counter.

Another example in the counter area is the use of gray counters instead of binary counters. Gray counters consume less power and produce less noise. Again a translator in front of the gray counter would handle appropriate gray-to-binary translation.

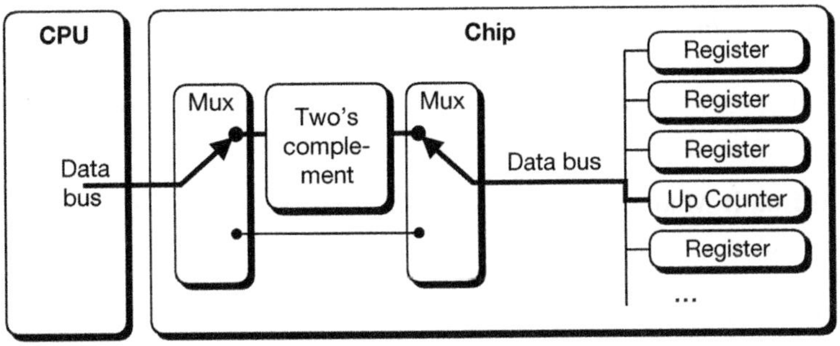

Figure 7.3: The countup counter is being accessed through the two's complement translator for countdown behavior.

☑   **Best Practice**

7.4.6 Use translator modules to optimize the firmware interface to a feature of the chip when the preferred hardware implementation of that feature is firmware-unfriendly.

7.5. Summary

In this chapter, I covered several aspects of hardware design. In the first section, I discussed the importance of ensuring that firmware was notified of any pertinent event that occurred in the block. I also discussed various ways of how firmware could know the task in the block was done. The most important way was to provide firmware with an interrupt bit that firmware can choose to use with interrupts disabled by polling the interrupt status bit, or by enabling that interrupt and waiting for the interrupt to occur.

In the second section, I discussed the how designs can impact the performance of the hardware/firmware interaction. I gave a few suggestions on how to improve that, such as increasing available buffer space.

I then discussed a few aspects of power-on and how firmware is not alive yet so the blocks must be designed to be self-sufficient until firmware can take over.

The last section gave several ways of making more efficient the ability for firmware to communicate with and control the block.

7.5.1. Supporting Principles

The concepts of this chapter support the principles of hardware/firmware interface design as follows:

1. **Balance the Load:** Many of the concepts are directed toward providing features for firmware to lighten its load but without necessarily adding extra load for hardware.

2. **Anticipate the Impacts:** Providing timer help and status bits indicating block events lessens the impact on firmware for handling timed delays.

3. **Design for Contingencies:** Adding features to the block, such as the DMA byte-swapping capability, could avert chip respins when problems are discovered.

Next is Chapter 8, Registers, which will cover several aspects in the design and assignments of registers and the bits in the registers.

CHAPTER 8

Registers

Registers are the interface that hardware provides to firmware; this is the primary means of communication between the two. Firmware reads from and writes to those registers. Hardware communicates information to firmware by making it available in registers for firmware to read. Firmware configures hardware and launches tasks in hardware by writing to registers. More specifically, each hardware block in the chip has a set of registers. Each block typically has a device driver within firmware that accesses that set of registers.

The term, register, has two slight variations in meaning that overlap each other. One is as an addressable portal through which firmware accesses hardware. The other is as a bank of flip-flops. Figure 8.1 illustrates the two types and the overlap.

Most portals have a bank of flip-flops behind them as illustrated in the middle section. An example is a configuration register where firmware sets or clears bits and the flip-flops retain those settings.

Some portals do not have a bank of flip-flops but have signals or combinatorial logic behind them, as illustrated by the left section. An example is a register where firmware writes a 1 that launches a state machine but no flip-flop is used to hold that 1 when the write operation is completed.

The shaded section on the right illustrates banks of flip-flops which are internal to the block and are not accessible to firmware. An example is an internal buffer that holds intermediate data in the block.

The term, register, as used in this book, is in the context of a firmware-addressable portal. Or in other words, in Figure 8.1, it is the left and middle sections with the white background, not the right section with the shaded background.

Another term used in the industry is CSR (control/status register).

This chapter discusses registers in great detail because the reading and writing of registers is where hardware and firmware meet, and therefore must mesh well together. I will discuss several aspects of registers, such as register addresses, locations of bits within a register, and types of bits. I will cover several problematic areas to watch out for, such as mixing types

DOI: 10.1016/B978-1-85617-605-7.00010-1.

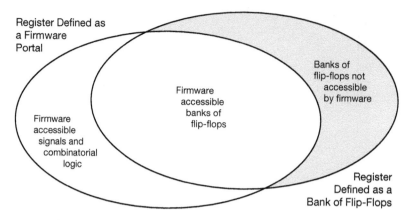

Figure 8.1: Two overlapping uses of the term "register."

of bits in a register, backward and forwards compatibility, and read-modify-writes. I will also discuss additional areas, such as ID codes and initiating block tasks.

All the points discussed in this chapter have the objective to improve the interaction at the hardware/firmware interface. By following the guidelines outlined in this chapter, many problems will be eliminated or mitigated.

8.1. Addressing

One or more chips exist within an embedded system that firmware must access. One or more registers exist within the chip that firmware must access. An address is used to select a chip and a register within the chip. This section discusses addresses.

Within this book, the terms processor and chip are used as separate entities, even though, technically speaking, a processor resides on a chip. The registers that firmware addresses may be on a die separate from the processor or on the same die as the processor such as on an SoC.

8.1.1. Processor Access

The method of the access by firmware depends on the architecture of the processor and the system. Two methods are commonly referred to as memory-mapped I/O and port I/O. I will add a third, multi-step I/O.

Memory-Mapped I/O

The same bus and instructions are used to access either main memory or chips. Different address ranges dictate whether main memory or chips will be accessed. This method provides firmware with transparent access to the hardware.

Listing 8.1: Memory-mapped access to registers.

```
void someFunction (void)
    {
    uint32_t volatile * regA = (uint32_t volatile *) REG_A_ADDR;
    uint32_t volatile * regB = (uint32_t volatile *) REG_B_ADDR;
    uint32_t offset = OFFSET;
    . . .
    *regB = *regA + offset;
    . . .
    }
```

Special sequences of instructions or handling of timing constraints are not required to get at the registers. This allows firmware to treat registers like it would treat its own variables and structures. Listing 8.1 illustrates a register being read from, regA, then adding to it the firmware variable, offset, and then writing the results to another register, regB.

Memory-mapped I/O is the preferred access method to the chip. The other methods may be necessary but memory-mapped I/O is the preferred method.

☑   **Best Practice**

8.1.1 Provide access to registers using memory-mapped I/O where possible.

Port I/O

With port I/O, processors have separate instructions, such as Intel's IN and OUT instructions, to access chips differently than main memory. Port I/O may be required in some cases, such as the processor selected or to avoid taking address space away from main memory. Depending on the design, separate address and/or data bus may be used.

Platforms that use port I/O forces firmware to use functions for reads and writes. The compiler then translates those functions into appropriate processor instructions.

Multi-Step I/O

This method of access requires multiple steps to get to the desired register. It boils down to using a combination of memory-mapped and/or port I/O access methods but multiple steps are required to do so. A list of examples of multi-port I/O access follows:

- Firmware has to go through one chip to get to another.

- Firmware has to switch in the desired page or bank of memory.

- Firmware has to switch modes within the chip.

- Address and data share the same bus.

- A protocol handshake is required.

- Addresses and data are shifted serially on a single wire.

- Timing delays are required to handle different chip speeds.

Firmware generally handles multi-step I/O through read and write functions. This ensures that all locations in firmware that are reading and writing will do so the same way. This is illustrated in Listing 8.2.

Listing 8.2: Multi-step access to registers.

```
uint32_t readReg (uint32_t addr)
    {
    uint32_t data;
    *regAccessPage = addr >> 16;      // Set up proper register page
    *regAccessAddr = addr & 0xFFFF;   // Address within the page
    *regAccessMode = ACCESS_READ;     // Setup mode
    while (!(*regAccessStatus & ACCESS_READ_READY))
        ;                             // Wait until ready
    data = *regAccessData;            // Get data
    return (data);                    // Return data
    }

void writeReg (uint32_t addr, uint32_t data)
    {
    *regAccessPage = addr >> 16;      // Set up proper register page
    *regAccessAddr = addr & 0xFFFF;   // Address within the page
    *regAccessMode = ACCESS_WRITE;    // Setup mode
    *regAccessData = data;            // Write data
    while (!(*regAccessStatus & ACCESS_WRITE_DONE))
        ;                             // Wait until done
    return;                           // Return
    }

void someFunction (void)
    {
    uint32_t offset = OFFSET;
    . . .
    writeReg (REG_B_ADDR, readReg(REG_A_ADDR) + offset);
    . . .
    }
```

The rest of this discussion on addresses refers mainly to memory-mapped I/O. But it extrapolates easily to port I/O and multi-step I/O.

8.1.2. Chip Base Addresses

In memory-mapped address space, each chip has a base address which is its offset in the memory address space. The chip base address is the starting address for the range of addresses of registers within the chip. This is illustrated in Figure 8.2.

Depending on the implementation of the chip and the system it will be used in, the chip base address may be static or dynamic. Static addresses are assigned during the design of the system based on the chips, boards, busses, and processors used. Static addresses are fixed and will not change, and can be hard-coded in the device driver.

Dynamic addresses are assigned at bootup or while running based on live hardware configuration changes, such as swappable parts. The firmware determines current configuration and makes address assignments as necessary. Addresses are likely to change when the system reboots or is configured differently. Device drivers make function calls to obtain the base address of their respective chips.

☑ **Best Practice**

8.1.2 Assign a unique base address to each chip.

Chip Addresses

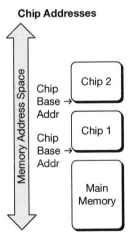

Figure 8.2: Chips mapped into memory-mapped space.

8.1.3. Block Offset and Base Addresses

A chip typically has more than one block, such as a USB device and a compact flash memory controller. Each block has its own address range, large enough to include all registers within that block. Each block has its own offset relative to the chip's base address, as illustrated in Figure 8.3. Regardless of whether the chip's base address is static or dynamic, the block offset is always the same.

The block offset is added to the chip's base address to get a block base address. If the chip's base address is static, then the block base address can be hard-coded at compile time by adding the block offset to the chip base address, as shown in Listing 8.3.

If this same chip is put on a different board and placed at a different address on that board, then only CHIP_BASE_ADDR in the device driver code needs to be changed.

If the chip's base address is dynamic, firmware will add the block offset to the dynamic address after calling a function to retrieve the dynamic address, as illustrated in Listing 8.4.

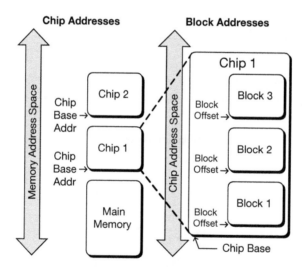

Figure 8.3: Blocks mapped into the chip's address space.

Listing 8.3: Generating the block base address from a static chip base address.

```
#define CHIP_BASE_ADDR      0xF00D0000
#define BLOCK_OFFSET        0x0000FEE0
#define BLOCK_BASE_ADDR     (CHIP_BASE_ADDR + BLOCK_OFFSET)
// The code can now use BLOCK_BASE_ADDR to get at registers
```

Listing 8.4: Generating the block base address from a dynamic chip base address.

```
#define CHIP_ID_CODE      0x1D
#define BLOCK_OFFSET      0x0000FEE0
#define BLOCK_BASE_ADDR   blockBaseAddr

uint32_t   chipBaseAddr;
uint32_t  *blockBaseAddr;

chipBaseAddr = getChipBaseAddr (CHIP_ID_CODE);
blockBaseAddr = (uint32_t *) (chipBaseAddr + BLOCK_OFFSET);
// The code can now use BLOCK_BASE_ADDR to get at registers
```

In either the static or dynamic case, the same block offset is used, BLOCK_OFFSET. From that, firmware calculates BLOCK_BASE_ADDR to access registers.

☑   **Best Practice**

8.1.3 Assign an address offset to each block relative to the chip's base address.

Assign each block its own address range to cover all of its registers. The address range of one block should not overlap that of another. Otherwise, firmware could inadvertently write to a register of another block.

☑   **Best Practice**

8.1.4 Allocate non-overlapping address ranges to each block in the chip.

Each block should allocate some room within its address range to add new registers in the future. The amount of space to allocate may vary, depending on the size of the block and anticipated expansion. But it can be padded out to where the next block starts.

☑   **Best Practice**

8.1.5 Leave room in the block's address range for future registers.

Assign blocks along 256-byte boundaries. This helps firmware engineers as they manage the memory map, write the firmware, and debug problems. Addresses that are examined will be easier for engineers to decode in their head. When written in hex format, the lower two hex digits will be 0x00. In other words, block offsets will be assigned at 0x0000, 0x0100, 0x0200, 0x0300, and so on.

On a 32-bit system, a 256-byte block has room for 64 register addresses. A small block that only needs 9 registers will have 55 unused locations before the next block starts. A block that needs 110 register locations requires two 256-byte chunks of address space and would have spare locations for 18 registers.

If address space is tight in the system, then maybe blocks needs to be aligned along 64-byte boundaries or some other alignment.

☑   **Best Practice**

8.1.6 Align the starting addresses of each block to a 256-byte boundary.

8.1.4. Register Offset Addresses

Each register within a block is assigned an offset relative to the block's base, as illustrated in Figure 8.4. To calculate the address of a register, the device driver adds the register offset to the block's base address (which is the block offset plus the chip base address). The device driver then uses this address to access the desired register.

☑   **Best Practice**

8.1.7 Assign an address offset to each register relative to the block's base address.

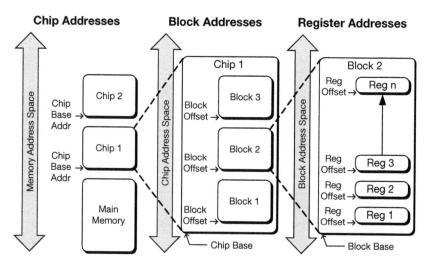

Figure 8.4: Registers mapped into the block's address space.

8.1.5. Sub-Blocks

A block may have logical subdivisions—sections where natural boundaries exist. Possible types of sub-blocks follow:

- **Used by multiple blocks:** A sub-block that needs to be instantiated multiple times in multiple blocks, such as a DMA controller.

- **Multiple instantiations:** A sub-block that needs to be instantiated multiple times, such as multiple channels and parallel pipelines.

- **Removable section:** A sub-block that could, if not needed, be left out when instantiated, such as support for a feature that the target product would not need.

- **Multiple design teams:** Each engineer or team designs their assigned sub-block with clear boundaries between them that, when assembled, will constitute the block as a whole.

Each of these sub-blocks should have its own address offset and range. This keeps the registers together within logical groups. Each sub-block should also have room to grow and should be aligned on a boundary, such as a 16-byte boundary.

☑ **Best Practice**

8.1.8 Assign each sub-block its own base address and address range, with room for expansion.

8.1.6. Bursting

Depending on the architecture of the chip, the CPU, and the system where it will be used, it may be slow to access non-sequential registers. To overcome that, some architectures provide a bursting facility which enables several words to be transmitted for sequential addresses. PCI Express is an example where random address access is much slower than sequential address access. If bursting might be required for the block, study the grouping and order of registers that firmware needs to access at the same time.

For example, to start a task, firmware may need to write to the following addresses in the following order:

- Address register

- Count register

- Control register

- Start register

Put those four registers in a group of sequential addresses. Those four words can then be transmitted in one burst. The address of the first register may need to be aligned to some boundary, such as a quad-word boundary. Other groups of related registers would be similarly grouped.

☑   **Best Practice**

8.1.9 Assign a burst-aligned sequence of addresses to related groups of registers if bursting is needed.

In the above list, the start register is listed last. Be sure to have it last in the address order. This ensures that the other registers are properly set up before the task in the block is launched.

☑   **Best Practice**

8.1.10 Assign the start register to the last position in the burst sequence of registers.

8.1.7. Unused Address Locations

Each block is assigned an address range and, most likely, some of the locations in that range are unused. The block must correctly handle any firmware accesses to any unused registers. Correct handling means that the block must ignore any writes to unused locations and return zeros for any reads from unused locations.

Why would firmware access unused locations? One reason may be due to a defect in firmware that addresses the wrong register. Ignoring writes and returning zeros for reads reduces side effects of buggy firmware.

Another reason is that the firmware might be designed to access an unused location because a register exists at that location on a different version of that block. For example, firmware might read that register to look for any pending conditions. On the version of the block where that register does not exist, reading the register will return all zeros. Firmware examines the return value and discovers that none of those conditions are pending and therefore will not take associated action in response to that. For this reason, it is important that the block drives zeros onto the data bus for reads and not let the lines float. It would confuse firmware if random bits in that register are randomly set, causing firmware to take the associated action when it should not have.

Another reason is that firmware may want to dump all registers or configure all registers by using a `for()` loop where it starts at an address and increments that address each time through the `for()` loop, accessing all registers in sequence, including any unused register locations in that range.

The block also needs to watch out for address aliasing. To illustrate with a simple example, suppose a block is assigned an address range for eight 8-bit registers, from address 0x00 to 0x07. However, the block only needs four registers at 0x00, 0x01, 0x02, and 0x03. For those four registers, only bits 0 (LSB) and 1 are needed and it would be easy to ignore bit 2. If bit 2 was ignored, then accessing locations 0x04–0x07 will instead access registers at 0x00–0x03. This is dangerous when firmware writes to address 0x04 because it will end up in the register at address 0x00, which could cause an undesirable response.

☑   **Best Practice**

8.1.11 Design the chip to return zeros for reads from unused address locations.

☑   **Best Practice**

8.1.12 Design the chip to ignore writes to unused address locations.

8.1.8. Changes in the Next Chip

The discussion to this point on addresses was in context of designing a new block in a new chip. This section discusses addresses with regard to making changes to the existing addresses for the next chip.

The static base address of the chip can change with little impact to firmware. (For dynamic base addresses, firmware is already set up to handle different addresses when necessary.) Likewise, the block offset within the chip can change. As new blocks are added, deleted, and changed, block offsets will be changed.

Changing the block base address (because the chip's base address changed and/or the block's offset changed) is typically a one- or two-line firmware change.

However, each register offset within its block should not change on the next version of the chip. If the register offsets do not change, no register address changes are needed in the device driver. Porting the device driver to new chips is easier and less prone to problems when all the register offsets stay the same. This also helps firmware engineers write device drivers that will work for multiple chip versions. Listing 8.5 is an example of how a device driver can service different chips.

Listing 8.5: A device driver that can service different chips.

```
// Details about the Banana chip
#define BANANA_CHIP_ID        0x00001400
#define BANANA_BASE_ADDR      0xF00D0000
#define BANANA_BLOCK_OFFSET   0x0000FEE0

// Details about the Potato chip
#define POTATO_CHIP_ID        0x00002700
#define POTATO_BLOCK_OFFSET   0x0000E000

// Variable for the block base address
uint32_t volatile *blockBaseAddr;

// Determine which chip and get its base address
uint32_t chipId = getChipId();      // Get chip ID
if (chipId == BANANA_CHIP_ID)       // If it is the Banana chip
    {                               // Chip has static address
    blockBaseAddr = BANANA_BASE_ADDR;
    blockBaseAddr += BANANA_BLOCK_OFFSET;
    }
else if (chipId == POTATO_CHIP_ID)// If it is the Potato chip
    {                               // Chip has dynamic address
    blockBaseAddr = getChipBaseAddr (POTATO_CHIP_ID);
    blockBaseAddr += POTATO_BLOCK_OFFSET;
    }
else                                // Driver can't support this chip
    {
    reportError (ERROR_UNKNOWN_CHIP);
    }

// The code can now use blockBaseAddr to get at registers
uint32_t volatile * regA = blockBaseAddr + 0x00;
uint32_t volatile * regB = blockBaseAddr + 0x04;
uint32_t volatile * regC = blockBaseAddr + 0x08;
// And the rest of the registers ...
```

Note that at the end of the above listing, the register addresses have the same offset, no matter which chip it is on. It is because the register offset from the block base address remains unchanged.

☑   **Best Practice**

8.1.13 Preserve the address offsets of the registers within the block when instantiating the block in a new chip.

When deleting registers, leave that address location empty. Do not move other registers into that place. When adding new registers, assign them to address locations that have never been used before. This avoids problems when device drivers for one version try to run on a block of a different version. Old device drivers accessing the old register locations have no effect and the new registers will not be inadvertently accessed. If new registers were put in at the same location as the old registers, unpredictable results will occur when the old device driver intends to access the old register but instead access the new. Leaving the space empty also leaves open the possibility of bringing those old registers back in a future generation of the block.

☑ **Best Practice**

8.1.14 Avoid reusing address locations of deleted registers in an existing block.

Although it is preferable to not change register offsets, at times it will be needed to make room for new registers to support new features. If many of the registers need to shift to make room, it may be an opportune time to make major adjustments, such as reordering the sub-blocks, putting gaps in between, and reclaiming locations of deleted registers. When needing to change register addresses, consult with firmware engineers for suggestions on how and what changes to make.

8.2. Bit Assignment

I have just discussed register addresses, how they are used to get at the desired register in a chip, and how they should or should not be organized and changed. I will now discuss the contents of registers and how bits should or should not be organized and changed. In this discussion, 32-bit registers are used but the concepts apply to 16- and 8-bit registers of any other size.

8.2.1. Assigning Bit Positions

When first populating a register with bits, start at LSB (Least Significant Bit), bit 0. If only 2 bits in a register are defined, starting at the LSB allows firmware to use the shorter 0x1 and 0x2, instead of the longer 0x80000000 and 0x40000000. As more bits are added, assign them to the left of existing bits.

This register map of the ABC Configuration Register shows 2 bits, A (Abort) and B (Bypass), in positions 0 and 1, respectively.

MSB							ABC Configuration Register—0x0020	LSB
Bits	31 30 29 28	27 26 25 24	23 22 21 20	19 18 17 16	15 14 13 12	11 10 9 8	7 6 5 4	3 2 1 0
R/W	- - - -	- - - -	- - - -	- - - -	- - - -	- - - -	- - - -	- - B A
Reset	0 0 0 0	0 0 0 0	0 0 0 0	0 0 0 0	0 0 0 0	0 0 0 0	0 0 0 0	0 0 0 0

A: **Abort**—Set this bit to abort the current task.

B: **Bypass**—Set this to put the block in bypass mode.

☑   **Best Practice**

8.2.1 Assign bits to the register starting on the right side at the least significant bit.

Keeping all the bits against the LSB side is a general guideline. There are cases when exceptions are appropriate and will be discussed. Here is one exception.

While assigning bits to a register, think about possible future needs and make room for them. In the register map, suppose the bypass might need to be expanded in the future to use 2 bits to be able to select one of up to four bypass modes. Leave the next position empty and assign the next bit after that.

This register map now shows bit 2 skipped over in case Bypass needs to expand to 2 bits. The next bit, C (Combine), is assigned to bit 3.

	MSB																ABC Configuration Register—0x0020														LSB	
Bits	31	30	29	28	27	26	25	24	23	22	21	20	19	18	17	16	15	14	13	12	11	10	9	8	7	6	5	4	3	2	1	0
R/W	-	-	-	-	-	-	-	-	-	-	-	-	-	-	-	-	-	-	-	-	-	-	-	-	-	-	-	-	C	-	B	A
Reset	0	0	0	0	0	0	0	0	0	0	0	0	0	0	0	0	0	0	0	0	0	0	0	0	0	0	0	0	0	0	0	0

A: **Abort**—Set this bit to abort the current task.

B: **Bypass**—Set this to put the block in bypass mode.

C: **Combine**—Set this bit to combine outputs.

📖   **Tales from the Trenches**

In a block, a 6th bit needed to be added in a register that had 5 other similar bits (among other bits). The engineer who first made the bit assignments allocated eight positions even though only five were needed at the time. Because he had done that, the 6th bit could be placed next to the other 5 without moving any other bits in the register. This helped keep the logic and device driver code neat and clean, making it less prone to confusion and defects.

☑   **Best Practice**

8.2.2 Reserve bits for future use, if needed.

8.2.2. Multi-Bit Fields

Besides 1-bit fields containing binary information, fields may contain more than 1 bit as needed. Small multi-bit fields can exist in the same registers as 1-bit fields.

This register map shows a 3-bit field, D (data width), assigned to positions 4 to 6.

	MSB			ABC Configuration Register—0x0020			LSB
Bits	31 30 29 28	27 26 25 24	23 22 21 20	19 18 17 16	15 14 13 12	11 10 9 8	7 6 5 4	3 2 1 0
R/W	- - - -	- - - -	- - - -	- - - -	- - - -	- - - -	- D D D	C - B A
Reset	0 0 0 0	0 0 0 0	0 0 0 0	0 0 0 0	0 0 0 0	0 0 0 0	0 0 0 1	0 0 0 0

A: **Abort**—Set this bit to abort the current task.

B: **Bypass**—Set this to put the block in bypass mode.

C: **Combine**—Set this bit to combine outputs.

D: **Data width**—Specify the number of bytes in a word. Valid values are as follows: 0x1=1 byte (default), 0x2=2, 0x3=4, and 0x4=8 bytes.

When engineers are working with registers containing multi-bit fields, they often are looking at hex values to mentally determine which bits are set. It is much easier if the fields were aligned along nibble boundaries to make hex/binary translations easier.

Suppose a register has four 5-bit fields: A, B, C, and D. If all the fields were put in the right-most position possible, this is what the 32-bit register would look like (where "-" means bit position not used):

Bits	31 30 29 28	27 26 25 24	23 22 21 20	19 18 17 16	15 14 13 12	11 10 9 8	7 6 5 4	3 2 1 0
R/W	- - - -	- - - -	- - - -	D D D D	D C C C	C C B B	B B B A	A A A A

Suppose all four fields contain the same value, 20 decimal, which is 0x14 in hex and 10100 in binary. The register would look like this (with 0 in the unused bits).

Bits	31 30 29 28	27 26 25 24	23 22 21 20	19 18 17 16	15 14 13 12	11 10 9 8	7 6 5 4	3 2 1 0
R/W	- - - -	- - - -	- - - -	D D D D	D C C C	C C B B	B B B A	A A A A
Contents	0 0 0 0	0 0 0 0	0 0 0 0	1 0 1 0	0 1 0 1	0 0 1 0	1 0 0 1	0 1 0 0
Hex	0	0	0	A	5	2	9	4

Since register values are more commonly written in hex form, this is how contents of the register would be written.

```
0x000A5294
```

It is very difficult to mentally look at that hex number and see that all four fields contain the same value. By aligning the four fields along nibble boundaries, the format of the register would look like this, making it much easier to read and see that all are the same, especially in hex form.

Bits	31 30 29 28	27 26 25 24	23 22 21 20	19 18 17 16	15 14 13 12	11 10 9 8	7 6 5 4	3 2 1 0
R/W	- - - D	D D D D	- - - C	C C C C	- - - B	B B B B	- - - A	A A A A
Contents	0 0 0 1	0 1 0 0	0 0 0 1	0 1 0 0	0 0 0 1	0 1 0 0	0 0 0 1	0 1 0 0
Hex	1	4	1	4	1	4	1	4

It is now easy to see that all four fields have the same value, 0x14. No mental bit shifting is required.

Aligning along nibble boundaries makes it easier to read the hex values. Alignment along byte boundaries can have some benefits in firmware performance. In the above example, not only are the four fields nibble-aligned, but they are also byte-aligned. Some CPUs have the ability to quickly read and write bytes within a 32-bit word (or 16- or 64-bit word, etc.). Although firmware may use the construct ((reg >> 8) & 0xff) to pull the 2nd byte out (using several assembly instructions), optimizing compilers can use the CPU's capabilities to do that in fewer assembly instructions. If alignment were not byte-aligned, the compiler could not take advantage of the CPU's byte-wise capabilities.

The number of bits in a bit-field dictates an advantageous alignment. Table 8.1 contains the alignment details based on the field size.

☑ **Best Practice**

8.2.3 Place bit fields of 1 bit anywhere as desired in the register.

Table 8.1: Alignment Based on Size of Bit Field

Bit Field Size	Alignment
1	Any bit, anywhere
2	Anywhere within a nibble
3–4	Nibble (4-bit) aligned
5–8	Byte (8-bit) aligned
9–16	16-bit aligned
17–32	32-bit aligned
33–64	64-bit aligned

☑   **Best Practice**

8.2.4 Place bit fields of 2 bits anywhere within a nibble.

☑   **Best Practice**

8.2.5 Place bit fields of 3 to 4 bits nibble-aligned, of 5 to 8 bits byte-aligned, of 9 to 16 bits 16-bit aligned, and so on.

8.2.3. Multi-Register Fields

Bit fields that are larger than the register size are accessible to firmware only via multiple register accesses. Suppose a 21-bit field is needed on an 8-bit chip. Which format should be used to distribute it across multiple registers?

```
---BBBBB BBBBBBBB BBBBBBBB -> Right-justified format
BBBBBBBB BBBBBBBB BBBBB--- -> Left-justified format
-BBBBBBB -BBBBBBB -BBBBBBB -> Spread evenly format
```

From a firmware point of view, right justified is less complicated to assemble. Listing 8.6 shows how it can be assembled into a 32-bit variable.

While the other formats can be similarly assembled, it is more natural to see shifts using 8, 16, and so on. It is more understandable to the reader that registers manipulation is involved. And often the CPU has optimized ways of manipulating bits in groups of 8.

As noted above, the low-order eight bits are in the register at address 0x00, the next 8 bits at address 0x01, then the rest at 0x02. If this block is ported to a 32-bit bus, the bits will already be in the right order when accessed as a `uint32_t`.

Listing 8.6: Assembling multi-register fields into a bigger integer.

```
uint8_t volatile * regA = 0x00;
uint8_t volatile * regB = 0x01;
uint8_t volatile * regC = 0x02;
uint32_t myField = ((uint32_t) *regC) << 16 |
                   ((uint32_t) *regB) <<  8 |
                   ((uint32_t) *regA;
```

Same rules apply when dealing with larger registers, such as putting a 50-bit field into 32-bit registers.

Right-justified also leaves room for expansion to a larger field while leaving the current bits in their current locations.

> ☑ **Best Practice**
>
> 8.2.6 Place bit fields with sizes bigger than a register with the less significant bits in the necessary number of registers and any remaining most significant bits right-justified in the last register.

8.2.4. Unused Bit Positions

Bit positions in a register that are not used should always return zeros. This is the same as discussed earlier with regard to unused address locations.

As an example, suppose block version A defines bits G, U, and H in bits 0, 1, and 2, respectively. Block version B defines bits G, U, and T in bits 0, 1, and 3, respectively. The device driver will be written to handle all four—G, U, H, and T—as illustrated in this diagram.

Bits	... 5 4	3 2 1 0
Block version A	... - -	- H U G
Block version B	... - -	T - U G
Driver supports	... - -	T H U G

The device driver is written to process any of these bits when set. Since unused bits always return zero, then bit 3 in version A will never be set, so bit T will never be processed on that version. And likewise, bit 2 in version B will never be set, so bit H will never be processed. Returning zeros in unused bit positions allows the same device driver to be used on multiple versions of the block without the device driver needing to know which version it is running on.

> ☑   **Best Practice**
>
> 8.2.7 Design registers to return zeros for reads from unused bit positions.

The block should also ignore bits written to unused positions. Again, this allows more flexibility for device drivers. If the device driver wants to set a certain bit that does not exist on all versions of the block, then it is ignored on blocks that do not support it. If the device driver needs to know whether or not that version supports it, the device driver can write a one to that position and then read it back. If it is a one, then that version of the block supports that bit. If it returns a zero, then that version does not support it and the device driver can adjust accordingly.

☑   **Best Practice**

8.2.8 Design registers to ignore writes to unused bit positions.

8.2.5. Changes in the Next Revision

After a block has been released in a chip, changes are often needed in the next revision. The next few sections talk about how to make those changes with minimal impact to firmware.

Don't Rearrange Bits

Leave the bit positions unchanged on the next generation of the block. Since the device driver often has to work on more than one version of the block, it is less complicated if the bits do not shift around.

If bits are shifted around, then the device driver has to add code to first determine which chip is being used. This assumes that the device driver can figure out which version it is running on. Listing 8.7 shows that code. However, it is just for 1 bit on two different chips. As more bits and chips have variations, the code becomes more complicated and error-prone.

It may appear to be simpler to define STATUS_MASK to be 0x100 for Rev A chips and then change it to 0x040 for Rev B chips, which will then update all places as necessary. But then the device driver will only work for Rev A or Rev B, but not both. A run-time switch,

---

Listing 8.7: Determine which mask to use based on the chip.

```
#define STATUS_MASK_REV_A    0x100
#define STATUS_MASK_REV_B    0x040

if (chipId == CHIP_ID_REV_A)
    status_mask = STATUS_MASK_REV_A;
else if (chipId == CHIP_ID_REV_B)
    status_mask = STATUS_MASK_REV_B;
else
    reportError (ERROR_UNKNOWN_CHIP);
```

as shown in Listing 8.7, is needed to get the same device driver to work on both versions of the chip. When Rev C is introduced, `CHIP_ID_REV_C` needs to be added in the `if()` statements and `STATUS_MASK_REV_C` needs to be defined, even if it contains the same value as `REV_B` or `REV_A`. And as more versions of the chip are developed, more masks will need to be defined. It is better to not move the bit in the first place, if possible. Then none of these `if()` statements are necessary, and just one define is needed, `#define STATUS_MASK 0x100`.

If you do have reasons to move bits around, consult with firmware engineers to get their opinions and suggestions on if and how to move them.

> ☑   **Best Practice**
>
> 8.2.9 Avoid changing bit assignments from one version of the block to the next.

Using Reserved Bits

When modifying a block for a next-generation chip, if it now needs to utilize a reserved space as predicted, then the space can be used with little impact to device drivers or other bits.

Continuing with this ABC Configuration Register, a bit was reserved next to B in case it needed to expand to a 2-bit field. Since space was reserved for it, B can expand to 2 bits without having to move any other bits in the register.

The description for bit B has been modified to reflect the change. Note that 0x0 and 0x1 are the same as the previous version. This allows legacy device drivers to still use this new version. An updated device driver is needed in order to take advantage of the high-speed bypass mode.

	MSB			ABC Configuration Register—0x0020				LSB
Bits	31 30 29 28	27 26 25 24	23 22 21 20	19 18 17 16	15 14 13 12	11 10 9 8	7 6 5 4	3 2 1 0
R/W	- - - -	- - - -	- - - -	- - - -	- - - -	- - - -	- D D D	C B B A
Reset	0 0 0 0	0 0 0 0	0 0 0 0	0 0 0 0	0 0 0 0	0 0 0 0	0 0 0 1	0 0 0 0

A: **Abort**—Set this bit to abort the current task.

B: **Bypass**—Specify which bypass mode to use: no bypass (0x0), legacy bypass (0x1), high-speed bypass (0x2), and not supported (0x3).

C: **Combine**—Set this bit to combine outputs.

D: **Data width**—Specify the number of bytes in a word. Valid values are as follows: 0x1=1 byte (default), 0x2=2, 0x3=4, and 0x4=8 bytes.

Dropping Obsolete Bits

If, on this next version of the block, some bits are being dropped, remove them but do not change the position of any remaining bits in the register. Again, this is to enable the device driver to more easily support multiple versions of the block.

In this register map, Bit C is now dropped from position 3 and the position remains empty. The other bits are not shuffled to close the gap. Note that the description for bit C is also dropped.

	MSB			ABC Configuration Register—0x0020				LSB
Bits	31 30 29 28	27 26 25 24	23 22 21 20	19 18 17 16	15 14 13 12	11 10 9 8	7 6 5 4	3 2 1 0
R/W	- - - -	- - - -	- - - -	- - - -	- - - -	- - - -	- D D D	- B B A
Reset	0 0 0 0	0 0 0 0	0 0 0 0	0 0 0 0	0 0 0 0	0 0 0 0	0 0 0 1	0 0 0 0

A: **Abort**—Set this bit to abort the current task.

B: **Bypass**—Specify which bypass mode to use: no bypass (0x0), legacy bypass (0x1), high-speed bypass (0x2), and not supported (0x3).

D: **Data width**—Specify the number of bytes in a word. Valid values are as follows: 0x1=1 byte (default), 0x2=2, 0x3=4, and 0x4=8 bytes.

Adding New Bits

As new bits are added in the next-generation block, assign them to the left of existing bits. Do not place them in any holes that may have been created by dropping other bits (unless there is no more room in the register). Again, this allows the device driver to be more portable across different versions of the block. It also reduces the chance of errors caused by a device driver inadvertently executing on one version as if it was on the other. Another reason for leaving those dropped bit positions empty is that it leaves open the possibility of bringing those bits back in the future.

	MSB			ABC Configuration Register—0x0020				LSB
Bits	31 30 29 28	27 26 25 24	23 22 21 20	19 18 17 16	15 14 13 12	11 10 9 8	7 6 5 4	3 2 1 0
R/W	- - - -	- - - -	- - - -	- - - -	- - - -	- - - -	E D D D	- B B A
Reset	0 0 0 0	0 0 0 0	0 0 0 0	0 0 0 0	0 0 0 0	0 0 0 0	0 0 0 1	0 0 0 0

A: **Abort**—Set this bit to abort the current task.

B: **Bypass**—Specify which bypass mode to use: no bypass (0x0), legacy bypass (0x1), high-speed bypass (0x2), and not supported (0x3).

D: **Data width**—Specify the number of bytes in a word. Valid values are as follows: 0x1=1 byte (default), 0x2=2, 0x3=4, and 0x4=8 bytes.

E: **Error buffer**—Turn on the error buffer to track several errors.

☑ **Best Practice**

8.2.10 Avoid reusing bit positions of deleted bits in an existing register.

8.2.6. Bit Types

I have just discussed how to assign bits within a register. I will now discuss different types of bits, how they behave, and how they should be assigned among registers.

Read/Write Bits

A common type of bit is the read/write bit. The read and/or write ability of the bit is documented from the firmware's perspective. Firmware can read the bit to see its value. Firmware can change the value of a read/write bit by writing 1's or 0's to the bit. The block, however, can only read the bit; it cannot change the value of the bit (except during power-on resets).

Common uses of read/write bits include:

- Control the actions of the block.

- Configure the behavior of the block.

- Enable interrupts.

- Control the level of output pins on the chip.

In all of these uses, firmware writes to read/write bits to configure the block's behavior.

Read-Only Bits

Another common type of bit is the read-only bit. This means that firmware can read the bit but cannot change the value of the bit by writing to it. Only the block can change the value of the bit. Any attempt by firmware to change the value is ignored by the block.

Common uses of read-only bits include:

- The status of an internal condition such as active, idle, full, empty, or error.

- The value of an input pin on the chip.

- The results of a timer/counter.

Write-Only Bits

Write-only bits are rare. It means that firmware can write to it and change its value but firmware cannot read back what the value is. Since firmware cannot read the register, it cannot confirm that the register contains what it wrote. If firmware needs to later on remember the value of what it wrote, it must keep its own copy of what it last wrote. Obviously, the block can read it and respond to it appropriately.

Reasons are very few to have write-only bits and should be avoided if possible. Here are two reasons where it might be appropriate:

- For security purposes, register might be rendered write-only so that rogue firmware modules cannot read the settings.

- The register might not have storage elements behind it. Writing to it causes some task to start, such as a state machine, but there is no need to keep a 1 in a flip-flop. Usually there is a status register that indicates that the task is now active.

Even if a register is deemed write-only, a read should still work and should return zeros.

□□   **Tales from the Trenches**

I was trying to configure a block to do something. Since accessing that block required multiple steps, I first tried to verify that the multiple steps worked by writing to three registers in the block and then reading them back.

The values returned by the read were incorrect. I spent time verifying that the multiple steps were correct. In the process, I noticed that the documentation labeled those registers as write-only. At first, I did not believe the documentation because it did not make sense. But after a while, I decided to believe the documentation. I wanted to see if the multiple steps worked by getting the block to respond in a manner that was visible by a scope probing one of the chip's pins. But the expected results did not occur. I thought maybe the addresses for those registers were wrong.

After many failed attempts, I consulted with the hardware engineer. The registers were indeed write-only, the addresses were correct, and the multiple steps were correct. The problem was that the block functionality was broken.

Had the registers been read/write instead of write-only, much time could have been saved, leading more quickly to discovering that the block was broken and that it could not be used at all.

☑   **Best Practice**

8.2.11 Avoid write-only bits whenever possible; use read/write bits instead.

☑ **Best Practice**

8.2.12 Design write-only registers to return zero when read.

Interrupt Bits—Write 1 Clear

With interrupt bits, the block sets a bit and firmware clears it. Firmware cannot set this bit, only clear it after the block has first set it.

Interrupt bits are used to inform firmware which event has occurred within the block. Firmware then acknowledges the interrupt by writing a 1 in that bit position to clear it. This behavior is also known as Write 1 Clear (W1C). This behavior permits more than one different interrupt to occur at different times while allowing firmware to clear one without risk of inadvertently clearing another. Interrupts will be discussed at length in the next chapter, Chapter 9, Interrupts.

Queue Bits—Write 1 Set

With queue bits, firmware writes a one in a bit position to set that bit in a register. But firmware cannot clear the bit. Only the block clears the bit. This is known as Write 1 Set (W1S).

Queue bits are typically used to queue some action in the block. When the block is done with that task, it then clears the bit. Firmware can read the bit, and if it is cleared, it knows that it can queue the action again. Firmware can queue any bit at any time, without regard to other bits in the register that may be set or that may about to be cleared by the block. Firmware writes a 1 to the desired position and a zero everywhere else. Zeros in the other positions do not affect the settings of the other bits. Queue bits will be discussed in more details later in this chapter in Section 8.5.2, Queuing Tasks in the Block.

Table 8.2 compares these five types of bits with regard to whether firmware and/or hardware can set and/or clear the bits.

Table 8.2: Comparing Types of Bits with Access Types by Firmware and Block

Bit Type	Firmware			Hardware		
	Set	**Clear**	**Read**	**Set**	**Clear**	**Read**
Read/Write Bits	√	√	√			√
Read-Only Bits			√	√	√	√
~~Write-Only Bits~~	√	√				√
Interrupt Bits (W1C)		√	√	√		√
Queue Bits (W1S)	√		√		√	√

Note: Write-Only-Bits is crossed out because it should be avoided.

Other types and variations of bits exist. The five discussed here are the most common.

8.2.7. Bit Types in Registers

Bits should not be grouped into registers without regard to their type. The different types are handled differently by firmware.

Bits of different writeable types (read/write, interrupt, and queue) should not be mixed in the same register. It forces firmware engineers to take extra, precautionary steps to make sure nothing is lost or inadvertently changed. Even if the initial firmware is verified as correctly written, defects could be introduced by someone not familiar with the register when they make subsequent maintenance changes or leverage the code.

To illustrate these complexities, I will show what is required if a register contains some read/write bits and some interrupt bits. Read/write bits are often handled by firmware with a read-modify-write sequence. Firmware sets bit 3 by reading the current contents of the register, OR'ing in 0x8, then writing the contents back out to the register. All the other bits are left the same—but bit 3 is now set.

Interrupt bits are often handled by firmware with a read-write-ack sequence. Firmware discovers that bit 18 is set, indicating a pending interrupt, by reading the interrupt status register which contains 0x40000. Firmware then acks that pending interrupt by writing just that bit, 0x40000, to the register.

Combining these two types of bits in the same register requires extra handling by firmware to avoid inadvertent changes of the read/write bits and inadvertent acknowledgment of interrupt bits. Listing 8.8 illustrates the extra handling.

Variations on the above algorithm is needed for read/write bits mixed with queue bits, interrupt bits mixed with queue bits, and with all three types mixed together in one register. These algorithms are not intuitive at first glance. Firmware engineers who have not previously seen mixed registers have to understand the implications of those combinations before they can start working on an algorithm. As is typical with any algorithm, first attempts are prone to defects, especially since these are not standard algorithms that are discussed in college classes or exist in books on algorithms.

Even though firmware can be coded to handle any of these combinations, it does make firmware prone to defects that should not be there. Assigning these writeable bits to separate registers eliminates the possibility that firmware can even have those errors.

Listing 8.8: Extra steps required to handle a register with read/write bits and interrupt bits.

```
#define REG_A_READ_WRITE_BITS    0x0000007F
#define REG_A_INTERRUPT_BITS     0x001F0000
uint32_t volatile * regA = (uint32_t volatile *) REG_A_ADDR;

uint32_t value;

// Turn on bit 3 in regA
value = *regA;    // Get the current register settings
value &= ~REG_A_INTERRUPT_BITS;   // Ignore any pending interrupts
value |= 0x8;    // Set bit 3
*regA = value;    // Write it back out

// Look for any interrupts
value = *regA;    // Get the current register settings
value &= ~REG_A_READ_WRITE_BITS; // Ignore read/write bits
// Look at value and discover that interrupt 18 is pending

// Ack interrupt 18 but no other interrupt that may be pending while
// leaving the read/write bits unchanged
value = *regA;    // Get the current register settings
value &= ~REG_A_INTERRUPT_BITS;   // Ignore any pending interrupts
value |= 0x40000; // A 1 to ack interrupt 18
*regA = value;    // Ack intr 18, but leaving r/w bits the same
```

☑   **Best Practice**

8.2.13 Do not mix different writeable bit types in any combination in the same register.

Mixing read-only bits in the same register with any one type of writeable bits is safe because the read-only bits are not affected by any type of write and reading those bits do not affect the behavior of the writeable bits.

But just because it is safe does not mean it should be done as a general rule. It still helps reduce confusion in the mind of engineers writing and maintaining the code and reduce the risk of introducing errors in firmware if read-only bits were kept in their own registers apart from any writeable bits.

☑   **Best Practice**

8.2.14 Assign read-only bits to registers with writeable bits only if necessary.

8.2.8. *Grouping by Operational Mode*

I just discussed grouping bits in registers by types. This section discusses grouping registers by how they are used, by their operational mode.

A few groups are listed in the following. You might find other groups for your particular application.

- **Boot up:** These registers are accessed only at bootup to configure the block in a manner that will never change while power is applied. Common uses include operating modes and timeout values.

- **Regular operation:** These registers are used all the time as the block does its job. Common uses include interrupt registers and data registers.

- **Test and debug:** These registers are only used during test and debug and are not intended to be used as part of normal operation. Common uses include snoop registers or test hooks.

Bits are assigned bits into appropriate registers in the appropriate group. For example, each of the above groups are likely to have their own read/write and read-only registers. Bits are then assigned to one of them based on the operational mode of the bit. Boot up read/write bits would be assigned to the bootup read/write register. And so on.

Depending on the nature of how the bits are used, there might be little risk in mixing bits of these different modes in the same register. But from an efficiency perspective, mixing usage is not efficient. Having to access regular operation bits that are scattered among bootup and test/debug bits across many registers is not efficient. Grouping them by themselves reduces the number of register accesses needed during normal operation.

Although the risk is small, there could be inadvertent changing. A bad value intended to change only regular operation bits could inadvertently change boot-up bits, causing the block configuration and behavior to change for no apparent reason and to never change back. This would be very difficult to debug. Unless necessary, do not mix bits according to their operational mode.

> ☑ **Best Practice**
>
> 8.2.15 Assign each bit to a register with bits used in the same operational mode.

8.2.9. Multiple Instantiations of a Block

If the chip contains more than one instantiation of a block, bits of each instantiation should be assigned to separate registers and registers for each instantiation should be in separate address spaces. This allows multiple threads of the firmware to operate on its own instantiation of the block without taking extra steps to prevent interfering with other threads.

For example, suppose there are two UARTs (RS-232 serial ports) in the chip. A UART handles 8-bit characters. Suppose that one 8-bit register is used to write out the character to be transmitted and another 8-bit register contains some control bits. If we are on a 32-bit processor, there might be the temptation to combine same functions into the same register in this fashion.

Offset	31 30 29 28	27 26 25 24	23 22 21 20	19 18 17 16	15 14 13 12 11 10 9 8	7 6 5 4 3 2 1 0
0x00	- - - -	- - - -	- - - -	- - - -	UART 2 Transmit	UART 1 Transmit
0x04	- - - -	- - - -	- - - -	- - - -	UART 2 Configuration	UART 1 Configuration

With this configuration, it is difficult for one thread to write a character in just eight of the 32 bits without inadvertently transmitting or writing over something in the other bits. And likewise, the control register is prone to being overwritten if both threads collide.

Another disadvantage is that it is cumbersome to make one device driver work for both. For every register read and write, the device driver first has to determine which UART it is working on and then do appropriate bit shifting and masking to access either bits 0-7 or bits 8-15.

A better way to do this is to set up each UART with its own set of registers, each with their own base address but with the same offset, as illustrated here.

Offset	31 30 29 28	27 26 25 24	23 22 21 20	19 18 17 16	15 14 13 12	11 10 9 8	7 6 5 4 3 2 1 0
0x00	- - - -	- - - -	- - - -	- - - -	- - - -	- - - -	UART Transmit
0x04	- - - -	- - - -	- - - -	- - - -	- - - -	- - - -	UART Configuration

This register map does not indicate whether this is for UART 1 or UART 2. But in the document, it will specify two different base addresses for the two UART blocks. Adding the register offset to the desired base address will access the register in the desired block. The registers in each copy are identical in number, content, and offset. But they are in different address spaces.

This allows two different threads of the firmware to operate, one for each UART. Since each copy of the block has its own set of registers, no coordination is needed between the two threads when accessing registers. It is easy to write one device driver that accesses both blocks. This is shown in Listing 8.9.

Listing 8.9: The same code is able to access either UART.

```
// Define UART base addresses
#define CHIP_BASE        0x90900000
#define UART_A_BASE      (CHIP_BASE + 0x1000)
#define UART_B_BASE      (CHIP_BASE + 0x1800)

// Define register offsets
#define REG_TRANSMIT  0x00
#define REG_CONFIG       0x04

// Declare an array with UART base addresses
uint32_t uartBase[2] = {(UART_A_BASE, UART_B_BASE};

// Function to write to a register
writeRegister (uint32_t addr, uint32_t data)
    {
    uint32_t volatile * regPtr = (uint32_t volatile *) addr ;
    *regPtr = data;
    }

// Transmit a character out the specified UART
char transmitChar (int uart, char data)
    {
    writeRegister (uartBase[uart] + REG_TRANSMIT, data);
    writeRegister (uartBase[uart] + REG_CONFIG, TRANSMIT_NOW);
    return (data);
    }
```

In this example, the function, `transmitChar`, is told which UART to use. That indexes into an array (of size two) of UART base addresses. The base address from that array is added to the register offset to get to the desired register in the desired UART.

☑ **Best Practice**

8.2.16 Assign all bits associated with a block instantiation to registers used only by that instantiation.

8.3. Data Types

Many registers contain multiple single-bit or multi-bit fields. This section covers registers with only one field but with several bits—bit fields used as numbers. I will discuss different types of numbers and how they should be implemented.

8.3.1. Integers

Bit fields used as integers should be assigned to their own register, especially if used by firmware independent of the other bits and if used regularly during operation.

To illustrate, Listing 8.10 shows how firmware adds 2 to the contents of a 12-bit integer. The first part is when the 12-bit integer is located at bits 8 to 19 in a register with other bits that must be preserved. The second part is when the 12-bit integer is in a register by itself.

☑   **Best Practice**

8.3.1 Assign each frequently used integer to its own register.

This best practice says to assign "frequently used integers" in separate registers. This assumes unsigned integers. Signed integers, whether used frequently or not, should be in their own registers.

Signed integers use the most significant bit to indicate the sign. When a register with a signed integer is using fewer bits than the size of the register, the unused bits must return the same value as the most significant bit of the signed integer. (This assumes, of course, that the integer is right-justified.) This sign extension ensures that the processor will interpret the signed number correctly.

A block that has an 8-bit signed number that is read by a 32-bit processor must make sure the sign is extended across the 24 unused bits. A +2 is 0x02 in an 8-bit register and 0x00000002 in a 32-bit register. A −2 is 0xfe in an 8-bit integer and 0xfffffffe in a 32-bit register. The unused 24 bits are the same as for bit 7 in the 8-bit portion.

Listing 8.10: Accessing a 12-bit integer with and without other bits in the register.

```
// Add 2 to an integer without changing other bits in the register
contents = *regA;          // Get the register contents
integer = (contents & 0x000FFF00) >> 8;    // Extract the integer
contents &= 0xFFF000FF;    // Erase the old integer keeping other bits
integer += 2;              // Add 2 to the integer
integer &= 0xFFF;          // Remove any overflow
contents |= integer << 8;  // Put new integer back with the other bits
*regA = contents;          // Write new contents back to the register

// Add 2 to an integer that is by itself in the register
*regA += 2;                // Increment the register contents by 2
```

According to a best practice specified earlier, all unused bits should return zeros. If that were done in this case, then a `0xfe` read by a 32-bit processor would be `0x000000fe`, which would be interpreted as a decimal 254, not a −2. Firmware can be written to handle this case so that the correct value, −2, can be obtained but it requires difficult and error-prone masking and integer size conversions to get it to occur.

In the other direction, when the processor writes `0xfffffffe`, the block would simply ignore the unused bits, correctly putting 0xfe in the 8-bit field.

Rather than thinking of the 24 bits as unused bits, think of them as sign-extended bits. They don't need to have a flip-flop behind them—they can just repeat the contents of the flip-flop for bit 7 across bits 8 to 31. And since those "unused" bits are used, a signed integer must be in a register by itself. Otherwise, some complicated bit shifting, masking, and type conversion must be done to make sure the correct signed values are read from and written to the desired location.

☑ **Best Practice**

8.3.2 Assign every signed integer to its own register.

☑ **Best Practice**

8.3.3 Always sign-extend a signed integer to the size of its register.

8.3.2. Real Numbers

Integers have no fractional portion. Real numbers do. (Note: Don't get real numbers consisting of an integer portion and a fractional portion confused with floating-point numbers consisting of a mantissa and an exponent.)

When assigning a real number to a register, one thing that must be decided is how many significant digits are needed in the fractional portion. In the decimal number, "5.36," the "5" is the integer portion and the "36" is the fractional portion with two significant digits. In this binary number, "101.0110," the "101" is the integer portion and the "0110" is the fractional portion with four significant digits.

To represent this binary real number, 101.0110, in a register, 4 bits (bits 0 to 3) are allocated for the fractional portion. Then at least 3 bits are allocated for the integer portion. More than 3 bits for the integer portion could be allocated if bigger numbers are needed.

To illustrate the nuances of real numbers in registers, I will use as an example a bicycle odometer which shows how many miles (1 mi = 1.61 km) the bike has traveled. In this register map, the real number is defined with 4 bits allocated for the integer portion, I, and 4 bits allocated for the fractional portion, F, as can be seen in this register map. The radix point (separating the integer from the fractional portion) is between bits 3 and 4.

	MSB						Bicycle Odometer Register—0x0034		LSB
Bits	31 30 29 28	27 26 25 24	23 22 21 20	19 18 17 16	15 14 13 12	11 10 9 8	7 6 5 4	3 2 1 0
R/W	- - - -	- - - -	- - - -	- - - -	- - - -	- - - -	I I I I	F F F F

In numbers, the radix is shifted to the left/right by dividing/multiplying by B^N, where B is the base and N is the number of digits to shift by. In decimal numbers (base 10), a number such as 1234.0 can have its radix shifted to the left two digits by dividing by 10^2, or 100, yielding 12.34.

The same steps apply with binary numbers (base 2). If the above register contains 01001000 in binary (72 decimal), then shifting the radix to the left by four binary digits yields 0100.1000. To shift a binary radix to the left by four binary digits, divide by 2^4, or 16. This then means that the register containing 01001000 represents 72/16 = 4.5.

In the C programming language, raising 2 to the Nth power is easily accomplished by using 1<<N. That is then divided into the value from the register to generate the real number. Listing 8.11 shows how firmware reads the register as an int, typecasts it to float, then divides it by 2^N using 1<<N.

With this 4-integer/4-fractional value, the max value is 11111111 (255 in decimal) which when converted ($255/2^4$) is 15.9375 mi (25.6489 km). A 4-bit fractional portion has a precision of 1/16th of a mile, which is 0.0625 mi, which is 330 ft (100 m). The 4-bit integer portion maxes out at 15.

Suppose that after releasing the bicycle odometer product, the customer feedback said that it is not good enough; it does not go far enough and it does not have a good enough precision. The next generation of the block must have better precision and a longer range value. The integer portion now has 8 bits and the fractional portion has 6 bits. The radix point has been moved from 4 to 6.

Listing 8.11: Convert a real number in a register to a floating-point number in C.

```
#define RADIX_POINT    4        // First bit after the radix point
float distance;
distance = ((float) *regDistance) / ((float) (1<<RADIX_POINT));
```

	MSB			Bicycle Odometer Register—0x0034											LSB
Bits	31 30 29 28	27 26 25 24	23 22 21 20	19 18 17 16	15 14 13 12	11 10 9 8	7 6 5 4	3 2 1 0
R/W	- - - -	- - - -	- - - -	- - - -	- - I I	I I I I	I I F F	F F F F

This now allows for a maximum of almost 256 mi (412 km) with a precision of 1/64th of a mile, which is 83 ft (25 m).

Firmware needs to be changed to accommodate the different location of the radix point. In the above Listing 8.11, RADIX_POINT needs to be changed to 6. This requires that the correct version of firmware be paired with the correct version of the device driver. If 0x00C0 (192 decimal) were read from the register, the old device driver with RADIX_POINT at 4 will divide it by 16 and interpret it as 12.0 mi (19.3 km). The new device driver with RADIX_POINT at 6 will divide it by 64 and interpret it as 3.0 mi (4.8 km). This register is not designed to allow firmware to be forward and backward compatible.

A better way to do this is to allocate more bits for the fractional portion, even though not all would be used by that particular version of the block. Suppose that 8 bits are allocated for the fractional portion even though only four will be used on the first version. The radix point is between bits 7 and 8. This is now what the first version would look like.

	MSB			Bicycle Odometer Register—0x0034											LSB
Bits	31 30 29 28	27 26 25 24	23 22 21 20	19 18 17 16	15 14 13 12	11 10 9 8	7 6 5 4	3 2 1 0
R/W	- - - -	- - - -	- - - -	- - - -	- - - -	I I I I	F F F F	- - - -

For this register, the firmware will be written with RADIX_POINT set at 8, causing it to divide by $2^8 = 256$. In this first version, though, the fractional portion only has 4 significant binary digits and is located at bits 4 to 7. The other four (bits 0 to 3) are not used and will always return zeros. And likewise, the integer portion is only bits 8 to 11, with bits 12 to 31 left unused, always returning zeros. The firmware using this version does not know that (nor does it need to know that), but it will not return values bigger than 15.9375 mi (25.6489 km) or have a precision less than 330 ft (100 m) simply because the register will not give it.

When the second version is made with an 8-bit integer portion and a 6-bit fractional portion, the register map now looks like this.

	MSB			Bicycle Odometer Register—0x0034											LSB
Bits	31 30 29 28	27 26 25 24	23 22 21 20	19 18 17 16	15 14 13 12	11 10 9 8	7 6 5 4	3 2 1 0
R/W	- - - -	- - - -	- - - -	- - - -	I I I I	I I I I	F F F F	F F - -

The radix point has not moved. It is still at 8. Firmware does not need to change for this second version. It still uses RADIX_POINT set at 8. But now with this version of the block, the maximum value that firmware will return is now just less than 256 mi (412 km) with a precision of 83 ft (25 m).

With the radix point at location 8 in both versions, firmware does not need to know which version of the block it is running on, allowing firmware to be forward and backward compatible. It will interpret the register the same way in either version. This reduces complications and potential defects by not having to do something different depending on which version it is running on.

When a register is first designed to contain a real number, the radix point must be placed somewhere to allow maximum expansion on both the integer and fractional portions. Exactly where that radix point should be depends on the real number that is being represented. To start with, pick a place and see what the maximum integer portion can be and what the precision is. If the maximum integer is not big enough, the radix point needs to be moved to the right. If the precision is not high enough, the radix point needs to be moved to the left. Adjustments are made until a good balance is achieved between the maximum integer and the precision.

In the bicycle odometer example with the radix point at location 8, the maximum integer with 24 bits is 16 million miles (26 million kilometers). That is enough to ride the bike for 35 round trips to the moon and back. That is big enough. With eight bits for the fractional portion, the precision is 20 ft (6 m). That may not be fine enough if technology for measuring distance on a bicycle improves.

What if the radix point was moved five places to the left, to location 13? The integer portion now has 19 bits, which is just over 500,000 mi (800,000 km), only one round trip to the moon and back, but still big enough. The 13-bit fractional portion generates a precision of about 8 in (20 cm). That should be a high enough precision to last for many years. The analysis shows that the radix point at location 13 for the bicycle odometer register should serve all current and future needs for max size and resolution. Firmware will then set RADIX_POINT to 13 and the register map for the first version of the block will then look like this.

	MSB								LSB
Bits	31 30 29 28	27 26 25 24	23 22 21 20	19 18 17 16	15 14 13 12	11 10 9 8	7 6 5 4	3 2 1 0	
R/W	- - - -	- - - -	- - - -	- - - I	I I I F	F F F -	- - - -	- - - -	

Bicycle Odometer Register—0x0034

☑   **Best Practice**

8.3.4 Place unused bits on both sides of a real number in a register to allow for future expansion, with bits on the left side for bigger numbers and bits on the right side for better precision.

Because unused bits on both sides of a real number are needed in conjunction with the real number, they should remain unused. In other words, real numbers should be in a register by themselves.

☑ **Best Practice**

8.3.5 Assign every real number to its own register.

8.3.3. Pointers

A common use of registers is to contain pointers to memory, such as to the starting address for the DMA operation. Memory is always addressed at the byte level—even if it is in a 16-, 32-, or 64-bit system. Addresses to memory in a 32-bit (4-byte) system progresses by 4s.

```
0x00000000
0x00000004
0x00000008
0x0000000C
0x00000010
0x00000014
 . . .
```

Pointer arithmetic in C handles that very nicely. If an address pointer to a 32-bit integer is incremented by 1, the value is actually incremented by 4. For an array of 32-bit integers, accessing the 11th element in the array is as simple as adding 10 to the pointer and C will actually add 40 (or 0x28 in hex). Note that the first element is obtained by adding zero. So the 11th element is obtained by adding 10. Listing 8.12 illustrates adding 10 to a 32-bit pointer.

Listing 8.12: Pointer arithmetic automatically taking into account size of element.

```
uint32_t * memPtr;              // Pointer to a 4-byte word
uint32_t cnt;                   // Amount to increment by
memPtr = (uint32_t *) 0xDAD08000;  // Addr to first in array
cnt = 10;
printf ("0x%08x + %d = 0x%08x\n", memPtr, cnt, memPtr+cnt);
// This will yield:
// 0xDAD08000 + 10 = 0xDAD08028
```

Listing 8.13: Pointer arithmetic to figure out number of 72-byte packets that have arrived.

```
someStruct_t * startStructPtr;        // Pointer to a 72-byte struct
someStruct_t * currentStructPtr;
uint32_t packets;                     // Number of packets transferred

// startStructPtr is already pointing to the start of the buffer
// The start of the buffer was already written to the block
// After the interrupt let's see how much has been transferred
// Read the register and convert the value to a struct pointer
currentStructPtr = (someStruct_t *) *regCurrPtr;
packets = currentStructPtr - startStructPtr; // Packets received
printf ("0x%08x-0x%08x = %d packets\n",
        currentStructPtr, startStructPtr, packets);
// This will yield:
// 0xDAD082D0 - 0xDAD08000 = 10 packets
```

The same will occur with elements of any size. For example, accessing the 11th element of an array of 72-byte structures by adding 10 to the pointer will cause the pointer to have 720 added.

This pointer arithmetic is handy when calculating sizes of buffers transferred. For example, suppose that an I/O block transfers packets that are 72 bytes long. Firmware gets an interrupt that several packets have arrived and have been put in memory. But how many packets have arrived? Firmware knows the starting address of the buffer in memory. But firmware will have to read a register in the I/O block to see where the address pointer is currently pointing to. Firmware can then use pointer arithmetic to figure that out, as illustrated in Listing 8.13.

In a 32-bit system, the lower two bits are always zero, and therefore could be considered as irrelevant. The hardware designer might be considering dropping those two bits and shifting the rest of the address to the right by 2 bits. But that is not a good idea, especially since pointer arithmetic in C handles everything as byte addresses.

Keep memory address pointers in registers at the byte level, even if the lower bits are unused. This register map illustrates that for a 32-bit system, bits 0 and 1 are unused.

	MSB						ABC Address Register—0x0030			LSB
Bits	31 30 29 28	27 26 25 24	23 22 21 20	19 18 17 16	15 14 13 12	11 10 9 8	7 6 5 4	3 2 1 0
R/W	A A A A	A A A A	A A A A	A A A A	A A A A	A A A A	A A A A	A A - -
Reset	0 0 0 0	0 0 0 0	0 0 0 0	0 0 0 0	0 0 0 0	0 0 0 0	0 0 0 0	0 0 0 0

A: **Address**—Starting address of the buffer.

> ☑ **Best Practice**
>
> 8.3.6 For registers containing pointers to memory, use units of bytes, even if memory is word addressable.

8.3.4. Constants

Some aspects of the design in the block have numerical values that are constants used for counters, timers, priorities, sizes, locations, and so on. The intent of the design is that those are constants, which, by definition, should never need to change.

However, as is often the case, some things need tuning after the fact. Instead of making those constants hard-coded into the hardware out of the reach of firmware, create a read/write register that has as its power-on default what the constant value should be. If everything is fine, firmware will not need to change it. But if there was a problem or if engineers need tune it or run experiments, firmware can write in different values to change the block's behavior.

> 📖 **Tales from the Trenches**
>
> The engine interface between the formatter board and the print engine of a LaserJet printer uses a proprietary protocol with a constant 10-ms timeout. I requested that the 10-ms constant be put in a read/write register and it was.
>
> For years, 10-ms timeout worked just fine. But one time, another engineer needed to perform an analysis and needed to use different values. Because the 10-ms constant was located in a read/write register, he was able to modify his firmware to put in different values for the analysis.

> ☑ **Best Practice**
>
> 8.3.7 Provide a read/write register that defaults to a value rather than hard-coding that value as a constant in hardware.

8.4. Hardware Identification

Pairing the correct firmware with the correct hardware can be difficult at times. Engineers must ensure that products in the field that get new firmware upgrades have the correct new firmware that will work with the old product hardware. In a development lab using

FPGA-based prototypes with frequent updates, new FPGA programming might not be accompanied by a corresponding upgraded firmware.

This section will discuss ways of helping firmware identify the hardware it is running on. This information permits the same version of firmware to run on these different versions. In other words, it provides forward and backward compatibility, where firmware can run on any known version of hardware.

8.4.1. Chip ID and Version

It is common for chips to have a read-only register that contains an ID code. Typically it consists of two parts, a vendor code and a device code. This gives a general view of what the chip is. From the ID code, firmware can know many things about the chip, such as the blocks it contains and their respective base addresses.

☑ **Best Practice**

8.4.1 Provide a chip ID register that uniquely identifies the chip.

In addition to an ID register, chips should also have a version register identifying the version of the chip. This is necessary to help firmware handle subtle differences if the chip rolls and more than one version of the chip have been sold to customers. This is especially important when FPGAs are used because many more versions are possible.

Care must be taken to ensure that this version number changes for every spin of the chip, even for small mask changes, and for every FPGA programming that is distributed.

☑ **Best Practice**

8.4.2 Provide a chip version register that uniquely identifies the chip revision or FPGA programming.

☑ **Best Practice**

8.4.3 Update the chip version register with every chip revision and with every FPGA programming.

Another chip variation used in the industry is to use the same die but with different bonding options when put in the package. This allows variations in the pins that blocks can access, including completely disabling blocks by removing all pin access.

Firmware needs to know how the chip is packaged in order to know which blocks are configured and how. Provide a read-only register that indicates to firmware which bonding configuration was used for the chip.

☑ **Best Practice**

8.4.4 Provide a die bonding configuration register that uniquely identifies the bonding configuration for dies that have multiple bonding options.

If, for some reason, a chip ID register is not provided, provide some means for firmware to distinguish one version of a chip from another. The following lists ideas on how to do that:

- A new read-only register that, when read, no longer returns zeros.

- A new read/write register that firmware can write ones to and then read it back and the ones are still there.

- A new read/write bit in a register that firmware can set then read to see if it is still set.

- A new read-only bit in a register that is stuck on.

Be sure to document which technique is used to help firmware identify the chip version.

☑ **Best Practice**

8.4.5 Identify the chip revision using new registers or bits from existing registers if no dedicated version register can be provided.

8.4.2. Block ID and Version

Taking the chip ID concept down farther, each block within a chip should contain its own ID and version registers. This allows firmware to base its versions on the block itself, and not have to decode which chip IDs map into which version of the block, especially when the same block is instantiated across many chips. This also allows existing device drivers to work on new chips, even though the new chip has a different chip-level ID and version. The existing device drivers do not need to be updated simply to add a new chip-level ID and version to its list.

This block-level ID and version is ideally suited for use on FPGAs, which are, by their nature, changing quite frequently. A chip-level version number has to change every time any one of the blocks makes a change. This impacts all device drivers, even those whose blocks did not change, causing each one to add the new chip-level version to its list. By using block-level version, only the blocks that changed need to have their respective device drivers change. This is especially useful if several versions of the FPGA code are being used throughout the development lab.

In order for the device driver to read the block ID and version registers, it needs to know where they are, even before knowing the version of the block. So the location of the block ID and version registers must always be the same in all versions of the block. It should be at or near the front of the address space for the block, such as offsets 0x0000 and 0x0004. When a device driver is given a base address for the block, it can check the block ID and version registers and know what version it is working on.

☑   **Best Practice**

8.4.6 Provide block-level ID and version registers for each block on a chip.

☑   **Best Practice**

8.4.7 Update the block's version number only when that block changes, not when other components on the chip change.

More was discussed about the block's version register in Section 6.2.5, Superblock Version Number.

8.5. Communication and Control

Imperative to proper operation as a system, hardware and firmware must work well together. This includes support from hardware to give firmware a wide variety of information it may need to make decisions (communication) and give firmware a wide variety of options for configuring and launching tasks in hardware (control). This section will discuss several aspects of communication and control.

8.5.1. Necessary Information

Firmware is best able to make proper decisions if it has necessary information to do so. The following is a list of some types of information:

- Current state of the block and I/O signals

- Performance data

- Buffer contents

- Error information

□□   **Tales from the Trenches**

An engineer from a startup company was adding an I^2C bus switch to an I^2C bus in an embedded power supply. The switch's data sheet cautioned that the upstream bus master should not switch in a downstream bus if the downstream bus was in the middle of a data transfer. The problem was that when the downstream bus was switched out, the upstream bus master could not know whether a data transfer was in progress. The bus switch did not provide any help to know that.

A bus monitor feature in the switch would have solved that problem. The switch could monitor the state of the downstream bus and know whether data transfers are active. The upstream bus master queries the switch regarding the current state of the switched-out bus and, when data transfer stops, then switch in the bus.

A good way to know what kind of information firmware would need is to collaborate with firmware engineers; ask them what they need to know or would like to know to help firmware operations.

☑   **Best Practice**

8.5.1 Collaborate with the firmware team to determine any internal information that each block should make accessible to firmware.

8.5.2. Queuing Tasks in the Block

Part of the functionality in blocks is to carry out tasks, such as an I/O transfer or data compression. A task is something that takes several clock cycles to complete. Configuration registers allow firmware to put the block in certain modes, but those mode and configuration changes happen immediately. A task takes time to complete, time to process data, time to wait on interactions with other blocks or devices.

A Task Life Cycle

Firmware initiates a task by writing to a register, monitors the task by reading bits, and eventually finds out that the task is done. Typically, these steps are accomplished using a queue bit, an active bit, and an interrupt bit. I will talk about this typical approach and other variations.

The fundamental purpose of these steps is to ensure that firmware and the block are in sync with each other and that firmware can know the current condition of the task. This is the handshaking between firmware and the block.

Four events occur with regard to the block when executing a task. The queue, active, and interrupt bits are changed during those events as follows.

1. **FW queues:** Firmware queues the task with the block by writing any necessary configuration information (such as modes, addresses, and counts) to appropriate registers, then setting the queue bit.

2. **Block starts:** The block starts the task and sets the active bit.

3. **Block finishes:** The block completes the task, clears the queue and active bit, and generates an interrupt.

4. **FW acks:** Firmware acknowledges the interrupt and reads any resulting values out of registers (such as end count, calculated results, and final addresses).

The time between events 1 and 2 is the queue time—the time it takes for the block to start the task. The time between events 2 and 3 is the active time—the time it takes the block to complete the task. The time between events 3 and 4 is the ack time—the time it takes for firmware to ack the interrupt. These events in the life cycle and their relationships with the queue, active, and interrupt bits are shown in Figure 8.5.

Firmware can monitor the progress of the task by reading the queue, active, and interrupt bits. If the queue bit is set but the active bit is not set (queue time), then the task is still pending—the block is currently held off from servicing the task. If the active bit is set (active time), then the block is currently working on the task. If the interrupt bit is set (ack time), which implies that the queue and active bits are cleared, then firmware knows that the task is done.

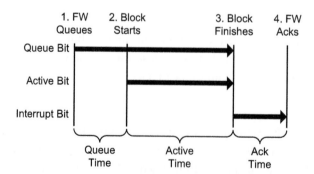

Figure 8.5: Bit settings during the life cycle of a task in the block.

☑ **Best Practice**

8.5.2 Design the block to set the active bit when it starts the task, and then clear the active bit and set the interrupt bit when the task is complete.

Don't Use a Read/Write Bit

The discussion on initiating tasks has been in the context of using a queue bit to initiate the task. A queue bit is set by the firmware and cleared by the block. This method ensures that the block sees the request one and only one time.

Problems will occur if a read/write bit is used to initiate a task; where firmware not only sets the bit, but must clear the bit. The problem is that firmware does not know how long to leave the bit set. If firmware does not leave it on long enough, the block could miss it because it was busy with something else. If firmware leaves it on too long, the block could finish the task, see that the bit is on, and start the task again.

📖 **Tales from the Trenches**

See Section 4.4.1, Document Defects, for a tale that applies to this situation.

☑ **Best Practice**

8.5.3 Provide a queue bit that firmware must set—and only hardware can clear—to initiate a task in the block.

Timing through the Life Cycle

The timing of this task life cycle sequence depends on the nature of the block. In some cases, the timing is a constant. In other cases, it varies depending on factors internal and external to the block.

In some cases, the queue time (from Figure 8.5) is instantaneous (within a few clock cycles). In other cases, the block must wait for something else to occur before it can start. For example, a resource that the block needs to use may not yet be available, the block needs an external event to start, or it may be busy executing the previous task. During this time, the queue bit is set but not the active bit. This allows firmware to know that the block received the request but is not yet working on the task.

The active time is a constant in some blocks and varies in others. Active time may vary due to the amount of data being processed or how long it must wait for external signals and handshaking. During this time, the active bit is set, allowing firmware to know that the block is working on the task.

The amount of ack time required depends on several factors in firmware, such as the priority of the interrupt and the priority of other firmware processes.

If the queue time and active time will never be very big, firmware engineers could choose to implement a polling response rather than an interrupt response. An interrupt response will take up CPU time due to task switching and interrupt decoding. In a polling response, firmware does not enable the interrupt but simply enters a loop after setting the queue bit. Firmware stays in that loop until the interrupt bit is set. (This assumes that the interrupt will be set, even though the interrupt is not enabled and therefore the interrupt will not propagate to the CPU.) When the interrupt bit is set, firmware can clear it and immediately move on. The ack time for a polling response is much shorter because firmware is ready and waiting.

A polling response is not good for long periods of time because firmware is tying up the CPU during this loop. Firmware engineers need to know the maximum possible queue and active times in order to make a decision on which to implement, the interrupt or polling response. Many factors dictate where the dividing line should be between interrupt and polling response, but a good rule of thumb is that anything more than about 50 to 100 clock cycles should use the interrupt response.

Clearing the Queue Bit

The queue bit is cleared when the block is able to receive another request from firmware to execute the next task. Firmware reads this bit to know if it can queue the task again.

☑   **Best Practice**

8.5.4 Design the block to clear the queue bit only after the queued task is launched and firmware is allowed to queue another task.

Figure 8.6 shows how the queue bit is not cleared until the end, and so a second task cannot be queued up until firmware is acknowledging the interrupt for the first one.

A variation is that the queue bit is cleared when the block starts the task. Both variations have different characteristics with regard to executing tasks one after another.

When the queue bit is cleared at the time that the task starts, the block is ready to receive another request even though it will not yet be able to execute it. If a task is already queued

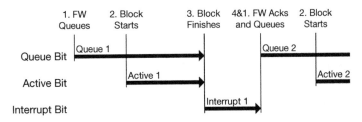

Figure 8.6: Timing of bits when the queue bit is cleared at the end.

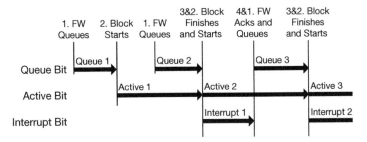

Figure 8.7: Timing of bits when the queue bit is cleared at the beginning.

in the block when the current task is done, the block can immediately start executing the next task without firmware intervention. This has an obvious performance benefit in that the block stays active all the time. Figure 8.7 illustrates this timing and shows the bit settings for three tasks.

Other variations of queue, active, and interrupt bits are possible, such as no active bit because it is so short, or no interrupt but because it is always quick. Whatever the variation is, make sure that firmware can know the state of the task that it launched.

Multiple Queue Bits

If a block has several tasks that could be launched, a question is whether or not they can be launched concurrently. If so, then their respective queue bits can be assigned to the same register. Examples of possible concurrent tasks include a data transfer task and a timer task.

If tasks cannot run concurrently, they should be assigned to different registers to eliminate the possibility that firmware could launch more than one at the same time. Example tasks that probably should not run concurrently are a data transfer task and a reset task.

☑ **Best Practice**

8.5.5 Assign queue bits to the same register only if their associated tasks are allowed to start concurrently.

8.5.3. Coherent Register Contents

Given the parallel and transient nature of the many states and operations within the block, it can be difficult to make sense of the information. In order to provide firmware with information that is accurate and makes sense, it may be necessary to provide shadow registers in hardware that holds information for firmware.

One example is a state machine that can detect error conditions in multiple states. Once an error is detected, the state machine traverses through error-handling states and generates an error interrupt. The block should record in a shadow register the state that detected the error and the levels of appropriate key signals. Firmware reads that shadow register and then uses it to respond to the error or gives it to engineers for diagnosis.

Another example is a wide register that requires multiple reads to get it out. To ensure coherency between multiple reads, a shadow register is needed to take a snapshot of the register on the first read so that the correct associated values are returned with subsequent reads.

Figure 8.8 illustrates a 48-bit counter that requires two 32-bit reads to retrieve all the contents. When the lower 32-bits are read, the upper 16 bits are copied into a shadow register for a subsequent read.

In this example, if the shadow register had not been there, firmware would have received 0x0030 for the upper 16, making 0x0030 FFFFFFFE for the whole 48 bits, which is incorrect.

☑   **Best Practice**

8.5.6 Use shadow registers to provide stable and valid snapshots of registers with rapidly changing values.

Besides providing content that is coherent, registers should provide coherent content all of the time.

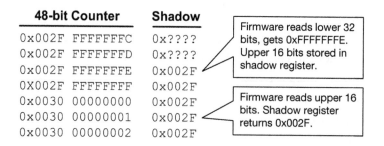

Figure 8.8: Using a shadow register to coherently read wide registers.

📖   **Tales from the Trenches**

We were having problems with a third-party block on our ASIC. Engineers tried to collect information by reading registers during block operation, but the information did not make sense. Upon reading the documentation from the third-party company, they discovered that it said that the contents of the block were only valid when the block was not active, and that when the block was active, the contents of the register were undefined.

That created a problem because firmware cannot always know what state the block was in or when the block changes state.

This tale illustrated a lack of coherency across time. If the block does not have anything to report while active, the register should be designed to return all zeros. One bit in the register should be a content-valid bit, allowing firmware to clearly know that the contents are valid, that the read happened during the proper time.

☑   **Best Practice**

8.5.7 Design registers to always return valid, accurate, and documented values, whether the block is idle or active.

8.5.4. Atomic Register Access

In registers containing several read/write configuration bits, firmware often needs to change 1 bit without changing the others. One technique is for firmware to keep a shadow copy of that register in its own data structures. Firmware modifies the desired bit in its copy, and then writes out the new value. Another technique is for firmware to first read the register, modify the desired bit, and then write out the new value.

If the register is only used by the one device driver, then either the shadow or the read-modify-write method can be used. However, for registers potentially used by more than one device driver, then each device driver must use the read-modify-write method. They cannot each keep their own shadow copy because they would quickly get out of sync. They must first read what is currently in the register to ensure they are working with a current and valid copy of the register.

Multiple device drivers accessing the same register can be dangerous. If the device drivers are not careful, one device driver could erase the changes of another device driver. This happens only under rare timing conditions. Since it is rare, it is very hard to debug, but it will eventually occur.

What Should Happen

Suppose the register in Figure 8.9 contains the value 0xBED. Driver A wants to modify the register, so it reads the register and ORs the contents with 0x400, which changes the value to 0xFED. Driver A then writes it out to the register, making it well-fed. Driver B then wants to modify the register so it reads the register, getting 0xFED. Driver B ANDs the contents with ~0x040 (the NOT of 0x040, which is 0xFBF), which changes the value to 0xFAD. Driver B then writes out the value, and now the register has the latest fad. Figure 8.9 shows what was just described.

What Should Not Happen

In contrast, this is what can happen but should not happen. The register in Figure 8.10 contains 0xBED. Driver A wakes up, reads the contents, ORs it with 0x400 getting the result 0xFED. However, before Driver A writes the results back out to the register, Driver B interrupts. Driver B reads the register, 0xBED, ANDs the content with ~0x040 getting 0xBAD. Driver B writes its results out to the register, and here is where it is bad. Driver B exits, and now Driver A can resume. Driver A does not know that it has been temporarily kicked off the CPU, nor would it know what other task was running, nor would it know that the other task just modified that register. It just simply resumes from where it left off. Driver A's next step is to write its contents, which is 0xFED, out to the register. It does so, making Driver B fed up that its changes were wiped out. Figure 8.10 shows what was just described.

This read-modify-write operation of firmware is non-atomic—it cannot complete these steps in one, non-interruptible step. Though this collision rarely happens, it can hang the system; when it does, it is very hard to isolate and track down.

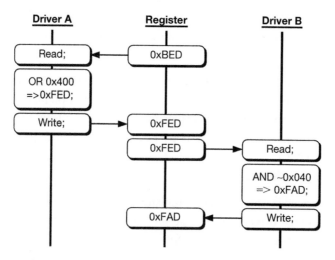

Figure 8.9: What should happen when two drivers modify the same register.

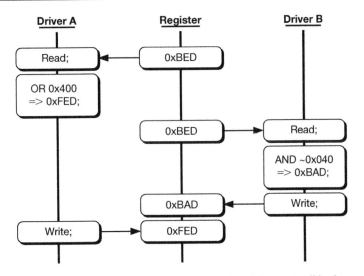

Figure 8.10: What should not happen when two device drivers modify the same register.

Registers with read/write bits are not atomically accessible. Registers with read-only, interrupt, and queue bits are atomically accessible. Read-only bits are, by definition, atomically accessible because firmware cannot change their settings. Interrupt and queue bits are atomically accessible because firmware can safely change 1 bit without changing the others and without prior knowledge of the current settings of the others.

Device Drivers Cannot Protect Against Collision

Device drivers try to fix this problem by disabling interrupts (or using mutexes) around their read-modify-write code of the common register. Had Driver A in Figure 8.10 disabled interrupts, Driver B could not have interrupted. Listing 8.14 shows how the two device drivers would protect their access to the register.

Listing 8.14: Protecting the read-modify-write of a register.

```
/* Driver A */                    /* Driver B */
disable_interrupts ();            disable_interrupts ();
*cfgReg |= 0x400;                 *cfgReg &= ~0x040;
enable_interrupts ();             enable_interrupts ();
```

However, disabling interrupts or using mutexes gives a false sense of security. Errors can be introduced into the code in many ways:

- Firmware code is leveraged, copied, and reused, and not necessarily copied from the right place.

- The protection must be done the same way in each place, whether disabling interrupts, using mutexes, or some other scheme.

- Each and every device driver has to implement this.

- Each of the different engineers must know how to do it.

- Engineers new to the code may not be aware of it.

If just one device driver does not disable interrupts when accessing the register, corruption can still occur. Unfortunately, the device driver that is being impacted is the one that is playing by the rules, the one that does disable interrupts. The device driver that is doing the damage is the one that did not play by the rules. In the above Figure 8.10, even if Driver B had disabled interrupts, Driver A can still overwrite it. Had Driver A disabled interrupts, Driver B would not have been able to interrupt until Driver A re-enabled interrupts after it was done.

Disabling interrupts only ensures that your device driver does not overwrite anybody else's device driver writes. But it does not ensure that your writes do not get overwritten.

If this situation is suspected, it can be a lengthy process to hunt through all of the code in all the device drivers to find the one spot that forgot to disable interrupts.

Because avoiding and diagnosing this situation is very difficult, the number of global registers that require access by multiple device drivers should be minimized.

☑ **Best Practice**

8.5.8 Avoid read/write registers that more than one device driver will access.

Atomic Registers

However, there are cases where global registers need to be accessed by multiple device drivers. Two common examples are the chip-level interrupt enable register and GPIO configuration registers. Fortunately, global registers in the chip can be designed to provide atomic access, allowing firmware to set or clear any bit as desired while leaving other bits unchanged. Here is one way of doing it.

Utilize two address locations that point to the same bank of flip-flops: one address for setting bits and one for clearing bits. The first address behaves as a Read/Write-1-Set, where firmware writes a one to set the desired bit. The second address behaves as a Read/Write-1-Clear, where firmware writes a one to clear the desired bit. Firmware can read from either address and get the same contents.

	MSB			GPIO Output Register—R/W1S 0x0280, R/W1C 0x0284						LSB
Bits	31 30 29 28	27 26 25 24	23 22 21 20	19 18 17 16	15 14 13 12	11 10 9 8	7 6 5 4	3 2 1 0
R/W1S	- - - -	- - - -	- - - -	- - - -	- - - -	- - - -	- - F E	D C B A
R/W1C	- - - -	- - - -	- - - -	- - - -	- - - -	- - - -	- - F E	D C B A
Reset	0 0 0 0	0 0 0 0	0 0 0 0	0 0 0 0	0 0 0 0	0 0 0 0	0 0 0 0	0 0 0 0

This register (two addresses but one bank of flip-flops) provides atomic access to firmware. Firmware does not need to use read-modify-write. But firmware can set or clear bits as desired without changing other bits and without having prior knowledge of the current levels of the other bits.

This type of atomic register is used in the PCI Express to Serial ATA Controller by Silicon Image for their Port Interrupt Enable Set/Clear register. (For SiL3531A Data Sheet, Document # SiL-DS-0208-C, revision C, 02/02/07, Silicon Image, Inc., see siliconimage.com/docs/SiL-DS-0208-C.pdf.)

☑ **Best Practice**

8.5.9 Provide atomic access to registers that more than one device driver will access.

8.6. Summary

This chapter has been about registers, the primary interface between firmware and the block. Since it is the primary interface, it has the biggest impact in getting firmware and the block to work together smoothly and efficiently.

Many concepts were given, which, if followed, will improve the interface. Although the concepts were varied, they share the following common purposes:

- Keep registers and bits in one block separate from other blocks to avoid collisions with other device drivers.

- When making changes to a block, make them such that device drivers can easily support both the old and the new versions of the block. Having the same device driver work on both versions reduces complexity, not only in firmware, but also in the maintenance and support of both the old and new versions of the block.

- Avoid complex interactions with firmware. Proper design in the block will, not only help reduce firmware errors, but also prevent some from ever occurring.

- Provide clear information to status, conditions, and versions. This helps firmware make decisions on how to handle (or not handle) various conditions and variations.

These purposes will help make decisions when faced with situations not discussed in this chapter.

8.6.1. Supporting Principles

The concepts of this chapter support the principles of hardware/firmware interface design as follows:

1. **Balance the Load:** Several concepts were taught that, just by how the registers were laid out, would ease the load and complexity for firmware without causing any additional burden on the hardware.

2. **Design for Compatibility:** Much of the chapter discussed techniques to allow device drivers to be forward and backward compatible.

3. **Anticipate the Impacts:** This chapter discusses being aware of impacts when making changes to the registers and bits for the next version.

Next is Chapter 9, Interrupts. There are enough issues and nuances associated with interrupts that they warrant a separate chapter.

CHAPTER 9

Interrupts

The previous chapter discussed registers, which is how firmware invokes action in the hardware. This chapter is about interrupts, which is how hardware invokes action in the firmware. Hardware uses interrupts to notify firmware that some event has occurred. When an interrupt occurs, firmware sets aside its current task and services the interrupt.

Because of the problems and confusion due to the variety of interrupt behaviors in use by the industry today, I have dedicated a separate chapter to this topic. These problems and confusion are due to a lack of consistency and clarity in the function and behavior of interrupts. What one chip calls Enable, another chip calls Mask. It may be that a 1 is written to "ack" (acknowledge) an interrupt on one chip, whereas a 0 is written on another.

This inconsistency leads to confusion and problems as firmware engineers write device drivers for different blocks, for different chips, and for chips from different companies. Leveraging skills and device driver code from one style of behavior to another leads to firmware defects, some of which are very difficult to debug.

Enforcing the same interrupt behavior in all blocks, in all chips, and across all companies will greatly reduce problems in firmware. As long as the behavior, whether logical or esoteric, is consistent throughout, engineers will know the method and understand it and will be able to leverage firmware code from one device driver to another.

Using a standard implementation has benefits. As an example, electrical engineers know what a flip-flop is, but because there are a variety of implementations in use, exact details are not known. But there are standard flip-flop types that are defined and understood, such as RS, D, and JK flip-flops. Once the type of flip-flop is specified, such as a D flip-flop, engineers know immediately how it works, its truth table, and how to wire it up. Standard flip-flops have fixed parts, such as a data and clock input, and it has optional parts, such as an enable or clear. These are also understood by engineers.

In contrast, an interrupt module can be implemented in many different ways, but no standard implementation exists.

In this chapter, I will discuss implementation variations and their impact on firmware. And I will state which variation should be part of an interrupt standard. If all companies that produce chips were to use this interrupt standard, many problems will be avoided in firmware, especially by those writing firmware for chips from various companies. Firmware functions and techniques that work with this interrupt standard can be written and distributed.

9.1. Design

In this section, I will discuss a few design guidelines regarding the interrupt module.

9.1.1. An Interrupt Supermodule

With the goal of providing consistency in the design of the interrupt module, it is logical to design the module to be instantiated wherever an interrupt module is needed. This lends itself to becoming a supermodule following the concepts discussed in Chapter 6, Superblock. The interrupt supermodule provides support for the superset of functionality and includes the following list of features:

- Consistency in the behavior of the module

- Consistency in the address offsets of the registers

- Consistency in the bit positions among the various registers

- The ability to specify the number of interrupt channels needed

- The ability to specify which optional registers are implemented

Each of these will be explained in greater detail in this chapter

☑ **Best Practice**

9.1.1 Design the interrupt module as a supermodule to provide the superset of all features needed by all chips instantiating the module.

Parts of an Interrupt Supermodule

To aid in the discussion in this chapter, I will describe the parts of an interrupt supermodule. Two major parts are registers and channels:

- **Registers:** An interrupt module contains several registers that firmware uses to manage interrupts. Some of the registers include pending, enable, and source status registers. More details follow in this chapter.

- **Channels:** One channel contains the necessary support for one incoming interrupt signal. It watches for when the interrupt occurs, latches that the interrupt has occurred, and contains controls for enabling and acking that interrupt. When an interrupt supermodule is instantiated, it will contain the number of channels necessary to support the number of interrupt sources.

From a visual perspective, registers could be thought of as horizontal components that intersect with channels, which are vertical components, as illustrated in Figure 9.1. Six channels are illustrated, indicating that six interrupt sources need to be managed.

Other parts of the interrupt module include the following:

- **Incoming source signals:** These come into the bottom of each channel, as illustrated. This is the signal that some event has occurred. It may come from a state machine, combinatorial logic, or an external signal.

- **Channel interrupt pending signals:** These come out of the top of each channel and is asserted if that channel has an interrupt pending.

- **Interrupt pending signal:** This is the OR of the channel interrupt pending signals. If it is true, one or more of the interrupt channels has an interrupt pending.

Each register spans each interrupt channel and is aligned with each channel. The pending status of channel 0 can be read from bit 0 in the pending register. Writing to bit 0 in the pending register will ack the pending interrupt in channel 0. Channel 0 can be enabled/disabled with bit 0 in the enable register. The current state of the incoming source signal for

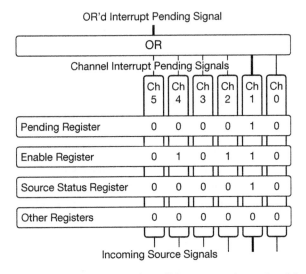

Figure 9.1: Registers spanning all interrupt channels with an interrupt shown for channel 1.

channel 0 can be read from bit 0 in the source status register. And other operations can be performed on channel 0 by using bit 0 in the other registers.

In this illustration, only six channels are instantiated, therefore only six bits in each register are used. The other bits (26 bits in a 32-bit system) are unused. Reading those unused bits always returns zeros, and writes to them are ignored.

With the values as illustrated in Figure 9.1, reading the pending register will show that bit 1 is set, indicating that there is a pending interrupt in channel 1, as illustrated by the bold signal line. With the registers spanning all channels, actions can be performed on channels at the same time. Writing 0x16 to the enable register will enable channels 1, 2, and 4, leaving the others disabled, as also illustrated.

Keeping this alignment of the same channel being in the same bit position across registers allows firmware to use the same masks no matter which register is being accessed. Listing 9.1 illustrates this by showing how the six interrupt masks are used. This example shows six example interrupts for a data I/O module.

☑   **Best Practice**

9.1.2 Assign each interrupt channel to the same bit position in the pending, enabled, source status, and other registers in the interrupt module.

9.1.2. Hierarchical Interrupt Structure

Interrupt modules are best used in a hierarchical fashion, with modules at the block level and at the chip level.

Each block has its own instantiation of an interrupt module. This allows the device driver for that block to have exclusive access to the registers in that block's interrupt module. The block's interrupt module is configured to support the necessary number of interrupt channels required for that block.

In the case that the block needs more interrupts than one module can support (e.g., more than 32 interrupts in a 32-bit system), then another module can be instantiated. The block-level interrupt module monitors all the interrupts for that block and produces one interrupt signal to be propagated up to the chip-level interrupt module.

☑   **Best Practice**

9.1.3 Instantiate the interrupt module in each block to support all interrupts for that block and that block only.

Listing 9.1: Using the same masks for all interrupt management tasks.

```
#define INTR_TX_FIFO_EMPTY      0x01
#define INTR_RX_FIFO_NOT_EMPTY  0x02
#define INTR_TX_TRANSMIT_ERR    0x04
#define INTR_RX_BAD_PARITY      0x08
#define INTR_RX_OVERFLOW        0x10
#define INTR_ABORT_DONE         0x20

// Enable all interrupts
*regIntrEnable = INTR_TX_FIFO_EMPTY | INTR_RX_FIFO_NOT_EMPTY |
                 INTR_TX_TRANSMIT_ERR | INTR_RX_BAD_PARITY |
                 INTR_RX_OVERFLOW | INTR_ABORT_DONE;

// Check pending interrupt
if (*regIntrPending & INTR_TX_FIFO_EMPTY) // If fifo empty
   {
   *regIntrPending = INTR_TX_FIFO_EMPTY;  // Ack this one only
   // Put new data in FIFO for transmit
   }

// Disable just one interrupt
*regIntrEnable &= ~INTR_RX_OVERFLOW;

// Is there more data in the Rx FIFO?
if (*regIntrSource & INTR_RX_FIFO_NOT_EMPTY)
   {
   // Process next data
   }
```

The interrupt module supports more than one interrupt source but only sends one signal up to the CPU. If any of the sources generate an interrupt, then the one signal to the CPU is asserted.

☑   **Best Practice**

9.1.4 Design the interrupt module to multiplex all its pending interrupts into a single interrupt line to be propagated upstream.

One interrupt module (or more if additional space is needed) is instantiated at the chip level. It monitors all the interrupt signals from the block-level interrupt modules and produces one interrupt signal to be propagated up to the CPU.

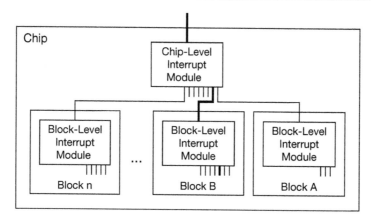

Figure 9.2: Hierarchy of block- and chip-level interrupt modules, with a pending interrupt shown.

☑ **Best Practice**

9.1.5 Instantiate an interrupt module at the chip level to collect the interrupt signal from each block interrupt module and produce one interrupt signal from the chip.

Figure 9.2 illustrates the block- and chip-level hierarchy. An example pending interrupt is shown with a bold line in the figure. An event occurs in Block B asserting the interrupt source line wired to the Block B's interrupt module which is assigned to the third interrupt channel, channel 2. The interrupt module captures the event and asserts its interrupt signal, which propagates up to the chip-level interrupt module. The interrupt signal from Block B is assigned to channel 1 in the chip-level interrupt module. The chip-level interrupt module then asserts its interrupt line, propagating the interrupt up to the CPU.

9.1.3. Interrupt Sharing

Interrupt sharing is used to allow more than one interrupt source to share the same interrupt channel. This is often done when multiple chips in a system need to share the limited interrupt lines into the CPU. Any device sharing the line can assert the interrupt into the CPU. When one of the devices interrupts the CPU, the interrupt handler polls all the devices sharing that line to determine which one asserted the interrupt. Once found, the device is then serviced so that it will deassert the line. If the interrupt line into the CPU is still asserted, then the interrupt handler continues polling the devices to find another interrupting device.

Sharing an interrupt line, however, has its disadvantages. When an interrupt occurs, firmware must individually poll each device to discover which one generated the interrupt.

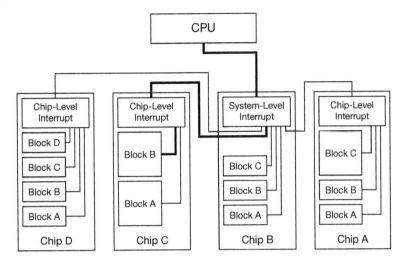

Figure 9.3: Muxing interrupts from several chips through a system-level interrupt module, with block B in chip C showing a pending interrupt.

An interrupting device must be serviced. It cannot be ignored because it can hide other devices, especially higher-priority devices, trying to interrupt the CPU.

A system-level interrupt module should be used to gather the interrupts from the various chips and mux them to make one interrupt into the CPU. One such module is the Programmable Interrupt Controller (PIC) common in old X86 platforms and is now part of the X86 Southbridge chipset.

Figure 9.3 illustrates how multiple chips are wired to a system-level interrupt module located inside one of the chips. The bold line shows how an interrupt from block B in chip C is propagated through the system-level interrupt module in chip B and then on up to the CPU.

> **Note:**
>
> As I stated earlier in this chapter, for the sake of consistency and to reduce defects, the same interrupt supermodule should be instantiated at the block and chip level. It should also be used for the system-level interrupt module. Depending on the design of the CPU, the interrupt supermodule could be instantiated there, too. However, other design requirements, such as having vectored interrupts, will require differences from the interrupt supermodule discussed here. It is beyond the scope of this book to address best practices within the design of a CPU but many of these concepts will apply.

A system-level interrupt module, whether a discrete chip or part of another chip, will avoid problems with multiple chips sharing interrupt lines into the CPU. Besides not sharing at the chip level, interrupts sources should not share interrupt channels at the block and chip level. Each should have its own channel.

☑ **Best Practice**

9.1.6 Assign each interrupt source signal to its own interrupt channel.

9.1.4. Source Signal Integrity

The signal coming into the interrupt module can come from a variety of sources, such as an external pin, an internal signal, or a state machine. Integrity of the signal must be ensured in order to have proper behavior of the interrupt module, to avoid false interrupt triggering but to be sure to trigger on all legitimate events.

I will divide this discussion into two areas; internal signals that come from within the chip and external signals that come from outside of the chip.

Internal Signals

Good chip design practice dictates that signals internal to the chip should be synchronized. This means that the incoming source signal into the interrupt module must be synchronized to the same clock that is driving the interrupt module. A signal might not be synchronized if it is coming from a different clock domain within the block or chip, or if it is a result of combinatorial logic.

Including a clock synchronization circuit inside the interrupt module ensures that incoming source signal will be synchronized to the interrupt module's clock.

☑ **Best Practice**

9.1.7 Provide a clock synchronization circuit in the interrupt module for the incoming source signals.

External Signals

External signals coming from pins on the chip are unsynchronized to the chip's clock. External signals will have different characteristics, based on where the signal comes from. If it is from a nearby chip on a well-designed board, the signal is fairly clean. If it is from a push-button switch, it will have bounce noise. If it is from a long wire from some external device, it is prone to cross-talk, ESD, slow rise and fall times, and other issues.

These problems could cause false, missed, multiple triggers, or other abnormal behavior, if wired directly into the interrupt module. Marginal conditions will cause problems only rarely, but those make it more difficult to diagnose and work around.

📖 **Tales from the Trenches**

I discovered that on rare occasions, the interrupt-pending register would show that an enabled interrupt for an external signal was pending but the CPU never received the interrupt.

The hardware engineer inspected the RTL code, which revealed that this external signal was not debounced nor was it synchronized to the clock used by the interrupt module. Under the right conditions, the noise and timing of the unfiltered, unsynchronized signal could result in the undesired behavior.

I had to insert a firmware workaround to monitor that line in case it became pending without generating an interrupt.

Each of the signals coming into the block needs to be dealt with appropriately with noise suppression, debouncing logic, and other necessary circuits. Once cleaned up, the interrupt signals can be fed into the interrupt module.

☑ **Best Practice**

9.1.8 Clean up all incoming external interrupt sources with debouncing, noise suppression, and other appropriate circuits.

9.1.5. Types of Interrupt Triggers

Interrupts are triggered in one of two ways: level-triggered or edge-triggered. Because slightly different definitions of these terms are in use, I will define them.

- **Level-triggered:** A level-triggered interrupt module always generates an interrupt whenever the level of the interrupt source signal is asserted. If the source signal is still asserted when the interrupt handler acks the interrupt, the interrupt stays pending, causing the interrupt handler to be re-invoked again. Level-triggered interrupts force firmware engineers to take into account what is generating the source signal and ensure that the source signal has been deasserted before they can ack the interrupt. In some versions of level-triggered interrupts, there is no "interrupt module" in between the source and the CPU that latched the source signal assertion. Clearing the interrupt source signal will cause the interrupt line all the way to the CPU to be cleared. And firmware engineers must understand those variations, too.

- **Edge-triggered:** An edge-triggered interrupt module generates an interrupt only when it detects an asserting edge of the interrupt source. The edge may be detected when the interrupt source level actually changes, or it may be detected by periodic sampling, noting when a sample of a deasserted level is followed by a sample of an asserted level. Generally the interrupt is generated only when the leading edge arrives, when the signal becomes asserted. Some designs will generate an interrupt on both the leading and trailing edges. Firmware can ack the interrupt anytime after the edge arrives, regardless as to whether the source signal is still asserted or has since deasserted.

Note

Another type of interrupt is the message signaled interrupt (MSI). Instead of an interrupt signal on a wire, a specialized message is sent via the normal communication bus. PCI Express uses this method. From a firmware perspective, MSI can be used as desired and firmware can accommodate it. This section discusses the issues regarding level- vs. edge-triggered interrupts. These issues do not apply to MSI-based interrupts, so MSI will not be discussed here.

Level- vs. Edge-Triggered Interrupts

With the goal of having one interrupt standard, is it possible to pick either level-triggered or edge-triggered interrupts and use it exclusively in all applications? It is possible to use either one; however, after examining several use cases, it will be clear that edge-triggered interrupts have the advantage.

Those who have written interrupt handlers for level- and/or edge-triggered interrupts have encountered situations that required special care in firmware to handle specific situations. It is not uncommon to think that the interrupt handler must be written a certain way to avoid those problems. Often the reason for that thinking is because by the time the interrupt handler is being written, it is too late to make any changes to the design of the interrupt module. It is cast in silicon, and firmware has to use it as is. But since the discussion here is about designing the interrupt module in hardware, we have the ability to optimize both the hardware and the firmware sides of capturing and responding to interrupts. It gives us the ability to examine new ways to architect the design.

The examination of level- vs. edge-triggered interrupts is best done by studying several different applications. I list several of them because these applications are what other engineers have brought up to me as we have analyzed the edge vs. level debate.

- **Source is a pulse:** This is when the interrupt source signal is simply a pulse with a very short duration, such that the source signal always deasserts itself before the interrupt handler can respond. In this scenario, there is no difference between edge- or level-triggered interrupts. The interrupt handler simply acks the interrupt without any additional work required.

- **Source indicates active condition:** This is when the source signal indicates that some condition is now active. It is cleared by firmware. For level-triggered interrupts, the condition must be cleared before the interrupt is acked. For edge-triggered interrupts, firmware has the flexibility to ack the interrupt before or after clearing the condition.

- **Source indicates idle condition:** This is when the source signal indicates that some task is complete. Firmware clears the signal by giving the block more work to do. For level-triggered interrupts, firmware must give the block more work before it can ack the interrupt. If there is currently no more work to do, firmware must disable that interrupt, and then re-enable later when there is more work to do. For edge-triggered interrupts, firmware simply acks the interrupt, whether there is more work to do or not.

- **Repeated event:** This source signal indicates that one or more events have occurred, and a counter or buffer is used to keep track of the number of occurrences. The source signal deasserts after firmware services each occurrence. With level-triggered interrupts, the handler can process one, ack the interrupt, and exit. If there are more, the interrupt is still pending and the handler will be re-invoked. With edge-triggered interrupts, the handler must loop until it services all occurrences. In this case, level has an advantage with cleaner code.

- **Source from another block:** This is a source signal that comes from a different block controlled by a different device driver. With level-triggered interrupts, the two device drivers must coordinate. If the interrupt source line will not be deasserted soon, the interrupt must be disabled to allow other interrupts to occur, and then re-enabled later after the other block deasserts the source signal. With edge-triggered interrupts, little coordination is needed—the interrupt can be acked immediately.

- **External source:** This is a source signal that comes in from outside the system for which firmware has no control of the signal. With level-triggered interrupts, when an interrupt occurs, it must be disabled until the external source signal deasserts itself, and then be re-enabled. For edge-triggered interrupts, no disable is necessary—the interrupt is simply acked.

- **Interrupt sharing:** Previously I discussed interrupt sharing and how it is not a good idea. But if it is needed, level-triggered interrupts have the advantage because the interrupt handler will be re-invoked as long as any device has its interrupt line asserted. For edge-triggered interrupts, the handler must poll all devices to be sure to catch all pending interrupts.

- **Interrupt nesting:** This is when a higher-priority interrupt occurs while servicing a lower-priority interrupt. In the level-triggered case, a higher-priority interrupt will be blocked until the lower-priority interrupt is serviced or disabled. For the edge-triggered case, the interrupt can be acked immediately, allowing higher-priority interrupts to occur, if necessary.

- **Interrupts during power-on:** When a system powers up, interrupt signals are unstable as the various parts of the system turn on. When firmware is ready to look at interrupt, it must determine if any pending interrupts are legitimate or due to power-on fluctuations on the source signals. In the level-triggered case, interrupts must be handled immediately or disabled. For the edge-triggered case, firmware can ack, allowing interrupts to be enabled, and then determine how to handle any pending interrupts.

This is not an exhaustive list of applications. But some patterns emerge. For level-triggered interrupts, several situations exist where the interrupting interrupt must be disabled because it cannot be acked yet. It must be disabled to allow continuation of other system functionality. When to re-enable that level-triggered interrupt varies, depending on the situation. However, interrupts do not need to be disabled for edge-triggered interrupts because they can always be acked immediately.

Level-triggered interrupts require that the firmware engineer understand the behavior of the source signal and accommodate the different types. Edge-triggered interrupts do not require as much understanding. This allows for more consistency in the handling style in the interrupt handler, which reduces complexity and increases the quality of the firmware.

☑   **Best Practice**

9.1.9 Make the interrupt module edge triggered.

Which Edge to Trigger On

Which edge should the edge-triggered interrupt trigger on? Before I answer that question, I need to clarify the naming convention of levels and edges. The reason for this is that some signals are designed using negative logic, where the 0 and 1 levels mean the opposite from positive logic.

- **0 vs. 1 level:** A 0 level means the voltage level of the signal line is at 0 V. A 1 means that the voltage level is at some positive voltage level. Actual voltage level depends on the voltage in the system and the chip technology being used. This is the same for positive and negative logic.

- **Asserted vs. deasserted levels:** The asserted level indicates the signal is true. In positive logic, it is at a 1; in negative logic, it is at a 0. The deasserted level is opposite.

- **Asserting vs. deasserting edges:** An asserting edge is when the level moves from the deasserted state to the asserted state. For positive logic, that is from 0 to 1. For negative logic, that is from 1 to 0.

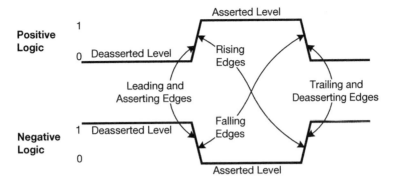

Figure 9.4: Definition of level and edge terms for positive and negative logic.

- **Leading vs. trailing edges:** This is the same as asserting vs. deasserting edges.

- **Rising vs. falling edges:** A rising edge is when the signal changes from 0 to 1, regardless as to whether positive or negative logic is used. A falling edge is when the signal changes from 1 to 0.

Figure 9.4 is a graphical illustration of these definitions.

It would be cumbersome to require that the edge-triggered interrupt module be instructed as to whether the incoming source signal is using positive or negative logic, especially since the module is likely to have a mix of both positive and negative logic source signals. The interrupt module is also not designed to interrupt on both edges of the signal. (See Section 9.6, Triggering on Both Edges, for a discussion on triggering on both edges.) For the sake of consistency and conformity to a standard, the interrupt module should be designed to interrupt on the rising edge, whenever the signal changes from 0 to 1.

Positive logic signals are wired directly to the interrupt module. Negative logic signals need to pass through an inverter before going to the interrupt module.

☑ **Best Practice**

9.1.10 Make the interrupt module rising-edge triggered.

Since these interrupt modules are designed to be hierarchical, the outgoing source signal that is propagated up to the next interrupt module will also use positive logic—it will change from a 0 to a 1 when an interrupt becomes pending. It will stay at 1 while one or more interrupts are pending.

☑ **Best Practice**

9.1.11 Make the interrupt module generate a 1 for the outgoing interrupt signal when one or more interrupts are pending.

9.2. Pending Register

A pending register contains a bit for each interrupt channel instantiated in the module. The bits are of the type, interrupt bit—write 1 clear. (See the section, Interrupt Bits—Write 1 Clear, in Section 8.2.6, Bit Types.) Firmware reads the register to see which interrupts are pending. Firmware writes a 1 to one or more positions to ack the interrupt in those channels. Zeros written to bit positions are ignored. Ones written to positions where there is no pending interrupt are also ignored.

> ☑   **Best Practice**
>
> 9.2.1 Provide an interrupt pending register that shows pending interrupts.

> ☑   **Best Practice**
>
> 9.2.2 Use the interrupt bit type in the pending register.

9.2.1. Acknowledging an Interrupt

The pending register reports which interrupts have occurred with a 1 in the appropriate bit position. When firmware acks the interrupt, the bit is cleared and the interrupt to the CPU is removed (assuming that no other interrupts are pending).

Write 1 Clear

In most chips, firmware writes a 1 to a bit position to ack the interrupt in that channel. This action is known as Write 1 Clear (W1C). On a few chips, firmware writes a 0 to clear, Write 0 Clear (W0C).

Fewer defects are introduced to firmware if it writes 1s to ack instead of 0s. With W1C, the contents read from the pending register can be immediately written to ack all pending interrupts. With W0C, an extra step is required of inverting what was read before writing. In some device driver architectures, interrupts are acked from different locations in the code. For W0C designs, defects can be introduced when engineers inadvertently forget to invert the value at one or more of the locations.

Listing 9.2 shows two columns, the left for W1C designs and the right for W0C. Each column shows two variations. Variation X has all pending interrupts immediately acked. Variation Y has the pending interrupts acked one at a time, as needed.

Listing 9.2: Writing 1s or 0s to ack.

```
01    // Writing 1s to ack, W1C       01    // Writing 0s to ack, W0C
02                                     02
03    // Variation X                   03    // Variation X
04    intr = *regPending;             04    intr = *regPending;
05    *regPending = intr;             05    *regPending = ~intr;
06    // Look for which intr          06    // Look for which intr
07    ...                             07    ...
08                                     08
09    // Variation Y                   09    // Variation Y
10    intr = *regPending;             10    intr = *regPending;
11    if (intr & INTR_A_MASK)         11    if (intr & INTR_A_MASK)
12       {                            12       {
13       *regPending = INTR_A_MASK;   13       *regPending = ~INTR_A_MASK;
14       // Service A                 14       // Service A
15       }                            15       }
16    if (intr & INTR_B_MASK)         16    if (intr & INTR_B_MASK)
17       {                            17       {
18       *regPending = INTR_B_MASK;   18       *regPending = INTR_B_MASK;
19       // Service B                 19       // Service B
20       }                            20       }
21    ...                             21    ...
```

In Variation X, the only difference is on line 05, where the contents of intr are inverted in the W0C case. In Variation Y, the only differences are on lines 13 and 18, where the mask is inverted in the W0C case when written to the register.

If you did not notice, there is actually a bug on the right side on line 18. INTR_B_MASK is not inverted when it should be. Since most chips are of the W1C style, defects could be introduced when firmware is ported from a W1C chip to a W0C chip. Or the engineer writing the code or maintaining and updating old code could inadvertently omit the inverting step.

📖 **Tales from the Trenches**

In one block on an ASIC, some interrupts had to be acked with a 1 and others had to be acked with a 0. I had to be careful to make sure that the device driver was writing 0s and 1s in the right places.

To help reduce confusion and lead to higher-quality firmware, the pending register should be of the W1C design.

☑   **Best Practice**

9.2.3 Design the pending register so that a 1 written to a bit position acks the interrupt at
that position.

Read Clear

Another variation for ack is used where the pending register clears (acks) the interrupt itself
as firmware reads the register. It saves time for firmware by not having to clear those bits
with a separate write. That may sound like a good idea, but it is dangerous.

The first read to occur after an interrupt is the only read that will get the list of pending
interrupts. In some firmware architectures, there is a need to read the pending register
multiple times before firmware is ready for interrupts to be acked. Each device driver might
be required to read the global interrupt pending register. Some device drivers are architected
to read its own block pending register multiple times during one interrupt. Firmware logging
code often reads several registers, including the pending register, to generate log traces.
Debuggers often scan the chip reading all its registers. Anytime these logging or debugging
tools read the read-clear pending register, they are at risk for reading and losing pending
interrupts.

An advantage touted for read-clear pending registers is when the CPU and the chip are
across buses, channels, bridges, and tunnels from each other. Some CPUs have a write
buffer that will hold up a write command for a short time. Write buffers and complex bus
architectures slow down how fast the CPU can access the chip. In these systems, there is a
time delay from writing the ack until it actually arrives at the chip so that it can lower the
interrupt line to the CPU.

If interrupt handler waits until its last step to ack the interrupt, it cannot immediately exit
out of the handler because the CPU will still be in interrupt mode since the interrupt line is
still active. The interrupt handler must wait until it knows that the line has been cleared
before it can exit. A common way to solve this problem is for the interrupt handler to read
the pending register right after writing the ack to the pending register. This forces the
handler to block until the read returns. When it does, the handler can safely exit.

A better way to handle this situation is to not wait until the last step to ack the interrupt. In
this edge-triggered system, acking the interrupt can be the second step in the handler, the
first step being to read from the pending register. By the time the handler services the
interrupt with other reads and writes to registers in the block, the interrupt line will be
deasserted and the handler can safely exit without delay.

Because of the dangers of a read-clear architecture, do not use that style to ack interrupts.

☑   **Best Practice**

9.2.4 Do not clear the pending register when firmware reads it.

9.2.2. Order of Interrupt Positions

When an interrupt occurs, firmware reads the interrupt register and then has to look, bit by bit, for which interrupt occurred. Once it finds a bit, it services that interrupt. Once that interrupt is serviced, it will continue to scan the rest of the bits for more pending interrupts.

CPU instructions easily test if a value is zero or non-zero, but not which bit or bits are set. Once the list of pending interrupts has been read into a variable, firmware will scan for a bit that is set. Once one is found, it will service that interrupt and then clear that bit. Firmware then tests if it is zero yet. If not, it will continue scanning, bit by bit. If it is zero, firmware knows it is done. Listing 9.3 illustrates this algorithm. In this example, a loop is used to scan the bits.

The loop will scan through the bits in order of their position in the register. Instead of a loop, a series of discrete if() statements could be used to check for each bit. The series of if() statements is commonly put in bit order but does not have to be.

To help firmware have flexibility, the position of the bits should be considered. In other words, what priority should be used to determine which interrupt should be put in which bit

---

Listing 9.3: Scanning for pending interrupts.

```
uint32_t intr;
uint32_t mask;
int i;

intr = *regIntrPending;    // Read list of pending intrs
*regIntrPending = intr;    // Ack all pending interrupts

for (i=0; i<INTRS; i++)    // For each interrupt position
   {
   mask = 1<<i;            // Puts a 1 in bit position i
   if (intr & mask)        // If intr i is pending
      {
      intrHandler[i]();    // Handle the interrupt
      intr &= ~mask;       // Clear that bit
      if (intr == 0)       // If there are no more intr pending
         break;            // Break out of the for loop
      }
   }
```

position? No specific criteria exist, but here are two guidelines than can be applied. You may have other criteria in your specific application.

- **Frequency:** Interrupts that occur most frequently should be first. A frequent interrupt assigned to position 0 will be caught in the first pass and then, most of the time, no other bits will be pending so it can quickly jump out of the loop. Catastrophic errors, since the system is going down anyway, can wait until it scans to the end of the list.

- **Urgency:** Interrupts that are urgent need to be serviced first so that they are not blocked by servicing less urgent interrupts that may also be pending.

The difficult decision is to weigh a frequent, non-urgent interrupt with an infrequent but urgent interrupt. Analyze what will happen if both are pending at the same time. Can the urgent interrupt wait for the worse-case service time for the frequent interrupt? If not, then put the urgent interrupt before the frequent interrupt.

☑   **Best Practice**

9.2.5 Assign interrupts to interrupt channel positions in the pending register in descending order of priority, starting at LSB.

9.3. Enable Register

The enable register allows firmware to control which interrupts will be allowed to propagate to the CPU. It is a regular read/write register that firmware configures as desired.

📖   **Tales from the Trenches**

On one of our ASICs, hardware engineers decided (and firmware engineers approved) that the chip-level interrupt enable register was not necessary because each block had its own interrupt enable register. The idea sounded good at first, but in hindsight it was not a good idea. There were two problems that could have been avoided had there been chip-level enables.

One of the blocks had a new interrupt added and the connection to the enable logic was omitted. This meant that firmware always had to service that interrupt since it could not be disabled at the block level or the chip level.

The other problem was that one of the chip-level interrupts was simply routing an interrupt from an external I^2C chip through this chip. Acking an interrupt on that external chip required writing across the slow, serial I^2C bus. Since the pass-through chip could not disable that external interrupt, the whole system had to stay inside the ISR for about 400 μs until that serial write was completed and the interrupt acked.

The engineers learned their lesson and put the chip-level interrupt enable register back in.

> ☑   **Best Practice**
>
> 9.3.1 Provide an interrupt enable register that controls which interrupts are propagated to the CPU.

9.3.1. A 1 Enables the Interrupt

As discussed in Section 5.7.2, Enabling and Acknowledging Interrupts, some chips use the term, Mask, for the register that controls interrupt propagation. Most chips that use that term are designed such that a 1 in a bit position allows an interrupt to propagate. However, some chips are designed such that a 0 allows an interrupt to propagate. This is confusing to firmware engineers and can lead to defective firmware.

As stated in that section, the term, Enable, is better than Mask. It is more intuitive to the reader that in the enable register, a 1 is used to enable an interrupt.

It also is more convenient for firmware so that the same constants can be used for managing interrupts in the pending, enable, and other registers. Listing 9.1 earlier in this chapter shows the constants used to enable interrupts.

> ☑   **Best Practice**
>
> 9.3.2 Design the interrupt enable register so that a bit value of 1 allows the interrupt at that position to propagate.

9.3.2. Enable Controls Interrupt

Two methods are in use that control how the enable controls the interrupt pending function. One method controls whether the interrupt pending flip-flop is enabled to capture edges in the source signal. If the interrupt is disabled, edges on the source signal are ignored. The other method is that the interrupt pending flip-flop is allowed to monitor for edges in the source signal, generating a pending interrupt signal, but the pending interrupt signal is not allowed to propagate upstream if disabled. Figure 9.5 illustrates these two methods.

In the enable-controls-capture method, the pending flip-flop will capture an edge only if it is enabled. After it is enabled, it will not capture a pending interrupt until the next rising edge occurs, even if the source signal is already asserted when it becomes enabled. If firmware wants to service any interrupts that may be asserted before it was enabled, it can read the source status register to see which ones are asserted.

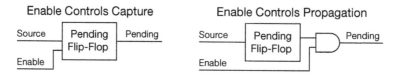

Figure 9.5: Two methods of how enable controls interrupts, by controlling capture or controlling propagation.

In the enable-controls-propagation method, the pending flip-flop will always capture the rising edge on the source. But it won't propagate upstream if not enabled. If an interrupt is pending when firmware enables the interrupt, the interrupt will propagate upstream immediately, interrupting the CPU. If firmware does not want that to happen, it can first ack the interrupt before enabling it.

The enable-controls-propagation method has the advantage that firmware, if desired, can know that an edge has occurred, even though it will not interrupt the CPU when it happens. This provides more information for firmware. If firmware does not need that information, it can simply mask it out. Listing 9.4 illustrates how firmware can handle this situation.

Another advantage of this method is that it will catch interrupts that occurred during bootup while interrupts are disabled. When firmware is ready to enable them, it can see if any interrupts occurred and either ack and ignore them or ack and service them.

Of the two methods, the enable-controls-propagation method is preferable because it gives firmware more information that it can optionally use.

☑   **Best Practice**

9.3.3 Design the interrupt enable register to control which pending interrupts are propagated, not which interrupts can become pending.

Listing 9.4: Acking all interrupts but only servicing enabled interrupts.

```
intr = *regIntrPending;    // Read all pending interrupts
*regIntrPending = intr;    // Ack all pending interrupts
LOG ("All intrs = ", intr); // Log all that are pending
intr &= intrEnabled;       // Remove non-enabled interrupts
// Examine intr to determine which enabled interrupts occurred
```

9.3.3. Default Settings for Enable

Standard practice in the industry is that when chips come out of power-on reset, that all interrupts are disabled. This is necessary to ensure that the CPU is not interrupted before firmware has a chance to boot up and get everything ready.

☑ **Best Practice**

9.3.4 Default all bits in the interrupt enable register to off (disabled).

9.4. Optional Registers

The pending and enable registers are the minimum that is required to have basic functionality for managing interrupts. This section discusses optional registers that may be beneficial for firmware to manage interrupts. In the supermodule concept, the existence of these registers will be specified with parameters when the module is instantiated.

This is not an exhaustive list of all possible optional registers. If engineers have others they need to add, the concepts taught here could be applied to other optional registers.

9.4.1. Source Status Register

The source status register indicates the current level of the incoming interrupt signal. This register has been mentioned a few times previously in this chapter. Since the interrupt module has a clock synchronization circuit built in, this register will reflect the synchronized signal.

This register is useful in several scenarios where the state of the incoming signal may be useful to know regardless of whether or not the interrupt is currently pending. Here is a brief list of possible scenarios:

- Indicate whether the incoming external signal is currently asserted or not.

- Indicate which external components need service due to edges missed because the CPU had been reset.

- If the interrupt was disabled, interrupts pending were acked and ignored. But when ready to enable interrupts, firmware can check for interrupt sources that are still asserted and need to be serviced.

- It can be used when servicing multiple occurrences of an interrupt between services, such as several incoming data packets located in the FIFO. The handler reads out one packet and then checks to see if the line is deasserted yet. If not, read another packet from the FIFO.

- At the chip-level interrupt module, it can be read to see which block-level modules are still pending even though interrupts at the chip-level have already been acked.

- If interrupt sharing were used (not recommended), check to see if other devices are holding the line asserted once one device has been serviced.

- For two interrupts, one for each edge of the same signal, the source status register will indicate which edge occurred last.

☑   **Best Practice**

9.4.1 Provide an interrupt source status register that indicates the current level of the incoming source signal.

With all these possible reasons for including the source status register, under what conditions would it not be needed? Many interrupts are due to events that occur within the block, such as task done or error detected. They are momentary events rather than a change of state which will eventually change back. They are short pulses on the interrupt source signal. In other words, it would be extremely rare for firmware to read the source status register at the one clock cycle that the source signal is active.

Instead of a short pulse, the signal may be on for several clock cycles, but its asserted level and its trailing edge is of no value or may be confusing to firmware without in-depth knowledge of the internal workings of the block.

Other possibilities would be signals that convey information available in other registers. An example is a Block Active bit in a read-only status register that conveys the state of the Block Active signal inside the block. When the Block Active signal is cleared, its trailing edge (inverted) is used to generate a Task Done interrupt. It may be confusing to have the Block Active signal visible in the source status register for the Task Done interrupt. While the block is not active, the inverted Block Active signal is still asserted and would show 1 in the source status registers; this would imply that Task Done is till pending, which may lead to confusion. Since the state of the block is available elsewhere, it is better to not make that available in the source status register.

For these and other types of uninteresting incoming interrupt source signals, do not make them visible in the source status register. Just leave those positions unused. If all bits are unused, then the source status registers does not need to be instantiated.

☑   **Best Practice**

9.4.2 Leave unused the bit positions in the source status register for uninteresting source signals.

9.4.2. Post Register

An interrupt is generated by some event in hardware. An interrupt post register allows firmware to cause the interrupt to be generated as if the hardware event occurred. Writing a 1 to a bit in the register generates a corresponding interrupt in the interrupt pending register and is treated like any other interrupt. It propagates up to the CPU (if enabled) causing the interrupt handlers to be invoked.

This is a write-only register with Write-1-Set (W1S) behavior. Firmware can read the pending register to verify the results of the write.

Engineers can use this feature to invoke their interrupt handlers in the interrupt handling context of the operating system. This can be used to test out firmware if generating the interrupt via hardware is difficult. Or it allows the same code to run, whether invoked by a hardware or firmware event.

☑ **Best Practice**

9.4.3 Provide an interrupt post register to allow firmware to trigger interrupts.

9.4.3. Atomic Enable/Disable Registers

As discussed in the section, Atomic Registers, in Section 8.5.4, Atomic Register Access, global registers that need to be accessed by multiple device drivers should provide atomic access for setting and clearing bits in those registers.

Interrupt modules instantiated at the chip level may need to be accessed by multiple device drivers, depending on the architecture of firmware. The enable register is the only read/write register in the interrupt module that would need to provide atomic access at the chip level. This is best implemented by adding two registers, the atomic enable register and the atomic disable register. These registers will not replace the enable register but be in addition to the enable register. The enable register should remain to provide firmware engineers the option of using either method.

Reads from any of the three locations (enable, atomic enable, and atomic disable) will return identical contents—the current list of enabled interrupts.

☑ **Best Practice**

9.4.4 Provide atomic interrupt enable/disable registers for interrupt modules accessed by multiple device drivers.

9.4.4. Masked Register

The pending register shows all pending interrupts, regardless as to whether they are enabled or not. A masked register is a read-only register that returns the pending register ANDed with the enabled register. In other words, it only shows those interrupts that have occurred and are enabled.

Firmware can do this ANDing by reading the pending and enable register or by reading the pending register and using its copy of the enable settings. This masked register is provided mainly for the convenience of firmware, if desired.

☑   **Best Practice**

9.4.5 Provide an interrupt masked register that indicates enabled interrupts that are pending.

9.4.5. Instantiation Register

Following the superblock concept, an instantiation register should be added to help firmware know which optional registers and how many interrupt channels are instantiated. The following register map shows an example instantiation register.

	MSB			Interrupt Instantiation Register—0x0000				LSB
Bits	31 30 29 28	27 26 25 24	23 22 21 20	19 18 17 16	15 14 13 12	11 10 9 8	7 6 5 4	3 2 1 0
R/W	- - - -	- - - -	- - - -	T T T T	- - - C	C C C C	r r r r	M A P S
Reset	0 0 0 0	0 0 0 0	0 0 0 0	0 0 0 0	0 0 0 0	0 0 0 0	0 0 0 0	0 0 0 0

S: **Source status**—This bit is true if the source status register is instantiated.

P: **Post**—This bit is true if the Post register is instantiated.

A: **Atomic enable/disable**—This bit is true if the atomic enable/disable registers are instantiated.

M: **Masked**—This bit is true if the masked register is instantiated.

r: **reserved**—These locations are reserved for future optional registers.

C: **Channels**—This contains a count of the number of interrupt channels instantiated. Note that it does not imply the bit location of those channels.

T: **Top channel**—This contains the bit position where the top channel is located. Positions are numbered starting with 0 at LSB. If all positions are filled from bit 0 to bit T, then T+1 = C. If there are some holes among the positions, then T ≥ C.

The instantiation register shown here assumes a 32-bit system. In a 16-bit system, Top Channel would not be included. In an 8-bit system, neither Channels nor Top Channel would be included. But firmware will still be able to get that information by writing 0xFF to the enable register, then reading it back and noting which bits are still set. Reading back 0x57 would indicate that C=5 (five channels) and T=6 (top channel is in position 6).

☑ **Best Practice**

9.4.6 Provide an instantiation register indicating instantiated registers and number of channels.

9.4.6. *Addresses of Optional Registers*

These optional registers may or may not be instantiated in a given block or chip. The instantiation register allows firmware to find out which ones are instantiated so that it knows what it available. Besides knowing which ones are available, firmware needs to know the addresses of each one. In order for that to be possible, the addresses of each optional register must be fixed, whether instantiated or not.

For example, suppose the source status register is at address offset 0x10. The address is an offset from the base of the interrupt module. For all interrupt modules in the chip, the source status register will be at offset 0x10.

If the source status register is not implemented, that address location will be left unused. Do not move any other registers into that location. Moving registers around depending on their instantiation configuration requires firmware to calculate their location based on some formula or algorithm. Leaving them in the same location will allow constants to be used for their offsets, as shown in Listing 9.5.

☑ **Best Practice**

9.4.7 Reserve an address for each optional register, whether instantiated or not.

Listing 9.5: Determine if the source status register is implemented and access it.

```
// Interrupt register base and offsets
#define ADDR_INTR_BASE            0xDD0B0380
#define ADDR_INTR_INSTANTIATION   0x00
#define ADDR_INTR_SOURCE_STATUS   0x10
. . . and other registers

// Instantiation bit positions
#define INTR_EXIST_SOURCE_STATUS  0x01
. . . and other positions

// Set up addresses to registers
#define INTR_ADDR(a) (uint32_t *) (ADDR_INTR_BASE + (a))
uint32_t * regInstantiation = INTR_ADDR (ADDR_INTR_INSTANTIATION);
uint32_t * regSourceStatus  = INTR_ADDR (ADDR_INTR_SOURCE_STATUS);
. . . and other registers

uint32_t instantiation;  // Copy of the instantiation register
uint32_t sourceStatus;   // Copy of the source status register

instantiation = *regInstantiation;    // Get instantiation
if (instantiation & INTR_EXIST_SOURCE_STATUS)
    {
    sourceStatus = *regSourceStatus;
    // analyze contents
    }
```

9.5. Interrupt Module Review

Up to this point in this chapter, I have been discussing the internal functionality and design of an interrupt module. The rest of this chapter will discuss using the interrupt module. But before I do that, I will give a brief, consolidated summary of the interrupt module.

As a reminder, I stated at the beginning of the chapter how there is no standard in the industry in the design, functionality, and management of interrupts. As I have discussed the various concepts of interrupts, I have stated what I think this standard should look like. It is beyond the scope of this book to propose the exact details of this standard, but it is an excellent starting place.

I will first review an interrupt channel and then how one or more interrupt channels are used with registers to make an interrupt module. The specific details of the design shown here are examples and not intended to state that it should be implemented this way in the standard.

9.5.1. Interrupt Channels

Figure 9.6 illustrates a schematic drawing of an interrupt channel and Listing 9.6 is its corresponding Verilog code.

This circuit contains six inputs and three outputs as follows:

- **Enable (I):** This comes from the enable register that firmware writes to and controls, whether or not a pending interrupt is allowed to propagate upstream.

- **Acknowledge (I):** This signal is true when firmware writes a 1 to the pending register to ack the interrupt. It clears the pending flip-flop.

- **Post (I):** This signal is true when firmware writes a 1 to the post register. It sets the pending flip-flop.

- **Reset (I):** This clears the pending flip-flop during the power-on reset.

- **Clock (I):** This is the standard system clock.

- **Signal In (I):** This is the incoming interrupt source signal. This signal is passed through a clock-synchronization flip-flop. A rising edge on this signal causes the pending flip-flop to be set, generating an interrupt.

- **Interrupt (O):** This is true if an enabled interrupt is pending. It is routed upstream to the CPU to generate an interrupt into firmware.

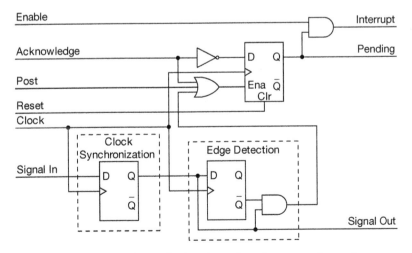

Figure 9.6: Schematic drawing of an interrupt channel.

Listing 9.6: Verilog code for an interrupt channel.

```verilog
module intr_channel_ckt(
    Enable,
    Acknowledge,
    Post,
    Reset,
    Clock,
    SignalIn,
    Interrupt,
    Pending,
    SignalOut
    );

// inputs
input  Enable;
input  Acknowledge;
input  Post;
input  Reset;
input  Clock;
input  SignalIn;

// outputs
output Interrupt;
output Pending;
output SignalOut;

// wires/regs
wire Interrupt;
reg  Pending;
reg  SignalOut;
reg  Q1;

always @ (posedge Clock) begin
    SignalOut <= SignalIn; // Clock sync
    Q1 <= SignalOut;
end

always @ (posedge Clock or posedge Reset) begin
    if(Reset) begin
        Pending <= 1'b0;
    end
    else if(Acknowledge) begin
        Pending <= 1'b0;
    end
    else if(Post) begin
        Pending <= 1'b1;
    end
    else if(SignalOut & ~Q1) begin
        Pending <= 1'b1;
    end
end

assign Interrupt = Pending & Enable;

endmodule
```

- **Pending (O):** This is true if an interrupt is pending, regardless as to whether or not it is enabled. It is readable by firmware.

- **Signal Out (O):** This is the synchronized version of Signal In and is made available to firmware.

9.5.2. Interrupt Module

The interrupt module consists of one or more interrupt channels and several support registers. Figure 9.7 illustrates this module with three interrupt channels.

The following describes the details of this interrupt module:

- **Interrupt channels:** An interrupt module has one or more interrupt channels. The illustration shows three channels.

- **Interrupt enable (R/W), atomic enable (R/W1S), and atomic disable (R/W1C) registers:** This is one bank of flip-flops accessed through three address portals to achieve different behavior. Firmware configures the enable registers like any read/write register. The flip-flops remember the setting to control the enabling of the interrupt. Firmware writes ones to specific positions in the atomic enable register to set (W1S) just those bits, leaving the other bits alone. Firmware writes ones to specific positions in the atomic disable register to clear (W1C) just those bits, leaving the others alone. The power-on default is 0 for all bits, disabled. Device drivers enable the desired interrupts when ready.

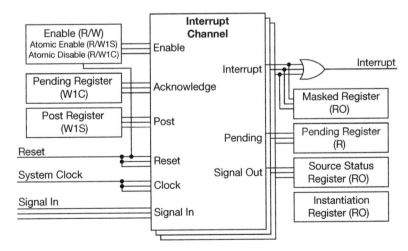

Figure 9.7: An interrupt module with three interrupt channels.

- **Pending register (W1C):** Firmware writes ones to specific positions in the pending register to acknowledge the desired interrupts. This register does not contain flip-flops. The ones last just long enough to ack the interrupt. (See Pending Register (R) in the following for the read half.)

- **Post register (W1S):** This is similar to the pending register except that it sets, not clears, the pending interrupt. This register does not support reads. If read, it returns only zeros.

- **Reset:** This is the chip's power-on reset which will clear all pending interrupts and clear the enable register.

- **System clock:** This is the system clock to clock the flip-flops and provide synchronization.

- **Signal in:** These are the incoming signal lines from various locations in the block. A rising edge on an incoming signal will generate an interrupt in the corresponding channel.

- **Interrupt:** This is the OR of all the interrupt signals from all the interrupt channels. If any one of them is true, then the interrupt signal out of the interrupt module is true.

- **Masked register (RO):** This returns the current list of interrupts that are both pending and enabled.

- **Pending register (R):** This is the same register as the Pending Register above, except this is for reads and the other is for writes. A read returns the current list of pending interrupts.

- **Source status register (RO):** A read from this register returns the current level of the incoming source signals.

- **Instantiation register (RO):** This contains the configuration settings of this instantiation of the interrupt module.

9.5.3. External Connections

Figure 9.8 shows the outside connections to the interrupt module and how it fits in with the address bus, the data bus, and other system connections.

- **Address:** The address lines are used to select registers within the module. Three bits are needed in this design to access all the registers. If wired in a 32-bit system, then it would be wired to address lines [4:2].

- **Data in and data out:** The number of data lines needed is determined by the number of interrupt channels implemented. If the module is configured for five interrupts, then data lines [4:0] would be connected. If not all packed together in consecutive positions, it would be connected as necessary, such as to bits 0, 1, 2, 4, and 6.

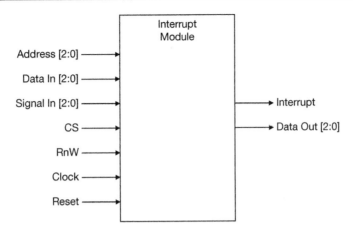

Figure 9.8: External view of the interrupt module.

- **Signal In:** These are the signals that the interrupt module will monitor for the rising edge. They can come from anywhere in the block/chip that needs to generate an interrupt to firmware. If five signals need to be monitored, then five lines will be connected.

- **CS, RnW, Clock, Reset:** These are typical support connections, chip select, read/write select, clock, and reset, needed for register and flip-flop operations.

- **Interrupt:** This is the one interrupt line that propagates the module's detected interrupts up to the CPU.

For the rest of this chapter, the discussion will be on how the interrupt module is used.

9.6. Triggering on Both Edges

In some applications, an interrupt is needed on both the leading and trailing edges.

9.6.1. Use Two Interrupt Channels

One possible solution is to modify the interrupt module to generate an interrupt on both edges. But from a firmware perspective, that solution hides which edge occurred and forces both edges to be enabled or disabled at the same time.

Instead of having both edges on one interrupt, use two different interrupt channels, one for the leading edge and one for the (inverted) trailing edge. This allows firmware to enable either one without having to enable both.

📖   **Tales from the Trenches**

In the engine interface block, five external signals were wired to five interrupt channels. One of the external signals generated an interrupt on both edges. Firmware did not need to know about the trailing edge. But since both edges were on the same interrupt, both had to be serviced. If one interrupt was not serviced soon enough, the second edge would occur and firmware would not know about it.

I had to write the device driver to check the source status register upon every interrupt to see the current level of source signal. The device driver would then know which edge occurred last. In the next version, we split the interrupt into two, one for the leading edge and one for the trailing edge, making the interaction much easier.

Figure 9.9 illustrates how the incoming source signal is wired to two different interrupt channels, one of them using the inverted signal.

☑   **Best Practice**

9.5.1 Use two separate interrupt channels, one for the leading edge and one for the (inverted) trailing edge, if interrupts on both edges of the source signal are required.

In the above tale from the trenches, the trailing-edge interrupt was not needed. So why was it implemented that way in the first place? It was because that was the definition of the protocol. In that particular application, the trailing edge interrupt was not needed but in other applications it was, so interrupts were generated on both edges.

In contrast to the above tale, this next one had the opposite problem.

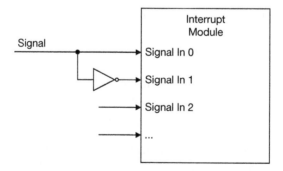

Figure 9.9: Wiring to trigger on both edges.

📖 **Tales from the Trenches**

In the engine interface block, five external signals generated interrupts, one of them on both edges. During development, system problems were encountered and one potential solution was to use the trailing edge of one of the other four signals as a workaround since it was too late to add pins to the chip and connectors. But, since the block was only capable of generating interrupts on the leading edges of those four, it was not a viable solution. In the next version of the block, all five interrupt signals had separate leading- and trailing-edge interrupts, allowing for such workarounds later.

Which signals should have interrupts on both edges? External signals are good candidates because firmware typically has no control over the external device controlling the signal. A door-open signal is one example. Firmware needs to know when the user opens the door. Firmware also often needs to know when the user closes the door, or in other words, the inverted door-open signal. It is easy to understand the need for firmware to know both the door-open and door-closed events. Another example is an item sensor that is used to count the number of items passing by. In that case, most likely only the leading edge is needed to indicate that a new item has appeared. But to be safe, if the trailing edge were also wired in, that gives more information to firmware for possible debugging, troubleshooting, and future enhancement needs.

GPIO pins are another possible example, since they are designed to be used as needed later on. Triggering on either or both edges will allow flexibility in how the incoming signal is used.

Signals that are short pulses, such as from a state machine or an error condition, do not need triggering on both edges.

Even if current designs do not call for trailing-edge interrupts, putting them in judiciously may help avert problems later.

☑ **Best Practice**

9.5.2 Consider assigning an interrupt channel to the trailing edge of any source signal that stays asserted for a while.

9.6.2. Channel Positions of Leading and Trailing Interrupts

For double-edge interrupts, the channel positions of the two edges should be considered in order to optimize firmware interaction.

If there are just a few among several other interrupts, put the trailing edge the next position up from the leading edge. This register map is an example illustration.

	MSB			Interrupt Register—0x0000				LSB
Bits	31 30 29 28	27 26 25 24	23 22 21 20	19 18 17 16	15 14 13 12	11 10 9 8	7 6 5 4	3 2 1 0
R/W	- - - -	- - - -	- - - -	- - - -	- - - -	- - - G	F E d D	C B a A

In this example, "A" and "D" have corresponding trailing-edge interrupts, "a" and "d." They are placed among other interrupts, as determined by their priority.

☑ **Best Practice**

9.5.3 Assign both edges to adjacent interrupt channel positions if there are a few double-edge source signals.

If there are several double-edge interrupts, it may be better to segregate the trailing- from the leading-edge positions, as illustrated in this register map.

	MSB			Interrupt Register—0x0000				LSB
Bits	31 30 29 28	27 26 25 24	23 22 21 20	19 18 17 16	15 14 13 12	11 10 9 8	7 6 5 4	3 2 1 0
R/W	- - - -	- - - -	- - f e	- c - a	- - - -	- - - -	- - F E	D C B A

In this example, "B" and "D" do not have corresponding trailing edge interrupts. The rest do. Holes are left in bits 17 and 19—the trailing-edge interrupts are not packed in together. This helps firmware define constants for these positions, as illustrated in Listing 9.7.

Listing 9.7: Defining constants for interrupt bits.

```
/* Define interrupt bit positions. */
#define BIT_A  0x01
#define BIT_B  0x02
#define BIT_C  0x04
#define BIT_D  0x08
#define BIT_E  0x10
#define BIT_F  0x20
#define FALLING_EDGE_SHIFT    16
#define BIT_nA (BIT_A << FALLING_EDGE_SHIFT)
#define BIT_nC (BIT_C << FALLING_EDGE_SHIFT)
#define BIT_nE (BIT_E << FALLING_EDGE_SHIFT)
#define BIT_nF (BIT_F << FALLING_EDGE_SHIFT)
```

The above listing shows that both the leading and trailing edges are in the same interrupt module. If, by the time trailing edges are added, there is not room to keep the same relative position, it may be better to use two separate interrupt modules, one for leading-edge interrupts and one for trailing-edge interrupts, as illustrated with these two register maps.

	MSB				Leading Edge Interrupt Register—0x0000					LSB
Bits	31 30 29 28	27 26 25 24	23 22 21 20	19 18 17 16	15 14 13 12	11 10 9 8	7 6 5 4	3 2 1 0
R/W	- - - -	- - Z Y	X W V U	T S R Q	P O N M	L K J I	H G F E	D C B A

	MSB				Trailing Edge Interrupt Register—0x0004					LSB
Bits	31 30 29 28	27 26 25 24	23 22 21 20	19 18 17 16	15 14 13 12	11 10 9 8	7 6 5 4	3 2 1 0
R/W	- - - -	- - z y	x w v u	t s r q	p o n m	l k j i	h g f e	d c b a

☑ **Best Practice**

9.5.4 Segregate leading-edge from trailing-edge interrupt channels if there are several double-edge source signals and assign them to the same relative channel positions.

☑ **Best Practice**

9.5.5 Assign the leading edge group to the lower half of the interrupt channel positions and the trailing edge group to the upper half if they will fit in the same interrupt module. Otherwise, use the same channel positions across two interrupt modules, one for each group.

9.7. Using the Interrupt Module

This last section gives a few guidelines as to when and how to use an interrupt module.

9.7.1. When to Allocate an Interrupt Channel

When an event occurs in the block that firmware needs to respond to, an interrupt must occur. But the block does not randomly decide when to generate the event. The task that generated the event was initiated somehow. Block tasks are either initiated externally or by firmware.

Externally initiated block tasks are when the tasks are launched by something outside of the block/device-driver pair. It may be a signal from another block on the chip or some I/O packet arriving on an I/O bus. It may generate an interrupt instantaneously, such as the assertion of a signal. Or it may require the block to do some work before generating the interrupt, such as bring in a block of data and compressing it.

Events generated from externally initiated tasks are asynchronous to both the block and firmware. Neither one is aware if and when it will occur. Therefore, an interrupt channel should be allocated for this event to notify firmware that it has occurred.

☑ **Best Practice**

9.6.1 Use an interrupt channel to notify firmware of any externally initiated events.

Firmware-initiated block tasks are when the firmware launches something in the block. Firmware knows that it launched the task but it may or may not know when it was completed. Tasks are either completed instantaneously (such as an abort that always completes in one or two clock cycles) or after some delay (such as a data compression task that requires several hundred clock cycles to complete). Even if it is known how many clock cycles a task will take, firmware has no good concept of time, and therefore an interrupt channel should be allocated for firmware-initiated tasks that will or could take time to complete.

☑ **Best Practice**

9.6.2 Use an interrupt channel to indicate completion of firmware-launched hardware tasks that will not always complete instantaneously.

Interrupts do not need to be allocated for instantaneous firmware-initiated tasks, but only if it will always be instantaneous. If it might delay under the right conditions, it should have an interrupt.

Instantaneous means something that will occur within one or two clock cycles, or at least be so fast that it will be impossible for firmware access the block again before the task is completed. In other words, firmware does not need to be delayed in order to wait for the block to finish the task before firmware can safely access the block again.

☑ **Best Practice**

9.6.3 Do not use an interrupt channel to indicate completion of firmware-launched hardware tasks that always complete instantaneously.

9.7.2. Repeated Interrupts

Interrupts occur either once or repeatedly. Interrupts that occur once require firmware to do something in order to get it to occur again. An example is a transmit-buffer-empty interrupt. That interrupt will not occur again until firmware puts more data in the buffer to transmit. Interrupts that can occur repeatedly are those that can occur without firmware intervention. An example is a data-packet-received interrupt where data packets are going to arrive whether firmware does something about it or not.

If repeated interrupts are not serviced by firmware, interrupts and/or data may be lost without proper hardware support. Some types of support include an interrupt overflow detector, an interrupt counter, and a buffer to store incoming data. The type of support needed depends on the application.

📖 **Tales from the Trenches**

In the Unity mono video block, there is a done interrupt and an underrun interrupt. Firmware had anywhere from 25 to 30 ms to respond to the done interrupt before the next done interrupt occurred. If firmware did not respond in time, the underrun interrupt occurred. Normally, everything worked fine. But occasionally some rogue process in firmware would disable interrupts too long such that the video block interrupt handler could not run. When it finally did, it read the interrupt pending register and both the done and underrun interrupts were pending. That meant that the interrupt handler had been held off for at least 25 ms. Not good! But at least the block detected the problem and generated a different interrupt so that the video block interrupt handler could respond accordingly.

Support should be provided generously. Firmware may, for the most part, be fast enough to handle the interrupts as they come. But there are occasional circumstances that force firmware to delay servicing the interrupt.

☑ **Best Practice**

9.6.4 Provide additional support, such as a buffer, a FIFO, an interrupt counter, or an overflow interrupt, for interrupts that could fire rapidly without firmware intervention.

9.7.3. Address Mapping

Hardware will interrupt firmware no matter what context firmware is in. When firmware gets the interrupt, it needs to quickly service the interrupt. This includes being able to quickly access the interrupt registers. In some architectures, register address space is limited, forcing designers to use techniques that will permit more registers than what the address space permits. One technique is having register pages that are switched in as needed. Another technique is to use indirection.

When the interrupt handler is invoked, it does not know the current context of registers. It has to go through extra steps to determine what needs to happen to make the interrupt registers accessible. And then, when it is completed, switch the context back so it is in the same state that the interrupted process assumes that it is still in. This design is prone to having firmware errors.

These problems can be avoided by assigning firmware registers to address locations that are always accessible.

☑   **Best Practice**

9.6.5 Place interrupt module registers in an address space that is always visible.

9.8. Summary

I stated at the beginning of this chapter that a major problem at the hardware/firmware interface is the inconsistency, variety, and limitations of interrupt designs in use today. There is no industry standard in the design of interrupts.

In this chapter, I discussed design variations with their pros and cons, and made my recommendation as to which design is better and should be part of a standard interrupt module. The key highlights to the proposed standard are as follows:

- Have a pending register that firmware reads to determine pending interrupts and that firmware writes 1s to ack interrupts.

- Have an enable register where a 1 allows the interrupt to propagate.

- Have the interrupt be rising-edge triggered.

- Make the interrupt module a supermodule that is instantiated at all locations and configured as appropriate.

Following such a standard leads to code reuse, not only in the RTL code in the chip but also in firmware code. Hardware and firmware engineers needing to write new RTL or firmware code will know the standard and know how to implement it. Simply following this standard will eliminate many errors in both the chip and in firmware. Other errors will be reduced and easier to find.

> 📖 **Tales from the Trenches**
>
> When enabling interrupts, firmware has to make sure that any pending interrupts are acked to avoid inadvertently invoking an interrupt handler. In one chip, the device driver had to ack before enabling the interrupt to prevent the interrupt line from asserting. But in another chip, the device driver had to wait until after enabling the interrupt before it could ack any pending interrupts. This subtle difference introduced a firmware defect that required some study before the firmware engineer realized there was a difference. Had a standard and consistent interrupt module been used, the firmware engineer would not have spent so much coding and debugging time supporting the two chips.

9.8.1. Supporting Principles

The concepts of this chapter support the principles of hardware/firmware interface design as follows:

1. **Set and Adhere to Standards:** There are too many flavors of interrupts used in the industry. In this chapter I strongly advocated defining a standard and I specified what it should look like.

2. **Balance the Load:** I discussed how edge-triggered interrupts were much easier for device drivers to handle than level-triggered interrupts.

3. **Design for Compatibility:** Having a standard for the interrupt module aids compatibility of interrupt handling code among different blocks and chips.

In this discussion on interrupts, I used several examples, many of which are errors and aborts. In the next chapter, I will discuss errors and aborts and ways to improve firmware's ability to respond to and handle them.

CHAPTER 10

Aborts, etc.

The design for aborting a task in a chip is too often an afterthought. It is not built into the design up front and is not thoroughly tested. This chapter discusses a few aspects regarding aborts with regard to its interaction with firmware.

Aborts come in a variety of designs and vary in the depth, extent, purpose, and naming of their functions. To establish a common base from which to discuss this topic, I will describe a hierarchy and functionality, and the terminology associated with it that will be used in this chapter.

10.1. Definitions

In general terms, this chapter is about stopping the block and returning the registers to a default state. The extent to which that is done varies by level. I define three levels; halt, abort, and reset. Halt has the smallest impact and reset has the biggest impact to the block. Figure 10.1 illustrates the relationship among these three levels.

I define these three levels for the purpose of this discussion. Block designs may implement anywhere from one to four levels. Different names are used as indicated in parentheses in Table 10.1. The table describes the use, tasks, and outcome for the halt, abort, and reset functions. For example, it shows how the reset function is used and why hardware and/or firmware would issue the reset command to invoke the reset task, which results in the reset outcome. These functions are invoked when the block asserts a signal or when firmware sets a queue bit in a register.

It is important to distinguish between an event and an action. An event invokes an action. For example, applying power to the system is a power-on event that invokes the reset action. A watchdog timer, a button press, or a firmware function are other events that could invoke the reset action. The block detecting an error is an event that invokes the halt action. Firmware detecting some condition is an event that invokes the abort action. When trying to map these concepts into your design, be sure to distinguish between events and actions so that the right event invokes the right action.

DOI: 10.1016/B978-1-85617-605-7.00012-5.

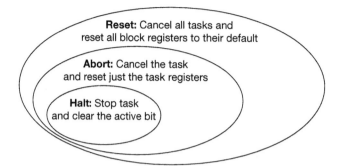

Figure 10.1: Relationship among halt, abort, and reset.

Table 10.1: The Use, Tasks, and Outcomes of Halts, Aborts, and Resets

Function*	Use	Tasks	Outcome
Halt (Stop, Pause)	The block invokes a halt when it detects an error, allowing for firmware to inspect the registers. Firmware may invoke this to stop block tasks and inspect registers. After a halt, firmware either resumes (if capable) or aborts the block.	Stops the task that the block is working on. The block may take a few clock cycles to get to a good stopping place so that it can resume if firmware wishes.	The registers are left unchanged except that the active (go) bit is cleared.
Abort (Soft Reset, Warm Reset)	Firmware issues an abort command when it needs to cancel the current task, even if the current task is not complete. Firmware can then load the registers for the next task and launch it. The block does not invoke an abort, only firmware.	Cancel the task and return all state machines to idle. Gracefully cease any interaction with other blocks leaving them in a ready state. Put the block in position to accept new tasks.	The registers associated with the task are cleared. The block is ready to accept another task.
Reset (Hard Reset, Cold Reset, Power-on Reset)	The reset is invoked at power up by power-on circuitry. Firmware may issue the reset command to clear problems that cannot be aborted. Firmware must then reconfigure the block after which firmware can launch a new task.	Abort all operations regardless of consequence.	All registers are reset to their default values. The block must be reconfigured, including re-enabling interrupts.

* Other terms in use appear in parentheses.

The abort function is the most complex of the three functions. Not only does it have to leave its own block ready for the next task, it must cleanly cease interactions with collaborative blocks and components so that they can work on the next task too. Most of this chapter discusses aborts. But I will first discuss halts and resets and then I will discuss aborts.

10.2. Halts

As discussed above, the block should have a halt facility that halts operations and leaves untouched all registers except for an active or go bit that needs to be cleared.

☑ **Best Practice**

10.1.1 Provide a halt function in the block that stops the current task, clears the task active (go) bit, and leaves all other registers and buffers unchanged.

If it makes sense for the given application, firmware should have the ability to invoke the halt operation. It may be useful for troubleshooting device drivers or for making changes to configuration values during the middle of operations (which is potentially dangerous).

Some blocks may be designed so that firmware can resume halted operations right where it left off. One possible application is a data compression block that is told it has a big chunk of data to compress even if it really doesn't yet. Firmware can halt it until more data are ready, and then tell it to continue.

In other applications, resuming is not feasible or possible. For example, in the case of laser printers, paper is moving and a mirror moving the laser across a page cannot mechanically stop in the middle of a page, especially if it has already entered the heated fuser. The laser and paper must continue to move, even if the rest of the page is left blank.

Once the halt is done, firmware must tell the block to resume operations or abort to clean up and get ready for the next task.

☑ **Best Practice**

10.1.2 Provide access to firmware to halt the block.

The difficult thing for firmware engineers writing device drivers for hardware blocks is that when things go wrong, there is very little visibility into the internal workings of the block. Any information that the block can provided will help engineers troubleshoot the problems.

When the block detects an error condition, it should invoke the halt function to stop the task but leave the registers untouched, allowing engineers to examine them to diagnose the problem. The following are types of problems that could be detected.

- The current address and byte count of a DMA controller may indicate if data transfer started, where it was in the middle of a transfer, or if it was done with the transfer.

- An examination of configuration registers will indicate if firmware programmed them correctly in the first place.

- An examination of status registers will indicate current settings.

- An examination of the current state of a state machine will indicate where it was at and what it was expecting.

- An examination of internal buffers could yield important information.

Once the examination is done, firmware should abort the block. Trying to resume operation when an error occurred is not likely to be feasible. Firmware should abort the block to clean up the problem and launch the next task.

☑ **Best Practice**

10.1.3 Design the block to halt when an error occurs.

10.3. Resets

The halt function has the smallest impact on the block. The reset function has the largest impact. It does not attempt to save any register settings, data in buffers, or current state. It does not attempt to gracefully terminate any interactions with collaborating blocks. It reboots the block restoring all registers to their default state, marking all buffers as empty, and sending all state machines to their initial state.

☑ **Best Practice**

10.2.1 Provide a reset function in the block that stops all tasks and resets all registers, counters, buffers, and state machines to their default state.

Unless required by the block, buffers that are cleared during a reset do not need to be zeroed out. That could take quite a bit of time for large buffers. But buffers simply need to be marked as empty by zeroing out the byte count and resetting any pointers back to the beginning.

Registers, on the other hand, should be reset back to a known and consistent default state. They should default to inactive, disabled, or idle settings. Especially for registers that control mechanical devices. A register controlling a stepper motor should default to off, not full speed ahead.

☑ **Best Practice**

10.2.2 Design every control register to come out of reset with its bits in a "safe" setting, such as inactive, disabled, idle, and so on.

The primary purpose of the reset function is to put the block in a known state after power is applied. This is necessary to put everything in a known state but also to put everything in an idle state until firmware can boot up and reconfigure it. The power-on circuitry in the system should be wired to a reset pin in all chips which is wired to reset all blocks within the chip.

☑ **Best Practice**

10.2.3 Design the power-on circuitry to invoke the reset function.

The exact nature of the reset function in a block varies depending on the requirements, conditions, and circumstances of the block. One characteristic is whether the function is invoked by a synchronous reset, an asynchronous reset, or both. Some designs require an asynchronous assertion but a synchronous deassertion of the reset signal.

The design of the reset function should allow for firmware to invoke the synchronous or asynchronous reset, or both if the reset function has both.

☑ **Best Practice**

10.2.4 Provide access to firmware to invoke synchronous and asynchronous resets.

10.4. Aborts

The halt function has the least impact, the reset function is the most invasive, but the abort function is the most complex.

10.4.1. The Need for Aborts

But why is an abort necessary? If the block is well designed, it should never need to be aborted, right? Aborts are necessary for two major reasons, internal errors and external conditions.

No matter how well designed or tested a new block is, internal errors within the block are very likely. There may be a malfunction or the block may find itself or be driven into an unknown state. The design engineer may focus too much on normal functionality, giving very little thought to error handling. An abort recovers from an internal error allowing the block to be used again with as little impact to the rest of the system as possible.

Some blocks require several settings, tables, and data to carry out a task. When that task is done, it is often easier to issue an abort to erase all residual data from the old task to ensure it does not impact the processing of the next task.

External conditions impact blocks that interact with components outside the block. Blocks must be able to handle external problems or changes, and aborts may be required to recover from that. The following lists several external conditions that could cause a block to be aborted:

- An external block or component producing data for this block has an error so it stops producing data. Alternatively, an external block or component consuming this block's data has an error that prevents it from consuming any more data.

- The memory buffer filled up, not allowing the block to accept any additional data.

- The incoming data has an error or is corrupted.

- A timeout occurred; interaction with an external component was taking too long.

- Firmware detected an error or other condition necessitating an abort.

- The user pushes a button on the device, which required the block to abort its current operation.

Two Tales from the Trenches are given here to illustrate two contrasting points. In the first, designing an abort functionality was an afterthought and the block had problems. In the second, an abort was used as part of normal operations.

📖 **Tales from the Trenches**

In a LaserJet printer, the video block reads memory over a bus to get raster data used to control the laser. The video device driver sets up the bus transaction to transfer large chunks of data. If the printer has a paper jam or if a user opens a door, the print engine immediately turns off the laser and stops all motors. If that happens while the video block is in the middle of a page, the video device driver needs to abort the block because the laser controller will not be consuming any more raster data.

While I was working on the abort use case for the video device driver, I asked questions to some hardware engineers and we discovered that the bus used to access memory had no provision for aborting an active (though stalled) transaction. Fortunately, there was still time to design that in before sending the design to fabrication. However, a few months later when the chips were back, a defect in the abort logic was discovered, necessitating a complex firmware workaround. In this situation, the abort function was not designed up front and the last-minute inclusion had a defect.

📖 **Tales from the Trenches**

In a LaserJet printer, the laser controller consumes the raster data from the video block until it reaches the bottom of the page. Because of the variability in paper movement, sizes, and where the raster line falls, the exact number of raster lines consumed by the laser controller is not always the same. The laser controller on about 60% of the pages for one particular product would not consume all the raster lines that the video block had, causing the video block to stall. When this condition occurred, the video device driver had to abort the video block.

There was no user-perceptible problem—the page printed fine—so the device driver simply aborted the video block and set it up for the next page. In this situation, abort was part of normal operation.

☑ **Best Practice**

10.3.1 Provide an abort function in the block that stops the current task and resets the associated task registers and state machines.

A block may have multiple tasks that firmware can invoke, such as a transmit and receive, and a compression and decompression. Some designs have a series of tasks in a pipe each of which processes the data as it passes through. Some may be as simple as a pulse generator that is set up at bootup and left alone. Each of these tasks should be able to be aborted by firmware.

> ☑   **Best Practice**
>
> 10.3.2 Provide abort functionality for all tasks in the block.

As stated earlier in this chapter, the block invokes the halt function when it detects an error, leaving all registers untouched to allow inspection by firmware. The power-on circuitry invokes the reset function, putting the block in a known state until firmware boots and can configure it as needed. But the block or the system should not invoke an abort. Aborts should be done only under firmware control.

> ☑   **Best Practice**
>
> 10.3.3 Provide access to firmware to abort the block.

10.4.2. Firmware's Interaction with Aborts

Aborting is very complex. It requires going from any condition back to a known condition. An abort consists of the following aspects:

- It requires that all state machines go from any state back to the home/idle state.

- It requires resetting certain counters and registers.

- It requires marking buffers as empty.

- It requires erasing residual data in buffers or memory that could impact the next task.

- It requires shutting things down in a specific order.

- It requires being aware of its interaction with surrounding blocks or components not being reset.

- And it requires doing anything else needed to get ready for the next task.

- But it also requires not resetting certain elements such as interrupts enabled and constants configured at bootup.

Some designs of abort functionality may necessitate firmware involvement, especially when several components are in a pipeline with data passing through. One on chip I had to abort the block, abort the DMA controller, wait for the DMA abort done interrupt, and then abort the block again to ensure that all buffers moving data from one stage to another got completely reset of any data that were still moving while aborting.

Ideally, firmware should only need to set one bit to abort the whole block. However, adding logic to the abort function to handle complicated abort procedures may add too much risk that could be avoided with help from firmware.

☑ **Best Practice**

10.3.4 Keep firmware's role in the abort process as simple as possible.

Depending on the nature of the block, the time it takes for the abort task to do its work may or may not be instantaneous. If it is as simple as resetting a few registers and returning the state machine back to idle, then it is quick. But there are cases where it could take some time, such as needing to finish the current data transfer with another block.

Since firmware must wait until the abort task is done before it can set the block up for the next task, it needs to know when the abort task is done. Assign an interrupt channel in the block's interrupt module to be an abort done interrupt.

If the abort task will always be instantaneous under all conditions, then no abort done interrupt is needed. But if the abort task could take some time under certain conditions, then an abort done interrupt is needed. For example, aborting an active block may take time because it is in the middle of a data transfer. But aborting an idle block may be instantaneous. However, firmware does not know if the block is active or idle so it needs to be prepared for either case.

The interrupt channel, as specified in Chapter 9, Interrupts, provides support for firmware to handle aborts that are sometimes instantaneous and sometimes not. After issuing an abort, firmware could leave the abort done interrupt disabled and check for the pending bit to be set. (Remember that in Chapter 9, I said that the pending bit will be set when the leading edge arrives even if disabled.) If, after a while, the pending bit does not become set, then firmware can enable interrupts and switch out to let other work be done while waiting. Listing 10.1 illustrates how this can work.

☑ **Best Practice**

10.3.5 Provide an abort-done interrupt if the abort task will not always be instantaneous.

Listing 10.1: Try first to see if abort is instantaneous. If not, then wait for interrupt.

```
#define INTR_ABORT_DONE    0x10
#define QUEUE_ABORT        0x02
#define MAX_ABORT_LOOP     10

int abortBlock (void)
  {
  int i;
  *regIntrEnable = ~INTR_ABORT_DONE; // Disable abort done interrupt
  *regIntrPending = INTR_ABORT_DONE; // Make sure pending is cleared
  *regQueue = QUEUE_ABORT;           // Issue the abort command
  for (i=0; i<MAX_ABORT_LOOP; i++)
    {
    if (*regIntrPending & INTR_ABORT_DONE) // If abort is now done
      {
      *regIntrPending = INTR_ABORT_DONE;   // Ack pending interrupt
      return (OK);                         // Return OK
      }
    }
  // If it got this far, it reached the max loop count, so set up
  // to wait for the interrupt
  *regIntrEnable = INTR_ABORT_DONE;  // Enable abort done interrupt
  semWait (&semAbortDone);           // Block until abort done intr
  return (OK);                       // Return OK
  }
```

10.4.3. Abort Behavior

Because aborting can be complicated and the exact steps may vary based on the current conditions, it is necessary that the block respond to aborts in a known and consistent manner every time.

The block must respond to the abort command every time firmware issues the command, even if the block is already in an idle state.

Why would firmware abort an idle block? Firmware cannot know at the very instance if the block is active or idle. Even if firmware verifies that the active bit is set, the block could easily go idle before firmware issues the abort command. Firmware must be able to issue an abort at any time and have the block respond appropriately.

Why should the block respond to an abort if it is already idle? It is so that it can clear the abort queue bit and generate an interrupt for firmware.

📖 **Tales from the Trenches**

When a state machine in the Unity mono video block received an abort command, it moves to an abort state to reset some bits, clear the abort queue bit, and generate an interrupt to the device driver. However, the state machine did not check for the abort queue bit while in the idle state, leaving the abort queue bit set.

When the device driver gave the block the next job, the state machine moved from the idle state, saw the abort bit, and then promptly aborted the job it was just given. The workaround was for the device driver to check whether the abort bit was still set. If it was, then the video block was given a dummy job to flush the abort bit.

The next version of the block was fixed to check for the abort bit in all states.

☑ **Best Practice**

10.3.6 Design the abort task to respond to an abort command under every condition, even while the block is idle.

The outcome of the abort task should be the same in all cases. In particular, if an abort task generates an abort done interrupt upon completion, it must do so in all cases, even if the abort task was completed instantaneously this time or if the block was already idle. Again, since firmware cannot know what the exact state the block will be in when it receives the abort command, firmware has to expect the same behavior all the time. If it were such that no interrupt was issued if the block was idle, then how does firmware know if it should wait for an interrupt or not? How long should it wait? What if the abort really is working but has a big buffer that it needs to finish transferring?

Make sure an interrupt is generated every time.

☑ **Best Practice**

10.3.7 Design the abort outcome to be the same no matter if the block is busy or idle.

I have just discussed a state machine that responds to an abort, clears the abort queue bit, and generates an interrupt. There may be several state machines running in the block to help with their part of the operation. They don't need to clear the abort queue bit or generate the interrupt, but they do need to respond by doing any necessary clean up and going back to idle.

> ☑   **Best Practice**
>
> 10.3.8 Ensure that all states in all the block's state machines, including all the idle states, will respond to the abort.

Unfortunately, aborts are not thought of as "normal" operation, the design and testing of the abort function is not given the same priority as the rest of the block. However, it must be given the same level of attention as the rest of the block. Otherwise, you will be relying on a poorly-designed and poorly-tested abort function to keep your well-designed and well-tested block going in case some defect slips through.

10.4.4. Abort Interactions between Blocks

As with the halt and reset function, the abort function should stay confined within its own block. Each block implements its own and is controlled by respective device drivers. Abort is complicated because blocks typically interact with other blocks or components and need to safely and cleanly abort so that the other blocks are left in a safe, clean, and ready state.

If one block needs to abort while it is collaborating with another block, the first block's own abort task should not reset, cancel, or erase anything in the other block. It should abort only its own block.

> ☑   **Best Practice**
>
> 10.3.9 Design each block with its own abort function that services just that block.

Figure 10.2 shows three possible ways that one block (Block A) can abort while leaving the other block (Block B) in a safe and ready state.

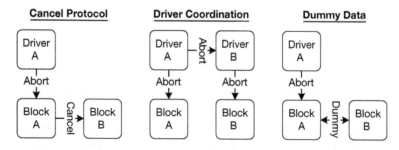

Figure 10.2: Three ways to safely abort interactions between two blocks.

The three ways are summarized here:

- **Cancel protocol:** The interaction protocol between the two blocks has an ability to send a cancel request. In this example, Driver A issues the Abort command to Block A. Block A then sends a Cancel request to Block B. They both terminate their interaction and Block A finishes aborting the task.

- **Driver coordination:** Driver A sends a message to Driver B that it is aborting and then both device drivers issue the Abort commands to their respective blocks.

- **Dummy data:** There is no provision to cut short any current interaction so Block A just sends Dummy Data over to Block B or takes data from Block B but ignores it, until the correct number of bytes have been transferred, completing that task for Block B. Block A then finishes aborting its task.

☑ **Best Practice**

10.3.10 Design the abort function so that it leaves any collaborative blocks in the ready state.

10.5. Summary

Canceling the operation of a block and restoring back to a known state has different levels and results. This chapter described three; halt, abort, and reset. Concepts were discussed regarding the design, the operation, and the outcome. Use these concepts as applicable whether your particular block defines one, three, or other levels of cancel operations.

Be sure to distinguish between events (power-on occurred, watchdog timer expired, firmware detected a condition, the block detected an error) and actions (halt, abort, and reset). Make sure the right event maps to the correct action.

Abort is the most complex due to the need to reset part of the block, cleanly terminate interactions with external blocks and components, and get ready to accept another task.

Several points were made regarding the importance of proper design in the hardware/ firmware interface: to make sure firmware can halt, abort, or reset as needed, to collaborate with firmware during the abort process, and to notify firmware when the abort task is done. Since firmware cannot know at a given instance what state the block is in, the abort function must respond correctly under all conditions, even if the block is already idle.

📖   **Tales from the Trenches**

In the Unity mono video block, the many defects made it very complicated to abort the block. The function in the device driver to abort the block was 250 lines long and contained some very complex logic with many cases and situations that had to be dealt with. I was getting details mixed up in my head while working on it, so I had to document what I was doing. I first started by adding comments to my code but that was too muddled. So I started to write a paragraph in the firmware code above the abort function but it was getting too detailed. I ended up using a word processor to document it. By time I was done, the document was 11 pages long and had three diagrams and a table. All that just to clearly explain those 250 lines of code. A few months later, I had to revisit that function and I was glad I had that document.

On the next version of the block, when all the defects were fixed, the abort function was reduced to about 10 lines.

10.5.1. Supporting Principles

The concepts of this chapter support the principles of hardware/firmware interface design as follows:

1. **Balance the Load:** The abort function should be designed to keep firmware's involvement as simple as possible. However, some blocks may have complicated abort procedures to get the various modules reset in an orderly fashion and it may be less risky to have firmware help walk through the abort steps.

2. **Anticipate the Impacts:** When aborting one block, anticipate the impact on other blocks interacting with the one block so that they are left in a safe and ready state.

3. **Design for Contingencies:** Things will go wrong in the block. Halts, aborts, and resets allow firmware to recover the block and keep the system going. The halt function allows engineers to inspect registers when things go wrong to try to diagnose the problems.

In the next chapter, I will present several ideas for test and debug hooks that may help diagnose and work around defects in both the device driver and the block.

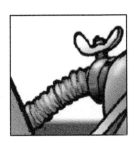

CHAPTER 11

Hooks

Try as we might, it is very difficult to consistently make perfect hardware. Defects and flaws will always exist. The challenge is to be able to understand and resolve them when we come across them. One of the better ways to do that is to add some test and debugging hooks in the block to help provide information on the defect.

The term "hook" refers to a mechanism that can be used to reach out or reach in to get something. In the context of this chapter, hooks in the chip allow firmware to reach in and get at something it would otherwise not have access to. It is a way of hooking in additional access to the chip.

Firmware has an advantage because code can be modified, re-compiled, and tested in a short amount of time. To diagnose defects, a debugger can be attached or debug statements can be added and compiled in. It is easy to add these debug hooks in firmware. This flexibility is available even when firmware is running on real hardware.

Silicon-based hardware does not have that luxury. Chips take millions of dollars and months to manufacture. Before incurring that time and expense, much testing is done to try to find and eliminate defects. However, simulators are slow, making them difficult to exhaustively run tests. Virtual prototypes, FPGA prototypes, and JTAG ports are better but still have limitations. They require extra hardware, run slower, and cannot be done in a buttoned-up system. Those techniques are valuable and useful in their application but are not within the scope of this book. This book is focused on the design of chips, not development tools.

In general, hardware engineers have very few chances to get it right. A flaw in the design that forces a respin can cost millions of dollars and months of delay.

Most of this book discusses techniques, concepts, and best practices that are intended to keep flaws out of the design. In contrast, this chapter discusses test and debug hooks that may help in diagnosing and working around flaws that do make it into the design.

Defects are not confined to hardware. Incorrect operation of the block may be due to defects in firmware because of incorrect settings of registers or due to corrupted data that the block is trying to process. The easy part is noticing that the block is not operating as it should.

DOI: 10.1016/B978-1-85617-605-7.00013-7.

The hard part is figuring out why. Debuggers in firmware with test and debug hooks in the block help collect information for engineers to diagnose the problem. In other words, test and debug hooks are not solely for dealing with defects in the block, but also defects in the firmware and system. Once the problem is identified, than a fix or workaround can be designed. Defects in firmware can be readily fixed. Defects in the block are often worked around by firmware.

11.1. Designing for Hooks

Since it is unknown where (hardware or firmware) defects will be, hooks need to be in place in various locations throughout the design in anticipation of possible defects that need to be addressed.

📖 **Tales from the Trenches**

A manager I met at a conference told me that his young design team announced that they were done with the design of the chip. He told them that in 6 months when the chip comes back, it will likely not work. He then asked them what they would need in the chip to figure out why. They had not thought about that—they had only concentrated on normal operation. So they went back to their desks and added some extra logic to help the test and debug phase.

But why should valuable silicon space be allocated for test and debug hooks when they are not needed for normal operation? The same question can be asked with automobile insurance—why pay for insurance (besides the fact that it is legally required) when you don't want anything in return? Because you will be glad you have it when you do get in an accident.

Test and debug hooks in the chip are insurance. The hooks are planned to not be used—but are there as a contingency for when something goes wrong. If only 1 out of 10 hooks is used, and that 1 hook averted a respin, then adding all 10 hooks was worth it. All 10 had to be added because it cannot be known in advance which one (or ones) will be needed.

Care must be taken to ensure that adding hooks does not add defects to the primary purpose of the design. Engineers should not have to debug the debug hooks.

Many of the hooks suggested in this chapter take up very little silicon space and are not very complex, keeping to a minimum the cost of adding and testing them.

☑ **Best Practice**

11.1.1 Allocate silicon space for test and debug hooks.

11.1.1. What Hooks to Add

How many test and debug hooks should be added is difficult to say. But use the same methods that the automobile insurance industry uses, look at past history. Insurance rates charged for a 16-year-old male with a new driver's license will be more than the rates for a 40-year-old female with a clean record. Parts of the block that are new and risky should have more test and debug hooks than parts that are mature and stable.

Many of the hooks in this chapter came because of defects I've encountered over the years. They are hooks that I had that were helpful, or hooks that I wish I had. Ask yourself where the problems have been on previous versions of the block. What test and debug hooks would have been useful?

☑ **Best Practice**

11.1.2 Design test and debug hooks based on lessons learned from previous hardware defects.

This is an excellent area to collaborate with firmware engineers. They had to develop firmware for previous versions without the benefit of simulator or logic analyzers to help debug. They would have ideas on what types of hooks would have been useful and what types they would like to see.

☑ **Best Practice**

11.1.3 Collaborate with firmware engineers on the design of test and debug hooks.

11.1.2. Adding Registers

Access to test and debug hooks is through registers. These registers do not need to follow the rigorous and formal process that normal registers do. They can come and go as required. Their bit and address locations can be rearranged. Any use of them by device drivers is "unsupported" and is not guaranteed to still be valid on the next generation of the block.

The address space for test and debug registers should be behind normal registers in the block to help keep them separated from the formal registers that must abide by stricter rules. It will also help keep firmware from accidentally accessing them. If the block's allocated address space is tight, debug registers can be assigned into a different page or accessed indirectly.

☑   **Best Practice**

11.1.4 Assign test and debug registers to their own address range or page in the block's register address space.

11.1.3. Looking for Potential Problem Areas

Potential problem areas should be looked for while designing the block. Analyze what would happen if the portion of the block being designed did not work as planned. If it didn't, is the whole block unusable? Or can it get by without it? If it is broken, how can firmware work around it?

Thinking about these questions can lead to changing the design to be more flexible. It may be that an alternative way of doing it is possible or a way of disabling that section and letting the rest of the block function without it.

Unfortunately, the more flexible the block is, the more combinations and permutations of modes that need to be tested. Good engineering judgment must be used to weigh risk vs. ability to test and debug.

☑   **Best Practice**

11.1.5 Design and document contingency plans to work around defects in blocks and sub-blocks.

11.1.4. Removing Workarounds

Resolving a defect in a chip may involve using a test and debug hook to make the chip usable without incurring the time and expense of respinning the chip. Using the test and debug hook is okay for the current version of the chip but should not be used on the next version.

While firmware workarounds are used to solve the problem, they are not perfect. For instance:

• Sometimes the workaround is very complex, making future support and changes very prone to errors, especially when done by someone else.

• Sometimes the workaround can only be 99.9% reliable and for some reason, there is no way to plug up that remaining 0.1%.

• Sometimes it is a performance impact because firmware has to do more work or because it cannot detect conditions as quickly as the block can.

- Sometimes it causes a loss of features. The workaround may have to be simply to never use that feature. The product can ship without it, but it would have been nice to have it.

- Sometimes it depends on not using the block in certain modes, which may be fine for this product but the next generation product may require those modes.

- Sometimes it depends on test and debug hooks which are "unsupported" and their existence and behavior is allowed to change on the next version.

If a hook was used to work around a defect in the block's logic, then fixing the logic will remove the need to use the hook. When working on the new version, look at defects in the previous versions and get them fixed so that firmware can quit using the hooks.

If the hook was used to work around a defect in the architecture of the block, then use of the hook may continue to be needed. In that case, that hook needs to be promoted to be a standard feature of the block, subject to the formal documentation, design, review, and testing imposed on normal features.

☑ **Best Practice**

11.1.6 Fix defects in each new version of the block to eliminate prior workarounds that used test and debug hooks.

When leveraging from a previous version of the block, consult with firmware engineers for workarounds used by their device driver that need to be addressed.

11.2. Peek...

What follows now for the rest of this chapter is a collection of several ideas for test and debug hooks. Some will work in your design—others will give you ideas for different hooks to add. This first section contains hooks that allow firmware to peek at what is going on inside the block without impacting operations within the block.

11.2.1. Internal Registers

A simple way to give firmware visibility to the insides of the block is to provide firmware-readable access to all internal registers, i.e., the banks of flip-flops that would otherwise not be accessible by firmware. Being read by firmware is not needed for the proper functionality of the block. But if made accessible, firmware can read current conditions.

Internal registers include those used to hold internal signals, conditions, and values. It could also be those used to hold shadow, working, or modified copies of firmware-accessible registers.

Whether every single internal register is accessible or not depends on the number of internal registers and the potential benefit to be gained by making them accessible.

☑   **Best Practice**

11.2.1 Provide read access to all internal registers.

11.2.2. Signals

Back in the old days when hardware was made out of discrete logic parts, it was easy to debug logic with a logic probe between gates, buffers, flip-flops, and other elements. But that is not possible with circuits confined on a single silicon chip.

Add a register that contains the current value of several internal signals, ones that would not normally be made available since they are not needed by firmware for normal operation. The following lists a few ideas:

- Busy/active signals.

- Signals between sections of the block.

- Signals feeding into and out of state machines.

- Signals feeding into and being generated by combinatorial logic.

- Signals used to enable counters.

- Signals used to control muxes.

- And any other signals you think might be interesting.

A 32-bit register can show 32 internal signals. If needed, more registers can be added to show more signals.

Even though internal signals are constantly changing when active, it can still provide clues to engineers trying to debug problems. If something is stuck, the signals show at what level. Firmware can do many successive reads to see if a particular signal is changing or not.

📖   **Tales from the Trenches**

A defect was found in a block where signal integrity issues caused extraneous interrupts. Fortunately an internal signal was made visible to firmware (per a firmware engineer's request) in the design of that block. That signal was true if the interrupt was valid. Since that signal was visible to firmware, it allowed firmware to determine whether the interrupt was valid or extraneous.

If more than one register is needed to show all the signals in a given set, it may be necessary to take a snapshot of all the signals at once then read them with the multiple register reads. This ensures that all the signals in the set are synchronized.

☑ **Best Practice**

11.2.2 Provide one or more registers that show the levels of key signals internal to the block.

Many blocks interact with other blocks and components through discrete signals other than the standard address and data bus. Those signals are used for control and handshaking, and must follow proper protocol in its signaling pattern. Bidirectional signals allow multiple components to drive the line. Are those I/O signals following proper protocol? Being able to read I/O signals allows engineers to diagnose I/O protocol problems.

☑ **Best Practice**

11.2.3 Provide one or more registers that show the current state of key input and output signal pins.

11.2.3. Memory

Address and counter registers are used to access external or onboard memory. Make those readable by firmware. During normal operation, they might be rapidly changing. If successive reads by firmware indicates constant changes, then firmware knows that the block is not stuck. But if successive reads are the same, then the block is stuck, stalled, or done. (A stalled bit next to an active bit could also be used to indicate when an active transfer is stalled.)

☑ **Best Practice**

11.2.4 Make counter and address registers readable even if they change rapidly.

A DMA controller is often use by blocks to transfer data from memory to the block and from the block to memory. The DMA controller itself is generally a mature and stable module but the block it services may not be. Problems may occur while data is being transferred. By reading the current address location in the DMA address register, firmware engineers can know where in memory the problems are occurring. DMA controllers with chaining capabilities could yield information regarding which link in the chain it is currently working on.

Following is a list of useful information that could be read from a DMA controller:

- Current address pointer

- Bytes left to transfer in this link in the chain

- Initial starting address for this link in the chain

- Initial byte count for this link in the chain

- Pointer to next link in the chain

Table 11.1 shows how this information can help diagnose data transfer problems.

☑ **Best Practice**

11.2.5 Provide read access to the parameters of DMA transfers in progress, including the initial and current data address and byte count, and the pointer to the next buffer in the DMA chain.

Blocks may have internal memory buffers, such as FIFO's, circular queues, stacks, and so on. As the block processes data, bytes will be consumed from buffers, and then produced and put in buffers as it moves to the next stage in the pipeline or awaits a memory transfer

Table 11.1: Diagnosing DMA Transfer Problems

DMA Register Status	Potential Problem	
	DMA from Memory	**DMA to Memory**
Both the address and byte count registers are unchanged from what firmware wrote.	The DMA transfer has not started; this may be due to an incorrect setup of the DMA registers.	The block has not yet given data to the DMA controller. The block may be set up incorrectly.
The address and byte count registers are one DMA burst size off.	One burst size from the beginning indicates that the DMA transfer has started but the block has not consumed the data. The block might not be set up correctly.	One burst size from the end of the buffer might indicate that a last byte is stuck somewhere inside the block.
The address and byte count registers are somewhere in the middle of the transfer.	The data read in may have had a corrupted spot causing the block to generate an error and quit. The current address register indicates the general vicinity where the corrupted data are in memory.	The block may have terminated early, stopping it from sending more data to the DMA controller. The byte count indicates how much was transferred to memory.
The address and byte count indicate a completed transfer but the block has not finished.	The block may be expecting more data than the DMA controller was programmed to transfer.	The block might have more data than the DMA controller was programmed to transfer.

via a DMA burst. Allowing firmware to inspect the head and tail pointers for the buffers, the byte count of the buffer, and possibly even the contents of the buffer will yield excellent clues as to what might have gone wrong.

When a byte is taken out of the buffer, it does not necessarily mean that the storage element that held the byte had been erased. Allowing firmware to read the whole buffer, whether empty, partially full, or full, allows firmware to read what was there and glean clues from that.

☑ **Best Practice**

11.2.6 Provide read access to internal memory and its support registers, such as FIFOs, buffers, head and tail pointers, and counters.

11.2.4. State Machines

Provide a register for firmware to read the current state of the state machines in the block. Even though the current state of a state machine may be rapidly changing during operation, if it were stuck in a state for some reason, then reading this register would permit finding out where.

Blocks with multiple state machines could have the current state of each state machine in the same register, space permitting. This register map shows the current state of three state machines. The X state machine has 3 bits, the Y has 5 bits, and the Z has 4.

	MSB			State Machine Register—0x0220					LSB
Bits	31 30 29 28	27 26 25 24	23 22 21 20	19 18 17 16	15 14 13 12	11 10 9 8	7 6 5 4	3 2 1 0	
R/W	- - - -	- - - -	- - - -	Z Z Z Z	- - - Y	Y Y Y Y	- - - -	- X X X	
Reset	0 0 0 0	0 0 0 0	0 0 0 0	0 0 0 0	0 0 0 0	0 0 0 0	0 0 0 1	0 0 0 0	

X: **Read state machine**—Current state of the read state machine.

Y: **Write state machine**—Current state of the write state machine.

Z: **Control state machine**—Current state of the control state machine.

Note that, following the guideline in Section 8.2.2, Multi-Bit Fields, the positions of each state machine are nibble-aligned. Actually, in this example, they are all byte-aligned because there is room and one of them, Y, is bigger than one nibble. This alignment makes it much easier to read the hex value and get the current state for that state machine without any mental bit shifting.

> 📖 **Tales from the Trenches**
>
> In the Unity mono video block, the state machine had several defects. However, we could not always verify that this was the case because we had no visibility of its current state.
>
> In the next version of the block, I requested a register to be able to read the current state. When the hardware engineer was turning on the new chip on a board, the block was not working. He read the state machine register and it indicated that it was stuck in a state waiting for an external signal. From that, he knew something was wrong with the signal line on the board coming into the chip. He looked and discovered that it was missing an in-line resistor, thus preventing the signal from reaching the chip. Soldering on an inline resistor fixed the problem. He said that the state machine register probably saved him 3 days of work. It proved useful in diagnosing problems outside of the video block.

When debugging complex state machines, not only is it useful to know the current state but to know what the next state will be. The next state is determined by current state and combinatorial logic of incoming signals. In addition, state machines produce outgoing signals as they traverse through the states. Exposing incoming signals, the calculated next state, and the resulting outgoing signals will help debug state machine logic, especially complicated ones. This register map illustrates those values for an example state machine.

	MSB				Main State Machine Register—0x0220			LSB
Bits	31 30 29 28	27 26 25 24	23 22 21 20	19 18 17 16	15 14 13 12	11 10 9 8	7 6 5 4	3 2 1 0
R/W	- - - -	- D R B	- - - -	- M A Q	- - - N	N N N N	- - - C	C C C C
Reset	0 0 0 0	0 0 0 0	0 0 0 0	0 0 0 0	0 0 0 0	0 0 0 0	0 0 0 0	0 0 0 0

C: **Current state**—Current state of the main state machine.

N: **Next state**—Next state of the main state machine.

Incoming Signals

Q: **Queue**—This incoming signal causes the state machine to launch a new task.

A: **Byte available**—This incoming signal indicates data is available to process.

M: **Mode**—This incoming signal controls which mode to use.

Outgoing Signals

B: **Busy**—This outgoing signal is true when the state machine is not in the idle state.

R: **Byte ready**—This outgoing signal is true when a byte is ready.

D: **Done**—This outgoing signal is true when the state machine is done and is used to generate an interrupt in the interrupt module.

☑ **Best Practice**

11.2.7 Provide one or more registers with nibble-aligned fields that show the current and next state and the incoming and outgoing signals of each state machine.

11.3. . . . And Poke

The previous section discussed test and debug hooks that allow firmware to peek inside the block. They are non-destructive peeks, in that the act of reading does not change the block's behavior.

This section discusses test and debug hooks that allow firmware to poke values into the block.

Warning:

These pokes will change the behavior of the block and they can be dangerous. The wrong value at the wrong time will cause the block to do the wrong thing. But when used with care, they can aid difficult testing and debugging efforts.

11.3.1. Destructive Reads and Writes

Reads are generally thought of as having no impact to the memory. However, reading from a FIFO causes data to be removed from the FIFO and the next one made available.

Giving firmware the ability to read from (empty out) and to write to (fill up) a FIFO will definitely change the behavior of current operations. While that is not desirous in normal circumstances, it is useful for testing purposes.

Small FIFOs are often used between stages in a pipe. One stage can be tested in isolation of stages before and/or after by having firmware write test data to the incoming FIFO of that stage and then read result data from the outgoing FIFO of that stage. Firmware can then examine the result data for correctness.

📖 **Tales from the Trenches**

The Unity mono video block had some FIFO buffers in a pipeline that were not getting emptied when an abort was issued. Fortunately, a read port for testing purposes existed in the middle of the pipeline behind those buffers. I inserted a workaround to read from the port during the abort process which had the effect of emptying the FIFO buffers, allowing for the abort process to complete so that the block could be ready to print the next page.

☑　**Best Practice**

11.3.1 Provide access points in each pipeline for firmware to extract data from and insert data into the pipeline.

11.3.2. Input and Output Signals

Blocks communicate with other blocks and components through input and output signals. The other blocks may be on the same silicon or they may be connected through a wiring harness to another component.

Test hooks for controlling those I/O signals are useful to allow the block to be tested without having to have the collaborating blocks or components connected or functional. Firmware can control the signals to test that the block is functioning correctly. Some signals require a specific waveform for proper operation so a waveform generator can be implemented to produce it.

These input and output signals hooks are also useful when trying to debug system issues by dividing the system into sections and testing for proper responses.

📖　**Tales from the Trenches**

A state machine in the Unity mono video block would occasionally get stuck waiting for more horizontal sync pulses from the laser scanning each raster line. However, at the end of the page, the laser would stop sending pulses. The abort signal did not work because those particular states were not looking for it, but only for the next sync pulse.

Fortunately, the block contained an artificial horizontal sync pulse generator for testing purposes. I modified the device driver so that when the state machine was stuck, the device driver would switch the block to test mode, have the generator generate a few pulses, and then switch back out of test mode and get the block ready for the next page. This generator intended for testing only ended up being used in normal operation.

☑　**Best Practice**

11.3.2 Provide means to simulate external input and output signals.

11.3.3. Overwriting Registers

Counters and state machine registers contain important data needed for proper operation of the block. Messing with those registers invites trouble, but when used with caution and understanding the implications, it can be useful.

Preloading registers can be useful to test certain responses. Proper response for a FIFO-full situation can be tested by preloading the FIFO counter with an almost-full count, and then writing the last few bytes to get it to be full. Putting the state machine in a difficult-to-reach state allows testing for proper response in those conditions.

This ability could also be useful as workarounds. If stuck in a state, writing a different state could get past that.

☑ **Best Practice**

11.3.3 Allow firmware to load any value into each counter or state machine in the block.

11.4. Monitor

The section on Peek hooks allows firmware to peek at existing flip-flops and signals inside the block. This section, Monitor, adds some logic to watch for events, collect data, and do some basic analysis that could provide useful information to firmware.

11.4.1. Event Tracking

While debugging problems, the following questions may be asked about the occurrence of an event:

• Did the event occur?

• If it did occur, how many times did it occur?

• Was it enough times?

An event counter can answer these questions. Firmware writes to the counter to reset it before starting the task. Then the task is performed. Afterwards, firmware can read that register to see if it occurred, and if enough or too many occurred.

For example, suppose an external line should pulse 512 times and only 512 times but there is problem somewhere. Firmware clears the event counter, performs the failing task, and then reads the counter. The following are possible values and reasons for the failure:

- **0:** No pulses occurred. The external line might not be connected properly or the component driving the line might be operating properly.

- **1:** One pulse occurred. A latch grabs the signal but is not getting cleared. A handshaking pulse is waiting for a response.

- **511:** One pulse got lost. An off-by-one problem.

- **512:** There were 512 pulses so the problem must be within the block.

- **513:** Noise on the line. An off-by-one problem.

- **1242:** Significant noise on the line. Maybe it is due to crosstalk. Maybe the input pin is not being driven and the pin is just floating.

Another use of this event counter is to measure performance. Sometimes an exact rate of occurrence is unknown and hard to measure. Firmware could reset the counter and then at some time later, such as 1 second, read it and see how many events occurred during that time.

☑   **Best Practice**

11.4.1 Provide firmware-readable and resettable event counters to track key events in the chip.

Knowing where bottlenecks are in the system will help diagnose problems. Is it the block itself? Is it the data bus? Is it memory? Is another block tying up the bus? It is hard to know because it is difficult to connect probes inside chips to find out. Summarized in the following list are a few ideas of probes that could be built into chips to collect data.

- **Bus utilization:** Busy counters and idle counters that show what percentage of the time the bus is busy. Another counter shows how many times one device wants the bus when it is already busy. These numbers will be very useful to determine bus utilization.

- **Memory bus utilization:** Counters to keep track of how often memory is being accessed. This will be useful to see if the bus is fast enough.

- **Block idle time:** An idle time counter keeping track of how much time the block is idle when it could be doing useful work. Counters indicating how much that block is accessing the buses and memory.

- **DMA blockings:** Counters monitoring how often each DMA is blocked waiting for access to the bus. This data could help adjust bus priorities.

- **Shared resource:** If there is a shared resource, such as one block that does either compression or decompression, or two blocks sharing the same DMA controller, monitor its utilization and how long one is blocking the other.

☑ **Best Practice**

11.4.2 Provide performance measurement hooks in the chip to collect data.

11.4.2. Timers

Many reasons exist for having timers that will generate an error interrupt if an event does not occur within a specific time limit. Typically, firmware has to write a timeout value to the register for the timer to use. Depending on what is being timed, the firmware engineer does not know what time is typical. So they have to be generous to allow for the worst possible case. But being too generous could impact system performance.

The information that the firmware engineer learns from this type of timeout is that the event was early enough or the event was too late. But if the event was early enough, was it barely early enough or way early enough? For one-shot timers, firmware launches the task then waits for the event interrupt or timeout interrupt. Firmware then processes it and then launches another task which restarts the timer.

The hook is to make the one-shot timer stop counting and hold its value when an early-enough event occurs. When the event occurs, firmware reads the counter and learns how close the event came to the timeout. The one-shot timer is reset and starts timing again when firmware launches the next task.

For example, if a one-shot timeout is set for 10 ms, but after much experimentation, it is learned that a good event always occurs in less than 2 ms, then the timeout could be adjusted to 3 ms to enable quicker detection and response to bad cases.

☑ **Best Practice**

11.4.3 Design each one-shot counter (timer) to stop and retain its count when an event occurs, and allow firmware to read it until firmware writes a new value or the counting is started again.

In some implementations, the timer is used to ensure that a periodic event keeps occurring. As long as the event keeps occurring, the periodic timer reloads the start value and continues counting down. When the periodic event stops occurring, then the timer will timeout and generate an interrupt.

Firmware cannot precisely read at the point in time to see how far the count got to and the register cannot stop since it must reload and start counting for the next event. For periodic timers, use a separate register to keep a snapshot of the timer when the event arrives. When the next event occurs, another snapshot is taken. As firmware samples the snapshot register, it can learn what typical values are for when the event arrives compared to the timeout value.

☑   **Best Practice**

11.4.4 Save a snapshot of the periodic counter (timer) register value to a separate register each time an event occurs.

11.4.3. Data Watching

When trying to debug state machines, it may not be sufficient to read the current state. What path did the state machine take to get to that state?

Add a buffer to store data that tracks the last few states leading up to the current state. To keep the buffer from filling up while spinning in one state (such as the idle state), add a counter to count how many clock cycles it was in that state. Table 11.2 illustrates the data collected of what a state machine trace might look like.

Some state machines would not be complicated enough to warrant space for a tracing capability. But complicated and high-risk state machines would and could be very useful to diagnose problems.

Table 11.2: Example Trace of Past Few States Visited

State	Count
1	1
2	1
8	104
5	1
6	23

☑ **Best Practice**

11.4.5 Add a simple trace facility for complicated and high-risk state machines.

Some data streams have issues besides simply transferring generic data. Error or control information may be contained in the middle of the data stream that is handled by the pipe.

A hook can watch for specified data in the data stream and then halt the block when it is seen. Data to watch could be good data (such as a boundary marker) or bad data (such as a null data). Once the pipe is halted, firmware can wake up to inspect and alter, and then resume or abort as needed.

☑ **Best Practice**

11.4.6 Provide a data transfer breakpoint facility that halts the transfer and interrupts firmware when specified data criteria are met.

11.5. More Hooks

This last section has a few more hooks to consider.

11.5.1. Bypass Paths

Blocks are often subdivided into sub-blocks with data or signals traversing from one sub-block to the next. Some sub-blocks are used only part of the time so some means is used to bypass that sub-block and move to the next. The sub-block may be designed to have the data or signal pass through it untouched. But a better design is to have a bypass path around the sub-block. Not only for sub-blocks that are used part of the time but for all sub-blocks, whether used some of the time or all of the time. Figure 11.1 illustrates several sub-blocks, each with its own bypass path.

When trying to diagnose problems, having a bypass path around each sub-block allows testing to be done for each sub-block in isolation from other blocks. Even though some sub-blocks are required for normal operation, being able to bypass it temporarily will allow testing and fault isolation.

Bypass paths might be needed to work around defects.

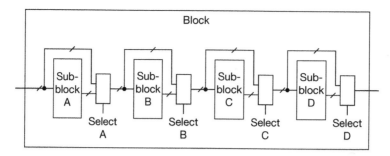

Figure 11.1: A pipeline with a bypass for each sub-block.

> 📖 **Tales from the Trenches**
>
> The Unity mono video block had a sub-block that interfered with the operation of another sub-block. The interfering sub-block could not be left disabled because its services were needed. Fortunately, the services of those two sub-blocks were not needed at the same time. I crafted an algorithm for the device driver to continuously enable and disable the bypass for the interfering sub-block during normal operation, thus allowing the services of both sub-blocks to be used.

A block with only one sub-block could also have a bypass path, allowing the testing of the DMA controllers bringing data in and out without interference from the block.

> 📖 **Tales from the Trenches**
>
> A decompressor block was generating errors on incoming compressed data. The block had a bypass path so that it was turned on to allow data to pass directly from the incoming DMA to the outgoing DMA. It was discovered that the incoming DMA was doing some unintended byte swapping, causing problems for the decompressor because the byte order was wrong. Engineers first thought that the problem was in the block, not the DMA, but the bypass path helped pinpoint the problem.

Besides being useful for test and debug purposes, bypass paths have other advantages. It provides a clean boundary that enables removing sub-blocks from the design. And data, bypassing around the sub-block avoids slow-down and congestion running through the block, similar to a freeway bypass running around a town where freeway speeds can be maintained rather than slowing down going through town.

> ☑ **Best Practice**
>
> 11.5.1 Provide a bypass path around each sub-block within a block, even if there is only one sub-block.

11.5.2. *Extra Resources for Test and Debug*

Resources are typically put on a chip only if there is a requirement for that resource as part of normal operation in the product. But sometimes those resources can be useful for test and debug purpose. However, those resources can only be used for normal operation or for test and debug but not both. Which means it is not possible to test and debug the use of that resource in normal operation.

To avoid the conflict, in addition to those resources for normal operation, additional resources should be added to the chip designated exclusively for test and debug purposes. Here are few examples.

GPIO Pins

GPIO pins are used in normal operation to provide basic I/O functionality. Their flexibility allows it to be used for one purpose on one product and another purpose on another product.

Besides normal operations, GPIO pins are well known for being useful for testing, debugging, and performance measurements. Firmware can toggle a pin and a scope could gather timing information. Sometimes GPIO pins are used to work around defects or add new enhancements. Add a few extra pins that have no assignment for normal operation.

> ☑ **Best Practice**
>
> 11.5.2 Provide extra unassigned GPIO pins to permit debugging and last-minute fixes.

Besides having a scope monitor firmware behavior via those GPIO pins, have the scope monitor internal signals. Select several internal signals as potential candidates for GPIO monitoring. Use a mux to have firmware select which one or ones are visible on one or more GPIO pins.

> ☑ **Best Practice**
>
> 11.5.3 Provide muxes that allow firmware to route a specified internal signal to a GPIO pin for monitoring.

Interrupt Module

Besides routing/muxing internal signals to a GPIO pin, also route appropriate signals to an interrupt module instantiated just for debug purposes. Possibilities include the following:

- Key internal signals as they change levels.

- Both input and output pins, such as protocol handshaking line.

- State machines when going idle or passing through some interesting state.

- Counters when it reaches zero or max.

All of these would default to being disabled. But when trying to solve problems, there is some useful information that can be gained from it. For instance:

- Did a particular internal signal ever change?

- Does the state machine ever make it back to the idle state?

- Did the counter ever make it to zero or was it constantly reloaded?

- Did the external device ever assert its ready signal on the input pin?

Even if a signal is changing too fast for firmware to respond to it without impacting the system, it is useful. For example, suppose it is unknown if a particular, high-frequency signal is active or not. Check and ack its pending bit and monitor if it keeps getting regenerated. That interrupt is not enabled so it will not interrupt the processor but firmware can tell that the signal is changing.

Under normal operation, most, if not all, debug interrupts will show pending because it shows activity. If one is not, then that signal might be broken or not yet turned on. At bootup, it will show which signals had changed by time firmware is ready to initialize the block.

Figure 11.2 shows that a test and debug interrupt module is separate from the block's own interrupt module. This method keeps all the pending "noise" out of the block's main interrupt module. Only when the test and debug interrupt module has one or more interrupts enabled will the block's main interrupt module show an interrupt pending from that module.

☑ **Best Practice**

11.5.4 Instantiate a test and debug interrupt module to generate interrupts from internal signals.

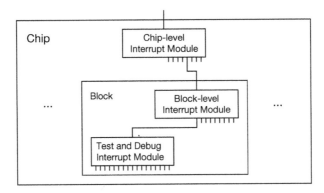

**Figure 11.2: A test and debug interrupt module wired into
the block's interrupt module.**

RS-232 Port

Some products need RS-232 serial ports for normal operation. Add an additional RS-232 UART dedicated for test and debug. The RS-232 serial port is the most basic of debug ports. Many devices can be connected to it; basic terminals, laptops & desktops, Windows and Linux machines. Even some old palmtop PDAs have terminal emulation that are 80 characters wide.

Since UARTs for RS-232 are plentiful, the IP to drop into the chip is small and trivial. Though it does require at least two I/O pins, they are pins well spent. Those pins could be muxed with other uses of those pins but then only one can have access to those pins.

RS-232 is slow and engineers must use caution to not transmit too much that it impacts the device being tested. That can be mitigated by adding a large buffer, such as 1 Kbytes or 4 Kbytes. Why so much in hardware when firmware can buffer all that? When debugging an interrupt handler, it may be necessary to send lots of information to the RS-232 port without having the RS-232 interrupt handler interrupt the interrupt handler being debugged.

☑ **Best Practice**

11.5.5 Include an RS-232 UART with generous buffer space for debugging purposes.

11.5.3. Dedicated Processor

SoCs with multiple processors are becoming more common. Add a processor dedicated for test and debug purposes. With the right architecture, it can monitor other processors, data flows, and signals. It could peek and poke into other parts of the SoC. And since it is used solely for that purpose, running debug code on that processor will not impact normal operation of other processors.

☑ **Best Practice**

11.5.6 Consider adding a dedicated debugging processor to monitor and poke other processors within a multiprocessor SoC.

11.6. Summary

Many test and debug hooks were discussed in this chapter. Some will be appropriate for your designs. You will also get ideas for others you can add. It may seem counterintuitive to "waste" silicon space for these hooks, but it will be worth it if just one hook allows you to get your product out the door without delays or respins.

Look for ways to have firmware peek and poke at the internals, to monitor activity, and provide extra tools. It is a guessing game as to which hooks should be added. But the more that is included, the more likely that the right tool will be in place when needed.

Since humans are not clairvoyant and cannot predict what defects and issues will appear, the challenge is to select the right set of hooks to include. Where would problems be likely to appear? New logic and complicated logic are two areas.

While test and debug hooks can generate some complex firmware workarounds, it can be a lifesaver to make the block usable.

📖 **Tales from the Trenches**

To get the Unity mono video block going, my device driver had to use four different test and debug hooks in six different ways in order to get the block functional. Had any one of those hooks not been in the block, the chip would have been useless; we would have had to spin the chip at a cost of millions of dollars and weeks of delay in product shipment. Instead, we were able to come up with firmware workarounds to make the block functional.

In the next generation of that block, every one of those defects was fixed. But we left in all the test and debug hooks as well as added others. And we ended up using some of them for a few new defects introduced and discovered.

Should test and debug hooks be taken out? Not unless it does not apply or if they take up too much silicon space. You never know when they might be needed.

Although the same rigor is not required for test and debug hooks as with the rest of the blocks, care must still be exercised to prevent defects in the hooks. It gets cumbersome to add test and debug hooks for the test and debug hooks.

11.6.1. Supporting Principles

The concepts of this chapter support the principles of hardware/firmware interface design as follows:

1. **Collaborate on the Design:** Be sure to work with firmware engineers for ideas on hooks that may be useful.

2. **Design for Contingencies:** This is the main message of this chapter, to prepare for contingencies by including many test and debug hooks throughout the chip.

3. **Plan Ahead:** It is unknown what defects and issues may arise. Adding these hooks just in case they might be needed is planning ahead.

The next chapter is directed toward firmware engineers. It has best practices to help them interface with hardware.

CHAPTER 12

Conclusion

Over 300 best practices are listed in this book. Remember that you are to use them only if applicable for your situation. Adopt them "as-is," adapt them as required, and generate your own.

But in order for your list of best practices to be effective, both the hardware and firmware engineers must collaborate together to come to an agreement on what that list should be. Even after you have generated a list, be sure to revisit it periodically to update it as your development environment evolves over time.

12.1. Key Points

Of all the points made in this book, the most important is collaboration. The hardware and firmware engineers must collaborate together to get their respective components to work together. By opening and keeping open the lines of communications between the teams, many of these issues will be brought up and discussed. The best practices will happen naturally. If you only remember one thing from this book, remember collaboration, and everything else will follow.

The most important collaborative tool is documentation. Place high importance on timely, accurate, and complete documentation. It is the primary reference for the firmware engineers for developing and debugging device drivers, for diagnosing hardware issues, and for troubleshooting hardware/firmware interaction problems. You, as a hardware engineer, have the advantage of being able to look at the RTL code to figure out what the hardware is doing. Firmware engineers generally do not have that access—they only have the documentation. Pay attention to the types of questions firmware engineers ask—it is an indication of areas in the documentation that might need more work. When the first draft of the documentation is ready, give it to firmware engineers for review and feedback. As the hardware is being designed, be sure to keep the documentation updated as the hardware design changes.

Establish and maintain internal standards in your development process, design methodologies, and coding guidelines. Standards will encourage consistency which will help

DOI: 10.1016/B978-1-85617-605-7.00014-9.

establish mature processes and designs. As your standards are followed, the quality of your product will increase.

Remember that designs cannot be perfect. But when there are problems, have the hooks in place to be able to diagnose and work around the defects. New designs and complicated designs should have more hooks. These hooks will not be used only for addressing defects in the block and its device driver alone, but also for system-level issues as all the components, modules, and pieces are integrated to work as a whole.

12.2. Benefits

Following the concepts in this book has several benefits:

- The engineering development time will be shortened because defects will be eliminated or mitigated.

- The hardware/firmware integration will be smoother because there will be fewer defects and hooks are available making it easier to diagnose and work around those that are there.

- Chips will have fewer respins due to functional problems because defects will be fewer due to correct-by-design construction and hooks will be available to work around defects that do make it in.

- The quality of the product will be improved because the system will be more stable when released to customers.

- The shorter development time, smoother integration, and fewer chip respins reduce development costs. On-time delivery to customers increases market share and revenue. And higher-quality products reduce warranty costs.

12.3. Seven Principles of Hardware/Firmware Interface Design

The following is a review of the seven principles:

1. The most important of these principles is **Collaborate on the Design**. Get your hardware and firmware teams talking to each other, formally and informally, locally and remotely. It is an area seen lacking many times. If you only concentrate on one principle, concentrate on this one. As you do so, many of the other principles will follow naturally and your overall development process and productivity will be greatly improved.

2. **Set and Adhere to Standards** and abide by them. This is not a time to be individualistic. The whole development process for this product and subsequent products will be much more efficient if you set and follow standards. Follow industry standards to the letter. Change and adapt your internal standards as needed, but make sure everyone is aware of it.

3. **Balance the Load** on both hardware & firmware. Adjust their work loads as needed. Again, one of the best ways to understand loading conditions is for hardware and firmware engineers to talk to each other.

4. **Design for Compatibility** to allow you more flexibility in the pairing of a version of hardware with a version of firmware. This will increase your productivity, especially as you work on future generations of products.

5. **Anticipate the Impacts** of your design and any changes to your design that you are making. Any impact you might be causing should be reviewed by engineers that would be impacted.

6. Take out an insurance policy by **Designing for Contingencies**. Include test and debug hooks in the chip to help diagnose and resolve problems, not only in hardware but also in firmware.

7. And finally, **Plan Ahead**. Do things right the first time so you don't have to do them again. Set up a direction and framework that will carry you through several generations of products.

12.4. It Finally Works! Let's Ship It!

Imagine a car that you have been working on. You encounter problems during the process but you manage to find ways to solve them or work around them. Finally you have it working and have a fully-functional car. Figure 12.1 illustrates such a car.

On the outside, the car looks and works great. However, what people don't see is what is really going on inside to make the car work great.

Imagine that the driver (device driver or car driver?) has to drive the car down the road, with its hood up, while reaching under the hood with a long pole to control the throttle. A lever is installed on the side of the car that will lower brake skids because the brakes do not work. The airbags are pre-inflated because the sensor does not work. That is okay because his head has to stick out the window anyway because the hood is up.

Figure 12.1: A car representing an embedded systems product that is finally working and can be shipped to customers.

An aerosol can horn is duct taped to the side to use as a horn because airbag is already inflated, making the horn on the steering wheel unusable. Another gas tank is installed on the roof with the fuel line snaking to the engine because the main tank has a leak. Plus the fuel line is bigger than designed because the engine needed more gas than expected. A bigger radiator and fan are installed up front because the engine runs hotter than expected.

A ladder is installed on the door for the driver to get in and out because the brake skid workaround will not allow doors to open. There is a panicked passenger, scared for having to ride with that driver in that car. The driver is leaning out of the window to see where to drive. He has a very jubilant look on his face; a look of great accomplishment. He says, "It finally works!!! Let's ship it!!"

This car is illustrated in Figure 12.2.

This car was able to be shipped because there were enough hooks in the hardware and firmware to get it functional. Although the car is not perfect, it worked, it got the passenger to the destination, and it can be sold to customers. The next generation car will fix up a lot of these problems.

Figure 12.2: A car humorously illustrating how hooks in the hardware and firmware saved the day; the car can be shipped to customers.

In the case study of the buggy video processor block, we were able to fix up the firmware to ship products with it. However, the customer never knew all that was necessary. It looked like a correctly-functioning printer to the customer. And we did it without having to incur the expense and delay of respinning the chip.

Hopefully you have learned from this book a few tricks and techniques that you can use in your work. And hopefully you will succeed in your product development.

Appendix A: Best Practices

This appendix brings together in one place all the best practices throughout this book with the intent of providing a checklist on a few pages for you to review.

As I have mentioned several times throughout the book, this is not an exhaustive list of best practices. Some will apply to your design, and some will not. And you will think of others to add to the list. Use this regularly while designing the chip and you will save some time, costs, and frustrations later, allowing for the development of the products faster, better, and cheaper.

Some of these best practices are not very clear if you have not read the associated background. The item number with each best practice will help you find where it is discussed in the book.

In the main part of the book, I used checkboxes with a check. Here I am using unchecked checkboxes so that you can check them as you complete them.

These best practices are also available online in an Excel® spreadsheet. (The best practices spreadsheet is available at the publisher's website, elsevierdirect.com/companions/9781856176057, and at the author's website, garystringham.com/hwfwbook.)

Make a copy of the Excel spreadsheet to keep one unchanged to match this book. But edit your copy as you see fit. Add columns as desired. Add, delete, and modify the best practices to fit your organization.

Chapter 2—Principles

☐ 2.1.1: Collaborate on the Design.

☐ 2.1.2: Set and Adhere to Standards.

☐ 2.1.3: Balance the Load.

☐ 2.1.4: Design for Compatibility.

☐ 2.1.5: Anticipate the Impacts.

☐ 2.1.6: Design for Contingencies.

☐ 2.1.7: Plan Ahead.

Chapter 3—Collaboration

☐ 3.1.1: Designate a member of the hardware team as best practice champion.

☐ 3.1.2: Designate a member of the hardware team as ambassador to the firmware team.

☐ 3.1.3: Designate a member of the firmware team as ambassador to the hardware team.

☐ 3.1.4: Hold a project kick-off meeting between hardware and firmware teams giving introductions and discussing schedules and procedures.

☐ 3.1.5: Collect and distribute contact information and spheres of responsibility of hardware and firmware team members across both teams.

☐ 3.2.1: Hold regular (weekly) meetings on relevant topics with appropriate firmware and hardware engineers in attendance.

☐ 3.2.2: Apply extra effort to meet when hardware and firmware teams are in different locations, such as using emails, teleconferencing, and other means.

☐ 3.2.3: Start collaboration between hardware and firmware engineers during the initial high-level hardware design phase.

☐ 3.2.4: Make sure that the firmware team is represented in the overall design of the chip, the detailed designs of the blocks, and the plans for testing.

☐ 3.2.5: Make sure that the firmware team is represented in reviews and signoffs of hardware checkpoints throughout the life cycle.

☐ 3.2.6: Use co-development activities, such as virtual prototypes, FPGAs, co-simulation, and old hardware to get firmware engineers involved in developing code and finding and resolving problems before the physical chips arrive.

☐ 3.2.7: Provide hardware engineering support to firmware engineers through to the end of firmware development.

☐ 3.2.8: Establish a repository for the hardware team's high-level and detailed design documents and provide appropriate access to it for firmware engineers.

☐ 3.2.9: Maintain a repository of chip defects that firmware engineers can easily access.

☐ 3.2.10: Notify all applicable firmware engineers of chip defects as they are identified.

☐ 3.3.1: Build bridges between teams to promote informal collaboration between hardware and firmware engineers.

☐ 3.3.2: Consult with firmware engineers when contemplating changes to the hardware/firmware interface.

☐ 3.3.3: Firmware: Initiate contact with the hardware engineer early in the design of the block to discuss the block, its device driver, and their interactions.

☐ 3.3.4: Firmware: Discuss with hardware engineers possible test and debug hooks to be added to the blocks that would assist firmware development. Review the best practices in the test and debug hook section for ideas.

☐ 3.3.5: Firmware: Work with the hardware engineer to find solutions to hardware/firmware interaction problems when they are discovered.

☐ 3.3.6: Involve both hardware and firmware engineers to determine the root cause of complicated defects and to then design a firmware workaround.

Chapter 4—Planning

☐ 4.1.1: Use existing industry standards where possible.

☐ 4.1.2: Use a de facto standard, if one exists, in the absence of an official standard.

☐ 4.1.3: Implement a standard exactly to the specifications of the standard.

☐ 4.1.4: Implement the full standard or a standard subset of the standard.

☐ 4.1.5: Clearly document any deviations from a standard, including motivations, justifications, and risks for each deviation.

☐ 4.2.1: Consult with other project teams to identify the latest version of the block to leverage for the next chip.

☐ 4.2.2: Consult with marketing and other partner teams to look into the near future for features that might be needed and add them to the block.

☐ 4.2.3: Add in necessary changes to support new requirements and features when leveraging a common version block from one generation to the next.

☐ 4.2.4: Develop internal design standards for the style and format of register layout, register access, interrupt modules, DMA modules, and other common elements.

☐ 4.3.1: Make changes to the new version of a block to be backward compatible with the old version of firmware where possible.

☐ 4.3.2: Minimize the impact on firmware when changes to a new version of the block cannot be completely backward compatible.

☐ 4.4.1: Document defects that exist in the chip, including description, chip version, how to reproduce, and workarounds.

☐ 4.4.2: Document all defects, even those deemed unlikely to occur and those for which cause and symptoms may be vague.

☐ 4.4.3: Review the list of defects to select those that should be fixed on the next version of the chip.

☐ 4.4.4: Develop and review hardware/firmware interface test plans with the firmware team to ensure that test cases for the block reflect actual firmware usage.

☐ 4.5.1: Avoid functional conflicts of shared pins by assigning them to separate pins if it is possible that they will be needed at the same time.

☐ 4.5.2: Analyze the design of each I/O block to ensure that it provides the proper buffer management support for status, control, interrupts, errors, and debug.

☐ 4.5.3: Keep interactions between the firmware and the block as simple as possible.

☐ 4.5.4: Evaluate prior silicon history, the existence of device drivers, and strong technical support when purchasing IP from third-party vendors.

☐ 4.6.1: Review the postmortem notes from the previous chip during the specification phase of the new chip and apply appropriate changes to fix defects and add design enhancements.

☐ 4.6.2: Conduct a postmortem review of the chip soon after product release.

Chapter 5—Documentation

☐ 5.1.1: Include in the chip documentation the specific details about each instantiated block including address offset, mapping of interrupt lines into global interrupt registers, and customizable parameter settings.

☐ 5.1.2: Distribute the block documentation to all applicable firmware teams, whether located in-house or with end customers and third-party developers.

☐ 5.1.3: Distribute the block unsupported specification only to in-house firmware teams.

☐ 5.1.4: Document in the block documentation the unsupported bits in supported registers with a note to say that they are unsupported and must use zeros when writing and be ignored when reading.

☐ 5.2.1: Develop documentation standards in content and format to be used across the whole block, across all the blocks in the chip, and across all chips produced by the organization.

☐ 5.2.2: Write the block documentation at the beginning of the design phase of the block.

☐ 5.2.3: Update the documentation regularly as the design of the block changes.

☐ 5.2.4: Review the documentation soon after the design is frozen to ensure accuracy and completeness and that it contains all design changes.

☐ 5.2.5: Use the documentation of a leveraged block as the baseline documentation for the new block.

☐ 5.2.6: Correct common documentation errors such as wrong register address, wrong bit position, old functions still listed, new functions not listed, and missing information.

☐ 5.2.7: Reduce obscurity and ambiguity of registers, bits, and functions by using clear names and descriptions.

☐ 5.3.1: Distribute the documentation to firmware engineers for the initial review after it is written at the beginning of the design phase.

☐ 5.3.2: Distribute the documentation to firmware engineers for subsequent reviews as the documentation changes due to updates, corrections, or design changes throughout the life cycle of the block.

☐ 5.3.3: Explicitly notate all changes in the documentation between current and previous versions distributed for reviews.

☐ 5.3.4: Firmware: Review the block's documentation and provide feedback to the hardware engineers regarding issues on the design, functionality, and documentation.

☐ 5.3.5: Firmware: Review the block's documentation and respond to the hardware engineers in a timely fashion.

☐ 5.4.1: Include detailed descriptions of the block that firmware engineers need or might need to know, such as details of its tasks, its registers and bits, and its limitations.

☐ 5.4.2: Include sufficient and clear information in the block documentation to allow others to take ownership of the block.

☐ 5.4.3: Include in the documentation a top-down description of the block that describes its theory of operation, its function in the system, and its parts.

☐ 5.4.4: Include in the block's documentation a document version history, indicating the various documentation releases and the changes made for each release.

☐ 5.4.5: Include in the block's documentation a block version history, indicating changes made and defects fixed.

☐ 5.4.6: Include in the block's documentation a chip-specific history, indicating instantiation details for each chip, such as base address, interrupt mask, and supported I/O pins.

☐ 5.4.7: Document the features that this block does and does not support.

☐ 5.4.8: Document the assumptions made of what firmware will do for this block.

☐ 5.4.9: Include a list of other documents to reference that may provide useful or necessary information for this block.

☐ 5.4.10: Provide both a reference section and a tutorial section in the block documentation.

☐ 5.4.11: In the tutorial section, describe the steps necessary to carry out each type of task.

☐ 5.4.12: Identify bit fields discussed in the tutorial section by register and bit-field name.

☐ 5.4.13: Define terms that may be unfamiliar in a glossary section.

☐ 5.4.14: Include an errata section, which describes where and how the block does not work as specified. Keep this updated, especially with defects found by firmware engineers.

☐ 5.5.1: Document all registers in the block, even test/debug registers.

☐ 5.5.2: Use automated register design tools to generate register and bit documentation from block design files.

☐ 5.5.3: Include table of registers in address order. Optionally include one in alphabetical order of the register names.

☐ 5.5.4: Document the register name and its address offset.

☐ 5.5.5: Document all interactions between registers.

☐ 5.5.6: Document the units of numbers in the registers, their minimum and maximum values, and the response for illegal values written to those registers.

☐ 5.5.7: Document what will be returned when reading address and count registers, whether original values written by firmware, the changing values while the block is processing, or the end values after processing.

☐ 5.6.1: Display the register map in a horizontal format in the block's documentation.

☐ 5.6.2: Put the LSB on the right side of the register map.

☐ 5.6.3: Number the bits starting with the LSB as bit 0.

☐ 5.6.4: Indicate the type of each bit—read-only, write-only, read/write—in the register map.

☐ 5.6.5: Document the power-on defaults for each bit in the register map.

☐ 5.6.6: Provide a detailed description for each bit under its register map.

☐ 5.6.7: Sort the bit descriptions under the register map from the LSB down to the MSB.

☐ 5.6.8: Document how each bit is affected—or not—by an abort.

☐ 5.6.9: Explicitly indicate each bit that is reserved for test and debug purposes.

☐ 5.6.10: For documents distributed to third-party developers, mark test and debug bits as bits that should be ignored and always contain zeros, but do not describe what they do.

☐ 5.6.11: Provide the warning in the document that the use of test and debug hooks is unsupported and may change in the next version of the block.

☐ 5.7.1: Document each interrupt as edge- or level-triggered.

☐ 5.7.2: Document if the interrupt is triggered on the rising or falling edge for edge-triggered interrupts or the high or low level for level-triggered interrupts.

☐ 5.7.3: Describe when and how to deassert the interrupt source to level-triggered interrupts.

☐ 5.7.4: Assign the name, "Enable," to the register that controls which interrupts will propagate.

☐ 5.7.5: Indicate the bit value—1 or 0—required to ack each interrupt.

☐ 5.7.6: Indicate which interrupts might occur before the task is completed.

☐ 5.7.7: Document which interrupts can be generated multiple times without being handled.

☐ 5.7.8: Document how quickly an unhandled interrupt could occur again.

☐ 5.7.9: Document what would happen if an unhandled interrupt occurred a second time before firmware serviced the first one (e.g., data loss, an error interrupt).

☐ 5.8.1: Document the minimum, maximum, and typical times for the block to start the task after its queue bit is set.

☐ 5.8.2: Document the minimum, maximum, and typical times for the block to complete the task, process the abort, or generate other time-delayed events.

☐ 5.8.3: Document the minimum and typical times that successive identical hardware events could occur.

☐ 5.8.4: Document the conditions and states that affect the variations of minimum, maximum, and typical times for each operation.

☐ 5.8.5: Document the duration of an operation in its primary unit of time, such as seconds or clock cycles.

☐ 5.9.1: Document the details of normal operation and what error checks are performed.

☐ 5.9.2: Document all error messages that the block could generate.

☐ 5.9.3: Document in detail all the conditions that could cause each error message.

☐ 5.9.4: Indicate whether an operation stops or continues in response to a given error.

☐ 5.9.5: Describe the state of the block after an error occurs.

☐ 5.9.6: Document the state of data—valid or invalid—after the error.

☐ 5.9.7: Describe how to recover from each error condition.

☐ 5.10.1: Describe how the block responds when configured to an invalid mode.

☐ 5.10.2: Document state machines that firmware engineers might need to know about.

☐ 5.10.3: Document the steps required to cleanly abort a block.

Chapter 6—Superblock

☐ 6.1.1: Design each block as a superblock—using a single set of design files—to provide the superset of all features needed by all chips instantiating the block.

☐ 6.1.2: Consolidate all versions of the same block from different chips into a superblock with all capabilities to be used in future chips.

☐ 6.1.3: Use the same set of superblock design files to instantiate the block one or more times in all chips.

☐ 6.1.4: Design each module (e.g., DMA, interrupts) as a supermodule with the superset of the features needed by all blocks instantiating the module.

☐ 6.1.5: Add new features to the common superblock rather than creating separate design branches of the block.

☐ 6.1.6: Retain all known low-overhead functionality in a superblock, even if current requirements do not call for it.

☐ 6.1.7: Leave in old functionality, if possible, until its replacement functionality has been proven.

☐ 6.1.8: Include low-impact, low-risk features in the design of the chip that could be used in future products or aid future development.

☐ 6.1.9: Increment the block version register whenever the superblock design changes, but not when the same superblock is instantiated in multiple chips.

☐ 6.2.1: Deactivate unused output signals from a block by leaving the signal unconnected at the block boundary, rather than changing the internals of the block.

☐ 6.2.2: Activate (deactivate) unused input signals to a block by tying the signal to its enabled (disabled) state at the block boundary, rather than changing the internals of the block.

☐ 6.2.3: Clearly document which I/O signals are active for each instantiation of the block.

☐ 6.3.1: Parameterize superblock configuration (e.g., buffer size, number of channels) as needed to allow the same block to be used one or more times in multiple chips.

☐ 6.3.2: Use parameterization only where it will significantly impact the silicon space used.

☐ 6.3.3: Review each large superblock for large optional sub-blocks to include or exclude using parameterization.

☐ 6.3.4: Use parameterization to include new features and exclude old features as the superblock evolves, allowing the same source files to produce instantiations of both current and previous block versions as needed.

☐ 6.3.5: Ensure that optional sub-blocks of a superblock have clean boundaries to the rest of the block.

☐ 6.3.6: Provide a fixed bypass path around the optional portion of a pipeline.

☐ 6.3.7: Store all parameter values for each instantiation in one or more firmware-readable instantiation registers.

☐ 6.3.8: Increment the block version register as new parameters are added to the superblock.

☐ 6.3.9: Do not change the block version register for different instantiations of the same version of the superblock.

☐ 6.3.10: Design optional registers to ignore writes and return zeros when the associated optional sub-block is excluded.

☐ 6.3.11: Design optional bits in fixed registers to ignore writes and return zeros when the optional bits' associated optional sub-block is excluded.

☐ 6.3.12: Design fixed and optional registers and bits to remain at the same position even when some optional registers and bits are excluded.

Chapter 7—Design

☐ 7.1.1: Always provide an indicator to firmware of any event or condition that firmware needs to know about.

☐ 7.1.2: Provide support in the chip—such as a general-purpose timer—that will generate an interrupt after short delays (less than 100 ms).

☐ 7.1.3: Use a status bit to indicate completion of tasks guaranteed to complete within an efficient polling period.

☐ 7.1.4: Use an interrupt to indicate completion of tasks not guaranteed to complete within an efficient polling period.

☐ 7.1.5: Use an interrupt channel to indicate completion of tasks that sometimes complete within an efficient polling period.

☐ 7.1.6: Use the interrupt module to provide both the status bit polling functionality and the interrupt functionality.

☐ 7.2.1: Size receive and transmit buffers appropriately for efficient communication between hardware and firmware.

☐ 7.2.2: Provide data buffering, queuing, and chaining to maximize data throughput.

☐ 7.2.3: Provide double-buffered registers so that firmware can queue the next task while the block is still running the current task.

☐ 7.2.4: Make the chip tunable so that firmware can adjust performance characteristics such as bus priorities and clock speeds.

☐ 7.2.5: Maximize performance margins to increase the potential for chip reuse in faster products.

☐ 7.3.1: Design the block such that it does not require firmware interaction immediately at power-on.

☐ 7.3.2: Design each block such that is still works at power-on even if its collaborative blocks are not ready yet.

☐ 7.3.3: Default GPIO pins to input.

☐ 7.3.4: Provide firmware-accessible power controls for each block.

☐ 7.4.1: When an error occurs, provide copious status information to firmware, including internal and external signal levels, state machine states, and counter values.

☐ 7.4.2: Include a byte-swapping capability in the DMA controller module instantiated throughout the chip.

☐ 7.4.3: Include a CRC and/or a checksum generator in the DMA controller module instantiated throughout the chip.

☐ 7.4.4: For each chip output pin connected to multiple blocks on the chip, multiplex the block output lines to select which block controls the signal on the chip output pin at any given time.

☐ 7.4.5: For each chip input pin connected to multiple blocks on the chip, multiplex the input line to select which block (or blocks) receives the signal at any given time.

☐ 7.4.6: Use translator modules to optimize the firmware interface to a feature of the chip when the preferred hardware implementation of that feature is firmware-unfriendly.

Chapter 8—Registers

☐ 8.1.1: Provide access to registers using memory-mapped I/O where possible.

☐ 8.1.2: Assign a unique base address to each chip.

☐ 8.1.3: Assign an address offset to each block relative to the chip's base address.

☐ 8.1.4: Allocate non-overlapping address ranges to each block in the chip.

☐ 8.1.5: Leave room in the block's address range for future registers.

☐ 8.1.6: Align the starting addresses of each block to a 256-byte boundary.

☐ 8.1.7: Assign an address offset to each register relative to the block's base address.

☐ 8.1.8: Assign each sub-block its own base address and address range, with room for expansion.

☐ 8.1.9: Assign a burst-aligned sequence of addresses to related groups of registers if bursting is needed.

☐ 8.1.10: Assign the start register to the last position in the burst sequence of registers.

☐ 8.1.11: Design the chip to return zeros for reads from unused address locations.

☐ 8.1.12: Design the chip to ignore writes to unused address locations.

☐ 8.1.13: Preserve the address offsets of the registers within the block when instantiating the block in a new chip.

☐ 8.1.14: Avoid reusing address locations of deleted registers in an existing block.

☐ 8.2.1: Assign bits to the register starting on the right side at the least significant bit.

☐ 8.2.2: Reserve bits for future use, if needed.

☐ 8.2.3: Place bit fields of 1 bit anywhere as desired in the register.

☐ 8.2.4: Place bit fields of 2 bits anywhere within a nibble.

☐ 8.2.5: Place bit fields of 3 to 4 bits nibble-aligned, of 5 to 8 bits byte-aligned, of 9 to 16 bits 16-bit aligned, and so on.

☐ 8.2.6: Place bit fields with sizes bigger than a register with the less significant bits in the necessary number of registers and any remaining most significant bits right-justified in the last register.

☐ 8.2.7: Design registers to return zeros for reads from unused bit positions.

☐ 8.2.8: Design registers to ignore writes to unused bit positions.

☐ 8.2.9: Avoid changing bit assignments from one version of the block to the next.

☐ 8.2.10: Avoid reusing bit positions of deleted bits in an existing register.

☐ 8.2.11: Avoid write-only bits whenever possible; use read/write bits instead.

☐ 8.2.12: Design write-only registers to return zero when read.

☐ 8.2.13: Do not mix different writeable bit types in any combination in the same register.

☐ 8.2.14: Assign read-only bits to registers with writeable bits only if necessary.

☐ 8.2.15: Assign each bit to a register with bits used in the same operational mode.

☐ 8.2.16: Assign all bits associated with a block instantiation to registers used only by that instantiation.

☐ 8.3.1: Assign each frequently used integer to its own register.

☐ 8.3.2: Assign every signed integer to its own register.

☐ 8.3.3: Always sign-extend a signed integer to the size of its register.

☐ 8.3.4: Place unused bits on both sides of a real number in a register to allow for future expansion, with bits on the left side for bigger numbers and bits on the right side for better precision.

☐ 8.3.5: Assign every real number to its own register.

☐ 8.3.6: For registers containing pointers to memory, use units of bytes, even if memory is word addressable.

☐ 8.3.7: Provide a read/write register that defaults to a value rather than hard-coding that value as a constant in hardware.

☐ 8.4.1: Provide a chip ID register that uniquely identifies the chip.

☐ 8.4.2: Provide a chip version register that uniquely identifies the chip revision or FPGA programming.

☐ 8.4.3: Update the chip version register with every chip revision and with every FPGA programming.

☐ 8.4.4: Provide a die bonding configuration register that uniquely identifies the bonding configuration for dies that have multiple bonding options.

☐ 8.4.5: Identify the chip revision using new registers or bits from existing registers if no dedicated version register can be provided.

☐ 8.4.6: Provide block-level ID and version registers for each block on a chip.

☐ 8.4.7: Update the block's version number only when that block changes, not when other components on the chip change.

☐ 8.5.1: Collaborate with the firmware team to determine any internal information that each block should make accessible to firmware.

☐ 8.5.2: Design the block to set the active bit when it starts the task, and then clear the active bit and set the interrupt bit when the task is complete.

☐ 8.5.3: Provide a queue bit that firmware must set—and only hardware can clear—to initiate a task in the block.

☐ 8.5.4: Design the block to clear the queue bit only after the queued task is launched and firmware is allowed to queue another task.

☐ 8.5.5: Assign queue bits to the same register only if their associated tasks are allowed to start concurrently.

☐ 8.5.6: Use shadow registers to provide stable and valid snapshots of registers with rapidly changing values.

☐ 8.5.7: Design registers to always return valid, accurate, and documented values, whether the block is idle or active.

☐ 8.5.8: Avoid read/write registers that more than one device driver will access.

☐ 8.5.9: Provide atomic access to registers that more than one device driver will access.

Chapter 9—Interrupts

☐ 9.1.1: Design the interrupt module as a supermodule to provide the superset of all features needed by all chips instantiating the module.

☐ 9.1.2: Assign each interrupt channel to the same bit position in the pending, enabled, source status, and other registers in the interrupt module.

☐ 9.1.3: Instantiate the interrupt module in each block to support all interrupts for that block and that block only.

☐ 9.1.4: Design the interrupt module to multiplex all its pending interrupts into a single interrupt line to be propagated upstream.

☐ 9.1.5: Instantiate an interrupt module at the chip level to collect the interrupt signal from each block interrupt module and produce one interrupt signal from the chip.

☐ 9.1.6: Assign each interrupt source signal to its own interrupt channel.

☐ 9.1.7: Provide a clock synchronization circuit in the interrupt module for the incoming source signals.

☐ 9.1.8: Clean up all incoming external interrupt sources with debouncing, noise suppression, and other appropriate circuits.

☐ 9.1.9: Make the interrupt module edge triggered.

☐ 9.1.10: Make the interrupt module rising-edge triggered.

☐ 9.1.11: Make the interrupt module generate a 1 for the outgoing interrupt signal when one or more interrupts are pending.

☐ 9.2.1: Provide an interrupt pending register that shows pending interrupts.

☐ 9.2.2: Use the interrupt bit type in the pending register.

☐ 9.2.3: Design the pending register so that a 1 written to a bit position acks the interrupt at that position.

☐ 9.2.4: Do not clear the pending register when firmware reads it.

☐ 9.2.5: Assign interrupts to interrupt channel positions in the pending register in descending order of priority, starting at LSB.

☐ 9.3.1: Provide an interrupt enable register that controls which interrupts are propagated to the CPU.

☐ 9.3.2: Design the interrupt enable register so that a bit value of 1 allows the interrupt at that position to propagate.

☐ 9.3.3: Design the interrupt enable register to control which pending interrupts are propagated, not which interrupts can become pending.

☐ 9.3.4: Default all bits in the interrupt enable register to off (disabled).

☐ 9.4.1: Provide an interrupt source status register that indicates the current level of the incoming source signal.

☐ 9.4.2: Leave unused the bit positions in the source status register for uninteresting source signals.

☐ 9.4.3: Provide an interrupt post register to allow firmware to trigger interrupts.

☐ 9.4.4: Provide atomic interrupt enable/disable registers for interrupt modules accessed by multiple device drivers.

☐ 9.4.5: Provide an interrupt masked register that indicates enabled interrupts that are pending.

☐ 9.4.6: Provide an instantiation register indicating instantiated registers and number of channels.

☐ 9.4.7: Reserve an address for each optional register, whether instantiated or not.

☐ 9.5.1: Use two separate interrupt channels, one for the leading edge and one for the (inverted) trailing edge, if interrupts on both edges of the source signal are required.

☐ 9.5.2: Consider assigning an interrupt channel to the trailing edge of any source signal that stays asserted for a while.

☐ 9.5.3: Assign both edges to adjacent interrupt channel positions if there are a few double-edge source signals.

☐ 9.5.4: Segregate leading-edge from trailing-edge interrupt channels if there are several double-edge source signals and assign them to the same relative channel positions.

☐ 9.5.5: Assign the leading edge group to the lower half of the interrupt channel positions and the trailing edge group to the upper half if they will fit in the same interrupt module. Otherwise, use the same channel positions across two interrupt modules, one for each group.

☐ 9.6.1: Use an interrupt channel to notify firmware of any externally initiated events.

☐ 9.6.2: Use an interrupt channel to indicate completion of firmware-launched hardware tasks that will not always complete instantaneously.

☐ 9.6.3: Do not use an interrupt channel to indicate completion of firmware-launched hardware tasks that always complete instantaneously.

☐ 9.6.4: Provide additional support, such as a buffer, a FIFO, an interrupt counter, or an overflow interrupt, for interrupts that could fire rapidly without firmware intervention.

☐ 9.6.5: Place interrupt module registers in an address space that is always visible.

Chapter 10—Aborts, Etc.

☐ 10.1.1: Provide a halt function in the block that stops the current task, clears the task active (go) bit, and leaves all other registers and buffers unchanged.

☐ 10.1.2: Provide access to firmware to halt the block.

☐ 10.1.3: Design the block to halt when an error occurs.

☐ 10.2.1: Provide a reset function in the block that stops all tasks and resets all registers, counters, buffers, and state machines to their default state.

☐ 10.2.2: Design every control register to come out of reset with its bits in a "safe" setting, such as inactive, disabled, idle, and so on.

☐ 10.2.3: Design the power-on circuitry to invoke the reset function.

☐ 10.2.4: Provide access to firmware to invoke synchronous and asynchronous resets.

☐ 10.3.1: Provide an abort function in the block that stops the current task and resets the associated task registers and state machines.

☐ 10.3.2: Provide abort functionality for all tasks in the block.

☐ 10.3.3: Provide access to firmware to abort the block.

☐ 10.3.4: Keep firmware's role in the abort process as simple as possible.

☐ 10.3.5: Provide an abort-done interrupt if the abort task will not always be instantaneous.

☐ 10.3.6: Design the abort task to respond to an abort command under every condition, even while the block is idle.

☐ 10.3.7: Design the abort outcome to be the same no matter if the block is busy or idle.

☐ 10.3.8: Ensure that all states in all the block's state machines, including all the idle states, will respond to the abort.

☐ 10.3.9: Design each block with its own abort function that services just that block.

☐ 10.3.10: Design the abort function so that it leaves any collaborative blocks in the ready state.

Chapter 11—Hooks

☐ 11.1.1: Allocate silicon space for test and debug hooks.

☐ 11.1.2: Design test and debug hooks based on lessons learned from previous hardware defects.

☐ 11.1.3: Collaborate with firmware engineers on the design of test and debug hooks.

☐ 11.1.4: Assign test and debug registers to their own address range or page in the block's register address space.

☐ 11.1.5: Design and document contingency plans to work around defects in blocks and sub-blocks.

☐ 11.1.6: Fix defects in each new version of the block to eliminate prior workarounds that used test and debug hooks.

☐ 11.2.1: Provide read access to all internal registers.

☐ 11.2.2: Provide one or more registers that show the levels of key signals internal to the block.

☐ 11.2.3: Provide one or more registers that show the current state of key input and output signal pins.

☐ 11.2.4: Make counter and address registers readable even if they change rapidly.

☐ 11.2.5: Provide read access to the parameters of DMA transfers in progress, including the initial and current data address and byte count, and the pointer to the next buffer in the DMA chain.

☐ 11.2.6: Provide read access to internal memory and its support registers, such as FIFOs, buffers, head and tail pointers, and counters.

☐ 11.2.7: Provide one or more registers with nibble-aligned fields that show the current and next state and the incoming and outgoing signals of each state machine.

☐ 11.3.1: Provide access points in each pipeline for firmware to extract data from and insert data into the pipeline.

☐ 11.3.2: Provide means to simulate external input and output signals.

☐ 11.3.3: Allow firmware to load any value into each counter or state machine in the block.

☐ 11.4.1: Provide firmware-readable and resettable event counters to track key events in the chip.

☐ 11.4.2: Provide performance measurement hooks in the chip to collect data.

☐ 11.4.3: Design each one-shot counter (timer) to stop and retain its count when an event occurs, and allow firmware to read it until firmware writes a new value or the counting is started again.

☐ 11.4.4: Save a snapshot of the periodic counter (timer) register value to a separate register each time an event occurs.

☐ 11.4.5: Add a simple trace facility for complicated and high-risk state machines.

☐ 11.4.6: Provide a data transfer breakpoint facility that halts the transfer and interrupts firmware when specified data criteria are met.

☐ 11.5.1: Provide a bypass path around each sub-block within a block, even if there is only one sub-block.

☐ 11.5.2: Provide extra unassigned GPIO pins to permit debugging and last-minute fixes.

☐ 11.5.3: Provide muxes that allow firmware to route a specified internal signal to a GPIO pin for monitoring.

☐ 11.5.4: Instantiate a test and debug interrupt module to generate interrupts from internal signals.

☐ 11.5.5: Include an RS-232 UART with generous buffer space for debugging purposes.

☐ 11.5.6: Consider adding a dedicated debugging processor to monitor and poke other processors within a multiprocessor SoC.

Appendix B: Bicycle Controller Specification

Document Version 3.2
Block Version C
22 Aug 2009

B.1. Introduction

The bicycle controller block provides functions necessary to support electric bicycles, a cost-effective, alternative energy transportation mode for millions of people worldwide. It monitors battery level, regenerative braking, pedal assist, and several performance parameters.

[This is actually an example specification used to illustrate several points in documenting the firmware interface to hardware blocks. It can be used as a template for generating other block specifications; the example can be used in parts, as a whole, rearranged, or otherwise modified to suit the needs and requirements of the organization. The bicycle controller as described in this example specification does not actually exist. The various aspects are contrived in order to illustrate various points. In addition, some areas are incomplete.]

B.1.1. Overview

B.1.1.1. System Overview

The bicycle controller block contains most of the necessary functions to coordinate tasks for the embedded bike. Figure B1 illustrates how it fits in with other blocks in the chip and components in the system.

The Bicycle Controller monitors some of the sensors on the bike. Other blocks are standard off-the-shelf blocks that are available to handle standard functions, such as monitoring the battery and controlling the display. The Bicycle Controller collects information from its own monitoring of the sensors as well as information gathered from other blocks to help it make

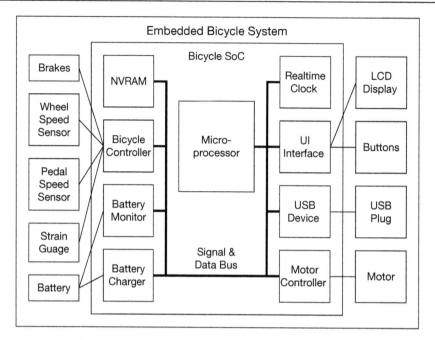

Figure B1: Overview of an embedded bicycle system.

decisions. It interacts with firmware running on the microprocessor which controls the whole system.

B.1.1.2. Block Overview

The bicycle controller block monitors events from other blocks in the bicycle SoC and from external sensors as shown in Figure B2. It monitors the wheel to track the speed and distance. It monitors the pedals to know when the rider is pedaling and when the rider is straining and needs an electric boost. It monitors the brakes to know when to engage regenerative braking to have it recharge the battery. It monitors events from the battery monitor and charger to know the level and to coordinate with the motor in using or generating power. It communicates with the microprocessor to receive instruction or to convey information. The microprocessor monitors button presses on the control panel and sends appropriate instructions to the various blocks. The microprocessor also retrieves information from the blocks to display on the LCD display.

B.1.2. History

B.1.2.1. Document History

Table B1 is a reverse-chronological list of changes made to the document since it was first leveraged from the previous release of this block. This tracks the changes made to the

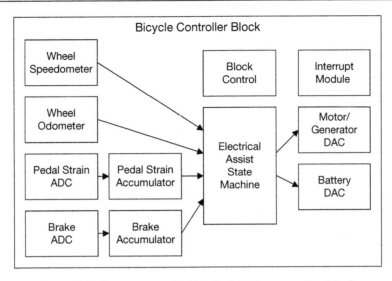

Figure B2: Components inside the bicycle controller block.

Table B1: History of Changes to the Block Documentation

Rev	Date	Changes	Who
3.2	21 Dec 08	Clarified description of the overheat error bit. Corrected the position of two interrupt bits to match how it is in the chip.	Harry Hardy
3.1	10 Oct 08	Made changes based on feedback from firmware review. Added the interrupt source register. Clarified programming description and example for battery monitor.	Harry Hardy
3.0	3 Aug 08	Initial release of this document for version C of the bike controller block. This document was leveraged from the latest document version (2.5) of the previous bike controller block version (B). Details about the wheel-size self-calibration feature were added. Change in the sampling rate of strain gauge was added.	Harry Hardy

document, which may or may not be associated with a change to the design of the block. See the next section for changes made to the design of the block.

B.1.2.2. Block History

Table B2 lists the changes that were made in the last several versions of this block, starting with the most recent version. This only contains changes that impact firmware.

B.1.2.3. Chip-Specific Details

Table B3 indicates how the block was instantiated into the various chips and lists the pertinent chip-specific details.

Table B2: History of Changes to This Version of the Block

Version	Changes
C	A different ADC is used for the pedal strain to accommodate a new strain gauge. The sampling frequency of the brake sensor was increased from 25 to 75 times per second. A wheel-size self-calibration feature was added. Added an interrupt source register.
B	An option was added in the controller block to convert speed and distance values to metric units. The internal clock was changed from 100 MHz to 125 MHz.
A	Original version.

Table B3: Chip-Specific Implementation Details of the Block

Chip	Block Version	Base Address	Interrupt	Buffer Size	Notes
Criterion ASIC	C	0xB1CE0000	0x00000008	128	
Time Trial SoC	C	0xBAB31000	0x00000040	64	Pedal strain input not tied to pin but tied low.
BMX SoC	B	0xB1CE0000	0x00000008	128	
Mountain SoC	A	0x0ABE8000	0x00000002	32	
Road ASIC	A	0x0BAD0000	0x00000002	32	

B.1.3. Features and Assumptions

B.1.3.1. Features Supported

Features of the bicycle controller block follow:

- Monitor pulse rate of wheel sensor and calculate speed in MPH and distance in miles.

- Monitor brakes for when and how hard brakes are applied to switch motor over to generator mode for regenerative braking. Also switch battery controller to charge instead of draw.

- Monitor pedal strain gauge and smooth out the pulsing readings into an overall rider effort applied.

- Monitor pedal strain and apply electrical assist if strain is too much for the rider.

- Coordinate with the battery and motor controller blocks.

- Provide a streaming of speed values to microprocessor for further data analysis and storage.

- Provide interrupts to the microcontroller on events such as brakes applied, motor engaged, generator engaged, battery control signals, speed and distance measurements, and others.

B.1.3.2. Features Not Supported

The following features are not supported:

- Does not monitor if bike is going up hill or down and so does not use that to determine electrical assist or regenerative braking.

B.1.3.3. Firmware Assumptions

This section lists the assumptions that are made of what firmware will do in the product.

- The block does not retain trip distance across power cycles. It is up to the firmware to monitor the distance traveled during this session and add that to a cumulative value stored in non-volatile memory.

B.1.4. References

Pertinent references that are related to this block.

- Application Notes ABC for the XYZ123 strain gauge for use with the pedals.

- Application Notes BCD for the XYZ125 pressure sensor for use with measuring amount of brake applied.

- Block specifications for the following blocks: Battery Monitor, Battery Charger, and Motor Controller.

B.2. Bicycle Controller Register Reference

The following lists all the registers in the block.

B.2.1. Register Table

Table B4 contains a list of registers in address order and includes the register name, address offset, and page number.

Table B5 is the register table in alphabetical order.

B.2.2. Registers

List the details about each the register.

B.2.2.1. ID and Version Register

This register identifies the block and its current version.

Table B4: Register Table in Address Order

Address Offset	Register Name	Page
0x00000000	ID version	5
0x00000004	Instantiation	7
0x00000020	Interrupt instantiation	8
0x00000024	Interrupt pending	8
0x00000028	Interrupt enable	9
0x0000002C	Interrupt source	10
0x00000040	Control	10
0x00000044	Configuration	11
0x00000048	Status	12
0x00000050	Current speed	12
0x00000054	Current distance	13
0x00000058	Trip log buffer address	13
0x0000005C	Trip log buffer byte count	14
0x00000070	Debug	14

Table B5: Register Table in Alphabetical Order

Address Offset	Register Name	Page
0x00000044	Configuration	11
0x00000040	Control	10
0x00000054	Current distance	13
0x00000050	Current speed	12
0x00000070	Debug	14
0x00000000	ID version	5
0x00000004	Instantiation	7
0x00000028	Interrupt enable	9
0x00000020	Interrupt instantiation	8
0x0000002C	Interrupt pending	8
0x00000024	Interrupt source	10
0x00000048	Status	12
0x00000058	Trip log buffer address	13
0x0000005C	Trip log buffer byte count	14

Table B6: Version Code Map

Code	Version	Note
0x04	C	
0x03	B	
0x02	-	This batch was going to be B but the chips would not boot. The next version is the fixed version.
0x01	A	
0x00	-	This was used for prototypes only; no chips were released with this code.

	MSB				ID Version Register—0x0000 0000					LSB
Bits	31 30 29 28	27 26 25 24	23 22 21 20	19 18 17 16	15 14 13 12	11 10 9 8	7 6 5 4	3 2 1 0
RO	I I I I	I I I I	I I I I	I I I I	- - - -	- - - -	V V V V	V V V V
Reset	0 0 0 0	0 0 0 0	0 0 0 1	0 1 1 1	0 0 0 0	0 0 0 0	0 0 0 1	0 1 0 0

V: **Version**—This identifies the current version of the bicycle controller block. See Table B6 for version codes.

I: **Block ID**—The block ID for the bicycle controller block is 0x0017.

Table B6 maps the version code in this register with the block version.

B.2.2.2. Instantiation Register

This register indicates how the configurable parameters were set when this block was instantiated in this chip. The power-on defaults for this register depends on how this block was instantiated in each chip.

	MSB				Instantiation Register—0x0000 0004					LSB
Bits	31 30 29 28	27 26 25 24	23 22 21 20	19 18 17 16	15 14 13 12	11 10 9 8	7 6 5 4	3 2 1 0
RO	- - - -	- - - -	- - - -	- - - -	- - - I	I I I I	- - - -	- - A M
Reset	0 0 0 0	0 0 0 0	0 0 0 0	0 0 0 0	0 0 0 X	X X X X	0 0 0 0	0 0 X X

M: **Metric support**—This bit is set if the metric conversion support was instantiated in this block.

A: **Wheel auto-calibration support**—This bit is set if the wheel size auto-calibration support was instantiated in this block.

I: **I/O lines**—This indicates which of the five I/O lines were instantiated. A 1 indicates that line is instantiated. The LSB of these five bits maps into I/O-0 and the MSB maps into I/O-4.

B.2.2.3. Interrupt Instantiation Register

This register indicates how the configurable parameters were set when this interrupt module was instantiated in this block. Defaults are known because this is not instantiated any differently in other versions of this block.

	MSB			Interrupt Instantiation Register—0x0000 0020			LSB
Bits	31 30 29 28	27 26 25 24	23 22 21 20	19 18 17 16	15 14 13 12	11 10 9 8	7 6 5 4	3 2 1 0
RO	- - - -	- - - -	- - - -	T T T T	- - - C	C C C C	r r r r	M A P S
Reset	0 0 0 0	0 0 0 0	0 0 0 0	0 1 0 1	0 0 0 0	0 1 1 0	0 0 0 0	0 0 0 1

S: **Source status**—This bit is true if the source status register is instantiated. This bit is always set; the Source Status register will always be available.

P: **Post**—This bit is true if the Post register is instantiated. This bit is always cleared; the interrupt post register is not available.

A: **Atomic enable/disable**—This bit is true if the atomic enable/disable registers are instantiated. This bit is always cleared; the atomic enable/disable registers are not available.

M: **Masked**—This bit is true if the masked register is instantiated. This bit is always cleared; the masked register is not available.

r: **reserved**—These locations are reserved for future optional registers.

C: **Channels**—This contains a count of the number of interrupt channels instantiated. Note that it does not imply the bit location of those channels. This will always contain 6.

T: **Top channel**—This contains the bit position where the top channel is located. Positions are numbered starting with 0 at LSB. If all positions are filled from bit 0 to bit T, then T+1 = C. If there are some holes among the positions, then T ≥ C. This will always contain 5.

B.2.2.4. Interrupt Pending Register

This register is used to view which interrupts fired and to ack pending interrupts. When read, bit positions with a 1 indicate pending interrupts. A 1 written to a position with a pending interrupt will ack that interrupt, clearing that bit. A 1 written to a position with no pending interrupt is ignored. Zeros written to a position, whether pending or not, are ignored.

These interrupts are edge-triggered, or in other words, this bit becomes a 1 when the interrupt source signal transitions from a deasserted to an asserted state. If this bit is acked while the interrupt source is still asserted, the interrupt will not re-trigger. It will not re-trigger until the interrupt source deasserts and then reasserts again.

When the interrupt source asserts, this bit will show interrupt pending, regardless as to whether or not the interrupt is enabled in the interrupt enable register. If it is not enabled, it will show pending but will not propagate to the CPU.

	MSB				Interrupt Pending Register—0x0000 0024			LSB
Bits	31 30 29 28	27 26 25 24	23 22 21 20	19 18 17 16	15 14 13 12	11 10 9 8	7 6 5 4	3 2 1 0
R/W1C	- - - -	- - - -	- - - -	- - - -	- - - -	- - - -	- - A F	C B S E
Reset	0 0 0 0	0 0 0 0	0 0 0 0	0 0 0 0	0 0 0 0	0 0 0 0	0 0 0 0	0 0 0 0

E: **Event stamp**—An event stamp has occurred and was put into the circular event buffer. This will continue to occur even without firmware intervention. However, if firmware does not handle it before the circular buffer fills up, the data in the buffer will be overwritten. This event will not occur faster than about 1 per second.

S: **Speed alarm**—This interrupt occurs when the speed of the bicycle is faster than the set speed limit value. This is used to alert the rider of the speed limit.

B: **Battery level low**—This interrupt occurs when the battery level is below 10%.

C: **Calibration done**—This interrupt occurs when the wheel size auto-calibration function has completed calculating the wheel size. This interrupt will never occur if the wheel auto-calibration support bit in the Instantiation register is not set.

F: **Calibration failure**—This interrupt occurs when the wheel size auto-calibration cycle failed to calibrate. This may be due to no sensor readings (the bike is stopped), erratic sensor readings, or results beyond permitted limits. It can also occur if the Metric bit in the configuration register is set. This error will never occur if the wheel auto-calibration support bit in the instantiation register is not set.

A: **Abort done**—This interrupt occurs when the abort process has completed and the block is ready to be set up again for the next task.

B.2.2.5. Interrupt Enable Register

This register controls which interrupts are enabled to propagate up to the CPU. A 1 in the position enables the interrupt to propagate. A 0 prevents propagation. If an interrupt is enabled when it is already pending, the interrupt will immediately propagate to the CPU. See the interrupt pending register for more details on these bits.

	MSB				Interrupt Enable Register—0x0000 0028			LSB
Bits	31 30 29 28	27 26 25 24	23 22 21 20	19 18 17 16	15 14 13 12	11 10 9 8	7 6 5 4	3 2 1 0
R/W	- - - -	- - - -	- - - -	- - - -	- - - -	- - - -	- - A F	C B S E
Reset	0 0 0 0	0 0 0 0	0 0 0 0	0 0 0 0	0 0 0 0	0 0 0 0	0 0 0 0	0 0 0 0

B.2.2.6. Interrupt Source Register

This register indicates the current level of the interrupt source signal. This interrupt module is edge-triggered, so interrupts will only occur on a deasserted to asserted transition of the interrupt source signal. This register allows firmware to read the current level of the interrupt source no matter if the interrupt is still pending or has been acked, or whether the interrupt is enabled or not.

Not all interrupts in the interrupt status register have their interrupt sources visible in this register. Only those whose interrupts source signals will stay asserted for a while. Those that are asserted just for one (or a few) clock cycles are not listed since firmware cannot purposely catch it asserted.

	MSB								Interrupt Source Register—0x0000 002C																							LSB
Bits	31	30	29	28	27	26	25	24	23	22	21	20	19	18	17	16	15	14	13	12	11	10	9	8	7	6	5	4	3	2	1	0
RO	-	-	-	-	-	-	-	-	-	-	-	-	-	-	-	-	-	-	-	-	-	-	-	-	-	-	-	-	-	B	S	-
Reset	0	0	0	0	0	0	0	0	0	0	0	0	0	0	0	0	0	0	0	0	0	0	0	0	0	0	0	0	0	0	0	0

S: **Speed alarm**—This will be 1 while the bike speed is above the speed limit. When the rider slows down below the speed limit, this will return back to 0.

B: **Battery level low**—This will be 1 while the battery level below 10%. When the battery is recharged and rises above 10%, this will go back to 0.

B.2.2.7. Control Register

This register is used to initiate various operations in the block. Firmware sets the desired bit to 1 to initiate that operation. The block will clear the bit when the operation is done. Only one bit is allowed to be set. If firmware writes a value with two or more bits set, the least significant set bit will take priority and the others will be ignored.

When firmware reads this register, it will be all zeros if no operation is in process, or only one bit will be set, indicating which operation is in process. Read the description for each bit below to see what happens if firmware tries to write ones to this register when an operation is in process.

	MSB								Control Register—0x0000 0040																							LSB
Bits	31	30	29	28	27	26	25	24	23	22	21	20	19	18	17	16	15	14	13	12	11	10	9	8	7	6	5	4	3	2	1	0
R/W1S	-	-	-	-	-	-	-	-	-	-	-	-	-	-	-	-	-	-	-	-	-	-	-	-	-	-	-	-	C	M	S	A
Reset	0	0	0	0	0	0	0	0	0	0	0	0	0	0	0	0	0	0	0	0	0	0	0	0	0	0	0	0	0	0	0	0

A: **Abort**—Set this bit to abort all activity in the block and reset several registers. This bit will stay set until the abort is completed and the abort done interrupt has been posted. Writing this bit will override any other bits that may be set, causing them to clear.

S: **Stop monitor**—Set this bit to cleanly stop the monitor activity. Writing this bit when the monitor bit is set will cause the monitor bit to clear. This bit will stay set until the monitoring has come to a stop. If the Monitor bit is not set or if the abort bit is set, writing this bit is ignored.

M: **Monitor**—Set this bit to activate the monitor function in the block that monitors bike speed, battery levels, rider's pedaling, and other events. If firmware tries to set this bit while any bit in this register is set, it will be ignored. This bit will stay set, and monitoring will continue to happen, until firmware sets the Stop Monitor bit.

C: **Calibrate**—Set this bit to initiate the wheel size auto-calibrate function. If firmware tries to set this bit while any bit in this register is set, it will be ignored. When the auto-calibration function is complete, this bit will be cleared and the calibration done interrupt will be posted. The wheel size auto-calibration function will not work if the metric bit in the configuration register is set. If it is set when trying to calibrate, the calibration failure interrupt will be posted. If the wheel auto-calibration support bit in the Instantiation register is not set, this bit will not exist and writing to it does nothing.

B.2.2.8. Configuration Register

This register is used to set configuration parameters in how the block should operate. None of these bits are changed when an abort is done.

	MSB				Configuration Register—0x0000 0044			LSB
Bits	31 30 29 28	27 26 25 24	23 22 21 20	19 18 17 16	15 14 13 12	11 10 9 8	7 6 5 4	3 2 1 0
R/W	- - - -	- - - -	- - - -	- - - -	- - - -	- - L M	r r B K	P T D S
Reset	0 0 0 0	0 0 0 0	0 0 0 0	0 0 0 0	0 0 0 0	0 0 0 0	0 0 0 0	0 0 0 0

S: **Speed**—Put speed events in the trip log buffer. Events are logged as the speed changes but no quicker than every 15 seconds.

D: **Distance**—Put distance events every 10th of a mile in the trip log buffer.

T: **Time**—Put time events in the trip log buffer every 15 seconds to time stamp other events. It will not log time events if no other events have occurred in the last 15 seconds.

P: **Pedal**—Put pedal events in the trip log buffer, such as when the rider is pedaling, not pedaling, and pedaling with or without battery assist.

K: **Brakes**—Put brake events in the trip log buffer, logging when the rider applies brakes.

B: **Battery**—Put Battery events in the trip log buffer, such as low (below 10%), charging, and full.

r: **Reserved**—These positions are reserved for future logging controls.

M: **Metric**—Set this bit to produce its result in metric units. Clear it to produce its results in British units. This bit must be cleared when doing the wheel size auto-calibration function.

L: **Log**—Set this bit to control the overall logging capabilities. If this bit is not set, then no events will be put into the trip log buffer.

B.2.2.9. Status Register

This register gives the status of various conditions in the system. The Monitoring and Calibrating bits will change to zero when an abort occurs; none of the other bits will change on an abort.

	MSB						Status Register—0x0000 0048							LSB
Bits	31 30 29 28	27 26 25 24	23 22 21 20	19 18 17 16	15 14 13 12	11 10 9 8	7 6 5 4	3 2 1 0
RO	- - - -	- - - -	- - - -	- - - -	- - - -	- - - -	- - - R	B P C M
Reset	0 0 0 0	0 0 0 0	0 0 0 0	0 0 0 0	0 0 0 0	0 0 0 0	0 0 0 0	0 0 0 0

M: **Monitoring**—This bit is set when the block is actively monitoring the bike systems.

C: **Calibrating**—This bit is set when the wheel size auto-calibration function is in operation.

P: **Pedaling**—This bit is set when the rider is pedaling.

B: **Braking**—This bit is set when the rider is applying the brakes.

R: **Regenerative braking**—This bit is set when the rider is applying the brakes and regenerative braking is being used to slow down the bike and charge up the battery.

B.2.2.10. Current Speed Register

This register indicates how fast the bike is moving. If the metric bit in the configuration register is clear, this register is in units of mph (miles per hour). If the metric bit is set, it is in units of kph (kilometers per hour). This number is represented as a real number with an integer portion (I) and a fractional portion (F). See Section B.3.3, Handling Real Numbers, to see how to translate the contents of this register into real numbers. The range is from 0.0 to 127.97 mph (or kph) in increments of 0.03.

This register will not contain a valid value until the monitoring bit is set in the control register. This register is refreshed every 10th of a second. When monitoring is stopped via the Stop Monitor bit, this register will no longer be refreshed and will retain the last value measured. Upon an abort, this register will be zeroed out.

	MSB		Current Speed Register—0x0000 0050					LSB
Bits	31 30 29 28	27 26 25 24	23 22 21 20	19 18 17 16	15 14 13 12	11 10 9 8	7 6 5 4	3 2 1 0
RO	- - - -	- - - -	- - - -	I I I I	I I I F	F F F F	- - - -	- - - -
Reset	0 0 0 0	0 0 0 0	0 0 0 0	0 0 0 0	0 0 0 0	0 0 0 0	0 0 0 0	0 0 0 0

I: **Integer portion**—This is the integer portion of the current speed.

F: **Fractional portion**—This is the fractional portion of the current speed.

B.2.2.11. Current Distance Register

This register indicates how far the bike has traveled since the monitoring bit in the control register has been set. If the metric bit in the configuration register is clear, this register is in units of miles. If the metric bit is set, it is in units of kilometers. This number is represented as a real number with an integer portion (I) and a fractional portion (F). See Section B.3.3, Handling Real Numbers, to see how to translate the contents of this register into real numbers. The range is from 0.0 to 4095.996 mi (or km) in increments of 0.004 mi or 21 ft (or, in metric units, 0.004 km or 4 m).

This register will not contain a valid value until the monitoring bit is set in the control register. This register is refreshed every 10th of a second. When monitoring is stopped via the stop monitor bit, this register will no longer be refreshed and will retain the last value measured. Upon an abort, this register will be zeroed out.

	MSB		Current Distance Register—0x0000 0054					LSB
Bits	31 30 29 28	27 26 25 24	23 22 21 20	19 18 17 16	15 14 13 12	11 10 9 8	7 6 5 4	3 2 1 0
RO	- - - -	- - - I	I I I I	I I I I	I I I F	F F F F	F F F -	- - - -
Reset	0 0 0 0	0 0 0 0	0 0 0 0	0 0 0 0	0 0 0 0	0 0 0 0	0 0 0 0	0 0 0 0

I: **Integer portion**—This is the integer portion of the current distance.

F: **Fractional portion**—This is the fractional portion of the current distance.

B.2.2.12. Trip Log Buffer Address Register

Firmware writes to this register the starting address in memory where the trip log events are to be stored. This is a circular buffer. When the buffer is full, the address and byte count are reloaded and new events are placed at the beginning of the buffer. Firmware must read the contents of the buffer before it is overwritten in the next pass. This is used in conjunction with the trip log buffer byte count register.

	MSB		Trip Log Buffer Address Register—0x0000 0058					LSB
Bits	31 30 29 28	27 26 25 24	23 22 21 20	19 18 17 16	15 14 13 12	11 10 9 8	7 6 5 4	3 2 1 0
R/W	A A A A	A A A A	A A A A	A A A A	A A A A	A A A A	A A A A	A A A A
Reset	0 0 0 0	0 0 0 0	0 0 0 0	0 0 0 0	0 0 0 0	0 0 0 0	0 0 0 0	0 0 0 0

A: **Address**—Firmware writes the starting address for the trip log events. This must be quad-word-aligned (16 bytes) so the lower four bits are ignored and treated as zeros. This must be written before launching the event logger. Writes to this register while the event logger is active are ignored. When read, this will return the next location where the next event will be stored in memory. When the block is aborted, the contents of this register will be left unchanged. This allows firmware to read and see where it is in the buffer.

B.2.2.13. Trip Log Buffer Byte Count Register

Firmware writes to this register the size in memory where the trip log events are to be stored. This is a circular buffer and the byte count is reloaded when it wraps around. This is used in conjunction with trip log buffer address register.

	MSB		Trip Log Buffer Byte Count Register—0x0000 005C					LSB
Bits	31 30 29 28	27 26 25 24	23 22 21 20	19 18 17 16	15 14 13 12	11 10 9 8	7 6 5 4	3 2 1 0
R/W	- - - -	- - - -	- - - -	- - - -	- - - -	- - - C	C C C	C C C C
Reset	0 0 0 0	0 0 0 0	0 0 0 0	0 0 0 0	0 0 0 0	0 0 0 0	0 0 0 0	0 0 0 0

C: **Byte count**—Firmware writes the size in bytes of the buffer for the trip log events. Since each event entry requires 12 bytes, this must be a multiple of 12 bytes. If not, results are unpredictable. The minimum value is 0x0C (1 event) and the maximum is 0xC0 (16 events). Writes to this register while the event logger is active are ignored. When read, this will return the number of bytes remaining for this pass. When the block is aborted, the contents of this register will be left unchanged. This allows firmware to read how much is left.

B.2.2.14. Debug Register

This register is used for testing and debugging only. For normal operation, the contents should remain 0.

Warning! The contents of this register may change in future versions of this block. Do not depend on using this for normal operation.

	MSB		Debug Register—0x0000 0070					LSB
Bits	31 30 29 28	27 26 25 24	23 22 21 20	19 18 17 16	15 14 13 12	11 10 9 8	7 6 5 4	3 2 1 0
R/W	- - - -	- - - -	- - - -	- - - -	- - - -	- - - -	- - - -	- E X D
RO	- - - -	- - - -	- - - -	- - - -	- - - -	- - M J	- - - -	- - - -
Reset	0 0 0 0	0 0 0 0	0 0 0 0	0 0 0 0	0 0 0 0	0 0 0 0	0 0 0 0	0 0 0 0

D: **Debug mode**—Set this bit to put the block in debug mode and enable the debug features.

X: **10X multiplier**—Set this bit to cause the speed and distance to measure ten times faster to help test speed and distance functionality.

E: **Debug events**—Set this bit to send additional debug tracking events to the trip log buffer. Since these events are many and frequent, the trip log buffer byte count register maximum size is increased by 16, or in other words, a maximum of 256 events, 3072 bytes.

J: **JustIn signal**—This indicates the current state of the JustIn internal signal. Consult with the block design specification for more details.

M: **ModSO signal**—This monitors the ModSO internal signal. Consult with the block design specification for more details.

B.2.2.15. All Other Registers

And similar sections will exist for all the other registers in the block.

B.3. Bicycle Controller Tutorial

This section gives a few examples of how to use the block.

B.3.1. Set Up Block and Monitor Events

This section describes how to configure the block, prepare the trip log buffer, and start monitoring activity.

- Allocate memory for the trip log buffer.

- Write the starting address in the trip log buffer address register.

- Write the byte count in the trip log buffer byte count register.

- Enable the desired events (bits 0 to 5) to log and turn on the log bit in the configuration register.

- Ack any stray pending interrupts in the interrupt status register.

- Enable all the interrupts in the interrupt enable register.

- Then set the monitor bit in the control register.

- As the event interrupt occurs, the CPU reads events out of the trip log buffer.

B.3.2. Wheel Size Auto-Calibration

This describes how to use the wheel size auto-calibration feature.

- Do this.

- Do that.

- Etc.

B.3.3. Handling Real Numbers

The current speed and current distance registers have the numbers represented as a real number with an integer portion and a fractional portion. Each register has a different number of integer bits and a different number of fractional bits. But the radix (the decimal period between the integer and fractional portion) for each register is at the same location, between bits 12 and 13. The unused bits will always return zero so they do not have to be masked off. These rules allow the same formula to be used for both registers. Listing B1 is C code that illustrates how a #define can be used to retrieve and convert both the speed and the distance register values.

B.3.4. Abort

Aborting in this block is fairly simple.

- Set the Abort bit in the Control register.

- Wait for the Abort Done Interrupt.

- Ack the Abort Done Interrupt.

The block is ready to set up again for the next task.

Listing B1: Converting from integer and fractional representation in the register to a float.

```
// Convert a register to a float. Assumes radix is at 13.
#define REG_2_REAL(reg) (((float)(readReg(reg))) / ((float)(1<<13)))
float distance, speed;
distance = REG_2_REAL(DistanceReg);
speed    = REG_2_REAL(SpeedReg);
```

B.4. Glossary

The following are terms that may be vague or unknown beyond the scope of this block. This is listed in alphabetical order.

- **ADC**—Analog to digital convertor.

- **DAC**—Digital to analog convertor.

- **Pedal strain accumulator**—The strain measurement of a rider pedaling is very up and down with every stroke. This smoothes out the measurement by averaging the reading across two strokes.

- **Regenerative braking**—The process of putting the motor into the electrical generator mode to charge the batteries. This can be used to slow down the cyclist when coming to a stop or to keep the speed down when coasting downhill.

B.5. Defects

This lists all known defect in the block for each chip and what firmware can do to avoid them.

B.5.1. Criterion ASIC

- A defect in the reset logic can leave the block in an unknown state. After power up, reset the block twice to get it into the known state.

Appendix D: Glossary

This book spans two disciplines, chip design and firmware programming, with each having its own vocabulary. Some terms in one discipline are unknown in the other. Some terms are common to both but have different meanings. And within a discipline, common meanings have different terms. This glossary contains terms and explains how they are used in the context of this book.

Abort Upon receiving an abort command, a block halts its operation and resets buffers, counters, and state machines. An abort does not reset configurations registers or clear memory that was set before the task started. Also known as a "soft reset."

Ack, Acked, Acking (Acknowledge) Used in the context of interrupts, as in to ack an interrupt.

Application Application in the firmware context is firmware that sits on top of the OS and goes through device drivers to get at the hardware. In the hardware context, it is used with ASIC and ASSP to denote hardware functionality specific to a particular purpose. See ASIC and ASSP.

ASIC (Application-Specific Integrated Circuit) A chip that has been designed for a specific purpose or application that is typically used in the products of just one company. Unlike FPGAs, ASICs must be fabricated to get the design on silicon.

ASSP (Application-Specific Standard Product) Like an ASIC, but designed for a standard application, such as a network or USB chip, that can be used in products by many companies.

Best Practice The best way to do something in a given situation.

Big-Endian See Endian.

Block A part of a chip that carries out an assigned task. A chip will have one or more blocks. Each block typically operates independently and may consist of one or more sub-blocks that all work together to carry out the task.

CAN (Controller Area Network) A two-wire network developed for communications among modules within an automobile that has since been expanded for other uses.

Chip The hardware component that is soldered on the board and consists of a silicon die in a package with many pins connecting the die to the board. Technically, a chip is any piece of silicon mounted on a board, whether it be a CPU with a few hundred pins or a little eight-pin, dual NAND gate. But for this book it is limited to large-scale chips that are not

CPUs or memory. Examples include ASICs, ASSPs, and FPGAs. Also known as integrated circuits.

Co-Development The hardware and firmware engineers working together to develop a chip and associated drivers before the chip is sent to fabrication to be turned into silicon. It typically means providing ways and means for firmware to test the drivers before silicon is received. Co-simulation and FPGAs are two forms of co-development.

Co-Simulation The means of running simulated driver code on simulated chip code, typically simulating down to the gate level for every clock edge. It is typically done before the chips are available. See Virtual Prototypes.

CPU (Central Processing Unit) The component that executes firmware, which controls the computer or embedded system. Although it does exist on silicon and in SoCs, and is in the discussion, it is not the focus for the best practices presented in this book. Used interchangeably with "microprocessor" and "processor."

CSR (Control Status Register) See Register.

Device Driver That part of firmware that directly interacts with blocks on a chip. It accesses the registers and handles the interrupts. There is typically one device driver for each block on the chip. Also known as "low-level firmware" or "BIOS."

Die The part made from silicon that has all the circuitry on it. It is mounted in a package that has pins and is soldered on a board.

Driver See Device Driver. Not to be confused with a current driver on a chip or a windows driver on a PC.

Embedded Device or Embedded System Any device that contains one or more microprocessors, zero or more customized chips, and some firmware to control it. Examples are cell phones, automobiles, and microwave ovens.

Embedded Software The same as firmware. See Firmware.

Endian Refers to the order of bytes in multi-byte words. In a 32-bit word, there are 4 bytes, bytes 0 to 3. If byte 0 is in the low end of the word (i.e., the least-significant byte), it is little-endian (3210). If byte 0 is in the high end of the word (i.e., the most-significant byte), it is big-endian (0123).

Fab (Fabrication) The foundry where chips are made.

Fabricate The multi-week process to make chips out of silicon.

Firmware Software that is inside an embedded system. It may be stored in ROM, flash, disc, or other such non-volatile memory device. Also known in the industry as "embedded software."

First Time Right The notion in the industry of designing a chip such that the first version that was produced at the fab shop works correctly. If there were defects in the chip that caused a second version to be made, it failed "first time right."

FPGA (Field-Programmable Gate Array) A chip that is already fabricated first and then subsequently programmed with a circuit. It has the ability to be programmed and reprogrammed. It is programmed and ready to go in a matter of minutes as opposed to several weeks for fabricated circuits.

Halt Stops operations but does not reset any counters, buffers, or registers. If allowed by the design, operation can be resumed to continue where it was halted. Also known as "stop."

Hard Reset This book uses the term, "reset." See Reset.

Hardware Although hardware includes many aspects such as printed-circuit boards, resistors, and connectors, the term is used almost exclusively in this book to mean chips, specifically chips that do specific tasks that are not processors or memory. See also Chip.

Hardware Engineer Although there are other fields of electrical engineering, in this book it refers to front-end chip designers.

HDL (Hardware Description Language) A language used for the design of chips. Examples include VHDL and Verilog. (See also RTL.)

Interrupt In this book, it is how the chip notifies firmware that some attention is needed.

Interrupt Channel One channel supports one interrupt source signal and represents one bit in an interrupt pending and interrupt enable register. Several channels make up an interrupt module. All enabled and pending interrupts from the interrupt channels are OR'd together and propagated upstream to the processor.

Interrupt Handler The functions in firmware that respond to interrupts generated by the chip. It is specialized functions that have to respond quickly and operate under limited resources.

IP (Intellectual Property) In the context of chips, it refers to the HDL code that describes a block or module. It is often used in the context of buying IP from another company to put into chips with other blocks.

ISR (Interrupt Service Routine) See Interrupt Handler.

Little-Endian See Endian.

LSB (Least-Significant Bit) The least important bit in a register. In a register, whether 8 bit, 16 bit, or any other size, it is Bit 0. See also MSB.

Microprocessor See CPU.

Module Used in this book to indicate a portion of a block or firmware. See also Sub-Block.

Mono (Monochrome) Video Block The block in Hewlett-Packard's LaserJet printers that uses raster data to control the laser painting the image on the paper. This block in HP's Unity ASIC is the subject of the case study in this book.

MSB (Most-Significant Bit) The most important bit in a register. In an 8-bit register, it is Bit 7. In a 16-bit register, it is Bit 15. And so on. See also LSB.

Power-On Reset The reset that occurs when power is applied. This is functionally identical to "reset." See Reset.

Processor See CPU.

Register An addressable portal through which firmware reads from and/or writes to the block. Although a bank of flip flops internal to the block and not accessible by firmware can also be called a register, it is not used in that context in this book.

Reset Stops all operations, clears out all memory, resets all state machines, and restores all registers and modes to their power-on state. A reset may be limited to one block or to the whole chip. Also known as a "hard reset" and a "power-on reset."

Respin To again fabricate a chip to correct design flaws.

RTL (Register Transfer Level) A term used to refer to the code that describes the logic design of chips. (See also HDL.)

Silicon The majority of chips are made on silicon. So the term is often used to refer to actual chips: "The silicon has arrived from the fab."

SoC (System on Chip) Refers to chips that have one or more processors along with several blocks on the same silicon die or FPGA. In some cases, the term PSoC (programmable system on chip) is used for an FPGA-based implementation.

Soft Reset See Abort.

Stop Used synonymously with "halt." See Halt.

Sub-Block A part of a block.

Superblock A block that contains a superset of all known capabilities for that block.

Unity ASIC An ASIC designed by Hewlett-Packard for use in their LaserJet printers. See Mono Video Block.

Verilog A language for specifying the logic design of chips.

VHDL (VHSIC (Very High-Speed Integrated Circuit) Hardware Description Language) Another language for specifying the logic design of chips.

Virtual Prototypes A software-based simulation of a hardware and firmware system. It is faster than co-simulation in that shortcuts are taken to not simulate every single gate change on every single clock edge. See Co-Simulation.

W1C (Write 1 Clear) A register with W1C bits is where firmware writes a 1 to clear the bit. Writing a zero does nothing.

W1S (Write 1 Set) A register with W1S bits is where firmware writes a 1 to set the bit. Writing a zero does nothing.

Index

Note: Entries referencing a figure are italic and followed by an f. Entries referencing tables are italic and followed by a t.

Printed and bound by CPI Group (UK) Ltd, Croydon, CR0 4YY

03/10/2024

01040339-0003